747266

D0495155

a 3 0 1 0 3 0 0 7 4 7 2 6 6 2 b

Resistance and Reaction

Resistance and Reaction

University Politics in Post-Mao China

Shirin Rai

University of Warwick

HARVESTER WHEATSHEAF

ST. MARTIN'S PRESS

First published in England 1991 by
Harvester Wheatsheaf
66 Wood Lane End, Hemel Hempstead
Hertfordshire HP2 4RG
A division of
Simon & Schuster International Group

First published in the United States of America in 1991
by St. Martin's Press, Inc., 175 Fifth Avenue,
New York, N.Y. 10010
ISBN 0–312–07187–6

© Shirin Rai 1991

All rights reserved. No part of this publication may be
reproduced, stored in a retrieval system, or transmitted,
in any form, or by any means, electronic, mechanical,
photocopying, recording or otherwise, without prior
permission, in writing, from the publisher.

Typeset in 10/12pt Times
by Photoprint, Torquay

Printed and bound in Great Britain by
Billing and Sons Limited, Worcester

British Library Cataloguing in Publication Data

Rai, Shirin
  Resistance and reaction: University politics in
  post-Mao China.
  I. Title
  378.51

    ISBN 0–7450–0903–4

Library of Congress Cataloging-in-Publication Data

Rai, Shirin
    Resistance and reaction: university politics in post-Mao China /
  Shirin Rai.
      p.   cm.
    Includes bibliographical references.
    ISBN 0–312–07187–6
    1. Education. Higher—Political aspects—China. 2. Higher
  education and state—China. 3. China—Intellectual life—1976–
  I. Title
  LA1133.R35   1991
  378.51—dc20
                                                              91–28959
                                                                  CIP

747266
UNIVERSITY OF
SUSSEX LIBRARY

For my parents – Satya and Lajpat

Contents

Acknowledgements

I would like to thank the various individuals and friends at Hangzhou and Beijing universities for their support during my research in China. I also owe a special debt to Clare Grist at Harvester Wheatsheaf for her enthusiasm for this project, and her gentle persistence that I finish it before too long. Molly Andrews, Bob Benewick, Jack and Maisie Gray, Cathy Hilman, Lajpat Rai, Jeremy Roche, and Gordon White have contributed greatly to the final shape of the book with their critical comments and editorial suggestions. While I benefited from their advice, the shortcomings of the book remain my own.

I would also like to thank my parents – Satya and Lajpat Rai – for their constant interest and concern for this project. Finally, it would not be far wrong to say that I would not have been able to complete this book in the time I did without the intellectual and emotional support of my husband Jeremy Roche.

Preface

Since the death of Mao Zedong in 1976, China has seen tremendous changes in its economic, political and social life. Both the scale of change and the rapidity with which it was introduced have been astounding. Not that the Chinese people have been unused to changes in policy. After all, it was Mao's favourite dictum that change is permanent, and stability only temporary. However, what has been exciting and startling about the post-Mao changes has been the new direction that they have given to China's economic and political life. Despite all the turmoil of the Cultural Revolution years – the marches, the mobilisations, the red flags, the radical rhetoric, and the chaos – the Maoist regime never diverged significantly either from a centralised, planned economic model, or from a political system based upon the Communist Party's monopoly of power. What the post-Mao leadership seemed to be offering was a change in both these areas. It was going to decentralise the economy by creating a market in land, labour, production and exchange. It was going to dilute the totalist control of the Party by separating the executive and political functions. It was further going to make the two reforms compatible by giving to the institutions of law the powers to enforce the contracts that a marketised economy and polity would need. The changes were monumental in a state socialist society. They were initiated by a leadership confident in the support it enjoyed among a people ready for change. It was a leadership that carried a twin legitimacy, personalised by Deng Xiaoping. First, that of participation in the revolution that had given to China a status in the world, and its people a pride in their modern history. Second, a legitimacy born of persecution by the radical left – the 'Gang of Four' – that was so hated after the chaos of the Cultural Revolution. This was a leadership that spoke in terms of moderation, pragmatism, and nationalism. It promised a better standard of living for the Chinese people, greater freedom from political orthodoxy, and a lessening of social tension with the withdrawal of radical rhetoric and political mobilisation. As the world looked on with interest, and some scepticism, the Chinese leadership set about putting its policies into practice.

The success of the reform policies introduced in stages, beginning in 1978, was not inconsiderable. The economy showed signs of almost immediate recovery from a period of stagnation, political life seemed to be moving towards greater openness, and there was a renewed vigour witnessed in the civil society. However, the very success of the post-Mao reforms has posed new questions for the leadership. These have been of two different types. First, with the progress of the reforms, new demands and new agendas have arisen that have become necessary for the leadership to address if this progress is to be maintained. These demands and agendas have differed in essence, making it easier for the leadership to meet them in some cases, and impossible in others. Second, as can happen with any policy decision, there have been some unintended consequences that have emerged during the implementation of the reform policy. To deal with these results the leadership has had to take new policy initiatives. The pace at which these initiatives have been taken has not always conformed with the expectations of those demanding them. The form that these initiatives have taken have also not pleased all sections involved, starting another spiral of demands upon the party/state.

The second problem that the Chinese leadership encountered on the road to success of its reform programme was the emerging gap between the text of the reforms and its interpretation by those who 'read' them. The subtext has been different for the reformist leadership, those who implement the reforms, and those affected by them. As a result of this, expectations among the people have risen sharply within the country. For example, while Deng Xiaoping talked of 'political restructuring' being crucial for the success of economic reforms, did he really mean to equate market reforms in the economy with pluralist politics? A move from 'totalism to authoritarianism' was all that was on the agenda as far as he was concerned. That some took this to be a call for the dismantling of the Chinese Communist Party's monopoly of power cannot be blamed on Deng. And yet the rhetoric of the reformers fashioned the responses to them.

However, the implications of the dynamic nature of the reforms themselves, and the expectations that they aroused, cannot be minimised. The fact that unforeseen results emerged, or that expectations outstripped policy initiatives, are problems that have become integral to the process of reform; they have to be addressed whether the leadership intended to or not. A refusal to do so will remain a source of future political instability, especially as the present leadership is determined to persevere with the economic reforms. The student movements that have caught the attention of the world since 1985, culminating in the Tian'anmen Square movement of 1989, are a pointer to the need to constantly readdress the reform agenda in the light of newly arising pressures and demands, as well as the cost of not doing so.

This book is a study of the reform policies in the sphere of higher education in post-Mao China. It is a study of the concrete conditions in Chinese universities, which gave rise to much social instability within the education system, which was then cast on to the national political scene. It focuses upon the nature of the educational reforms, their impact on the lives of various interest groups within the universities in China, and the different opportunities that these groups found for articulating their demands, anxieties, and fears. It seeks to understand the necessity for, as well as the nature and progress of, the reforms in higher education. The book addresses two issues. First, the nature of the pressures and interests arising out of the structure and functioning of higher education in China and post-Mao reforms. Second, the ways in which these pressures and interests have been allowed to be aired in the political system, and with what results. It is thus a study of the levels of participation allowed to different sections of the university population by the authorities. It explores the realm of non-authorised participation by those denied access to the public sphere within and outside the university. While unpacking the process of policy implementation in China, it also studies strategies of overt and covert subversion, tactics of resistance through non-action, and of open opposition by those affected by the reform policy. It points to the political consequences of the failure of institutions and organisations when they are unable to or incapable of representing the interests of their membership. It is, in short, a story of a process of recognition of special interests, and a demand for a system that will allow for their articulation.

As the post-Mao reforms in higher education have unfolded, the Chinese intellectuals have gone through a cycle of rising expectations. Euphoria about the imminent realisation of these expectations gave way to anxiety and disappointment about the pace of the reforms, suspicion of, and anger with, the reformist leadership they saw as being unable to free itself from its own past, and finally an open defiance and opposition to the regime. Throughout this period the intellectuals have been ready and willing to participate in the process of reform. They have felt and expressed a sense of responsibility in the project of modernising China. In this they have acted in the best traditions of the Confucian literati – an engagement with, not a withdrawal from, public life has characterised their behaviour. The Communist Party, for its part, has moved through a phase of recognising the importance of the intellectuals to the modernisation of the Chinese economy, to wanting to build bridges with this section that had been so reviled during the Maoist period, and giving it a special position in the Chinese public sphere – one of limited but important participation in policy-making, as friendly critics of the regime. On both sides there was real enthusiasm and understanding for the necessity of change. What neither side had envisaged was the kind of pressures that the reforms would result in. For both the intellectuals and the party/state the progress of the reforms in the economy, political system, and educational establishment produced certain unforeseen problems. These pressures created demands on both sides – for an increased role in the public space by the intellectuals, for a greater restraint and conformity by the party/state. As these demands began to clash, dialogue turned into accusation. As channels of communication froze up, the mutual suspicions and anger led to collision, and the suppression of political reform in China.

The primary data for the book were collected in 1987 in Hangzhou and Beijing. Much has happened since then in China. The 'political restructuring' that Deng Xiaoping had offered has been shelved. Zhao Ziyang, the ex-premier, has, in the short run, lost the battle for the leadership of the Chinese Communist Party to the hard-liners. Many intellectuals have had to flee the country for fear of persecution, many others have faced politically managed trials for their role in the Tian'anmen Square movement. However, the changes have not been as momentous as one might expect after the upheaval in Tian'anmen Square. The Chinese leadership has decided upon continuing with its economic reform policies. The western nations, after initial moral indignation gave way to hard-headed business sense, have renewed trade with China. In its turn the Chinese leaders have reiterated their 'open door' policy. What also remains unchanged in the Chinese polity are the pressures that continue to accumulate as the economic reforms proceed; the different interests that continue to emerge and consolidate. The articulation of these interests remains an unresolved question for the Chinese political system. How this question will be answered remains as yet unclear. This book provides no models for a future China. It seeks only to understand the processes, choices and pitfalls in the way of a reforming state socialist society.

Abbreviations used for source materials

Australian Journal of Chinese Affairs	AJCA
Beijing Review	BR
China Daily	CD
China Now	CN
The China Quarterly	CQ
China Report	CR
Chinese Education	CE
Foreign Broadcasts Information Service	FBIS
Guangming Ribao	GMRB
Hongqi	HQ
Issues and Studies	I&S
Joint Publications Research Service	JPRS
Modern China	MC
Renmin Jiaoyu	RMJY
Renmin Ribao	RMRB
State Education Commission	SEC
Summary of World Broadcasts	SWB
Xinhua News Agency	NCNA

1

Introducing the issues

Introduction

In 1978 China embarked upon a new adventure of reforming a centralised economic and political system from within. It was to be another Long March – to economic prosperity, military strength and political stability. It was to be a 'revolution from above', led by those who had been discredited by Maoist radicalism, and who now sought to create a new legitimacy for the Communist Party of China (CPC) by appealing to realism, moderation, and efficiency. By 1989 the reforms were a decade old. The successes had been many, and accolades great. The economy was recovering from stagnation, the education system was beginning to fulfil the needs of the economy, and the leadership enjoyed broad political support. However, the period was not without problems, some more intractable to resolution than others. The communal fabric of the economy was rapidly unpicked. But as the threads of centralised economic control loosened, they released pressures and problems unintended and unforeseen by the leadership. As the value-system created by the Maoist regime crumbled, nothing appeared to replace it; as old certainties died, they left a vacuum that the post-Mao leadership seemed unable to fill.

The Maoist experience of radical politics had satiated the people's appetite for new movements, and had made them cynical about the old style of politics managed and controlled by a single party. The post-Mao leadership promised them new vistas of economic prosperity, and seemed to promise a limited political liberalisation. As the new economic policies took effect and resulted in not only tremendous growth but also unintended socio-economic contradictions, the demand for greater freedom for articulation of interests and opposition gathered momentum. The opposition movement that confronted the leadership in Tian'anmen Square was symptomatic of this growing democratic impulse. Many inspirations, many intellectual traditions and lived experiences clashed in it to make its demands seem extremely broad, and even unfocused. It was, however, a powerful critique of the existing political system. It was a challenge not to the power of the leadership but to its authority. Most of the students who were involved in the Tian'anmen demonstrations were impelled by frustrations felt at the non-fulfilment of the very expectations aroused by the leadership's promises of reform – a 'political restructuring' that did not seem to happen – and by an idealism that resulted from their nationalism.

One of the central concerns of the intellectuals of China who supported the movement in Tian'anmen Square has been that of political participation. They demanded that they be let in on that process of reform – not just as objects of policy-making but as subjects participating in implementation, critique and re-evaluation of the policies affecting them. 'It was the typical view', writes Li Lu, one of the leaders of the movement, 'of the reformers within the Party – that reforms were the responsibility of the Party and government leaders. People should be confident that everything would be done well. They should not interfere.' (Li Lu, 1990: 113) There are two issues that arise from this concern: first, the issue of the autonomy and participation of individuals and groups, and interest-representing organisations in policy implementation in China. Second, the question of the implications that this process has for the political system in terms of the opening of the public sphere to citizen and group participation, and democratisation of the procedures of decision-making.

Participation: a conceptual framework

A concern with political participation in the large modern nation states has been considered as misplaced on the ground that it is an unrealistic project: the full participation by citizens in the public political sphere is impossible given the size of the population, and the complexity of the process of policy formation and implementation faced by national governments today. Interest in participation has also been regarded as utopian in another sense – the majority of the people do not want to be bothered with politics, even less with practical politics (Dahl, 1961). This, in turn, is said to indicate their acceptance, nay, approval of the status quo (Almond and Verba, 1963). The Rousseauist concern with participation as important to psychological growth of the citizen is denied, and indeed considered at best arrogant, at worst dangerous (Huntington and Nelson, 1976). The danger comes from a sense of mass participation as uncontrolled power, easily misled and manipulated by an interested and articulate élite which comes to represent the interest of the inchoate 'masses' (Schumpeter, 1947; Converse, 1964). The masses are characterised as ignorant, intolerant, indifferent, and irrational in comparison with the 'leaders', the élite, who are educated and trained to be objective in making decisions (Lipset, 1960; Berelson, Lazarusfeld and McPhee, 1954). Another criticism of the concept of participation that is particularly relevant to the study of Chinese politics again comes from Huntington. In his book *Political Order in Changing Societies* (1968), Huntington points to the process of institutionalisation of democratic processes as a prerequisite for inclusion of 'new social forces' into politics. A neglect of this condition, he feels could actually lead to 'political decay', destabilisation, and therefore prove dangerous to democracy itself. As we shall see below, this is an argument that has been taken up by economic reformers in China who argue for a clear political space to implement economic policies unhindered by democratic critique. The concept is also considered as too loosely constructed to be helpful in understanding actual political reality. While on the one hand, political participation can be seen as a conceptual subset of the idea of democracy, on the other, it is not as precise as the idea of representation which finds concrete form in interest representation by groups and organisations, electoral processes, and élite political practice.

A defence of the concept has to take on board this mountain of criticism. While technology can overcome the constraints of spread of information, it cannot answer the need for conceptual regeneration. There is a need to make the construction of the concept more sinewy, its usage more rigorous. There is a need to narrow it down, to isolate characteristics that are essential to it, and those that cannot be included. This is particularly important when studying political systems like China where the 'masses' were repeatedly mobilised to participate in political life and where that 'participation' was repeatedly manipulated by the various factions of the ruling élite in its own interest. The 'masses' became the legitimisers, their mobilisation a referendum, and its expropriation a mandate to rule.

One defence of the concept is the strength and the resilience of the idea itself – despite the barrage of criticism, it refuses to lie down and die. It resurfaces time and again, whenever the 'apathetic mass' of the élite theory sits up and takes notice of what is happening around and above it. The 1960s were such a time – the whole world seemed in a vortex of participatory politics. There was the students' revolution in Paris which ignited little fires across Europe, there was the Prague Spring – the brave attempt to thaw the Russian-imposed political winter; there was a quarter of humanity apparently making a Cultural Revolution to create a 'new socialist person': all this reaching a new high with the anti-Vietnam War movement in the United States which soon became global. With the decline of the students' movements, many declared that participation as a political concept was in a decline too. But as the '60s merged into the 1970s the demand for extension of participatory rights to the people, and a deepening of their existing rights, did not abate – there arose the revolutionary movements in Indonesia, the students' movement in Sri Lanka, the Naxalite movement in India and the Democracy Wall movement of 1979–81 in China itself. Later, in the 1980s, there were the revolutions in Iran and Nicaragua, and then the breathless change in Eastern Europe that has led to a strange sense of 'change in permanence' in the international political arena. In all these movements we find reflected a deep concern with the idea of political participation. It was the same with the recent students' movement in China.

Furthermore, while seeming too elastic to be useful, participation is a concept that can help explain certain relevant processes in various areas of public life – social, economic and political. By examining participatory practice in these different spheres we can make systemic analysis more rigorous, and critique more possible.

It also provides a yardstick by which to judge existing public political practices – the openness or otherwise of the processes of decision-making and of the institutions involved in implementing public policy. Further, the concept enables us to draw 'into the debate institutions which are not themselves part of the official political sphere.' (Graham, 1986: 166) While including representation within its boundaries, it also allows the possibility of analysing a broader scope of public activism of individuals in society, thus presenting a more realistic picture of socio-political interaction.

In defining participation more rigorously we can study it across a space covering social, political, and economic structures and systems. We can also study it in terms of 'depth' – it has the potential of progress from a generic use of the term to a more rigorous and particular political process. In this way the looseness of the concept that its critics disfavour can be minimised and its applicability to various social and political realities increased.

Participation occurs at various levels of social life. While economic participation refers to the 'right and ability of members of an economic institution . . . to play a role' in its management, social participation involves the right and ability of individuals and groups to articulate, represent and organise for their interests in the realm of 'civil society'. Political participation concerns itself with the right and ability of citizens to influence the direction of local and/or national policy and control policy-making bodies through various political processes and institutions – elections, recall, demonstrations, activities of political parties (White, 1988: 6).

We can identify three levels of participation (see Pateman, 1970). People can be *mobilised* to participate in the public sphere. This is done by institutions that remain outside the effective control of those mobilised. Mobilisation might be in support of the mobilisers or against their opponents. In either case decisions are taken by authority structures not accountable to the people. Mobilisation also involves more than just discussions about the decisions to be taken: it suggests *active* participation – demonstrations, 'struggle meetings', rallies, sit-ins, mass meetings. The Cultural Revolution was an example of mobilised participation. The next level can be called *licensed participation* (Strand, 1989: 54) which 'allows a degree of open or thinly veiled negotiation or bargaining to take place between the regime and the group, and shifts the sole burden for success or failure of particular policies away from [the authority structures]' (*ibid.* pp. 54–5). Such a process allows for only a critical élite to bargain with the incumbent leadership for particular and/or more general demands. It is a controlled process of political participation. Finally, there is *autonomous participation*. It is not limited to the necessity of equality of decision-making power; it emphasises the opportunity to be able to do so. It bases itself on individuals, but insists upon an autonomous space for groups of individuals that come together in interest-representing organisations. Autonomy implies the possibility of demands being made by these organisations upon the authority structures, and the availability of mechanisms for holding them responsible. It extends the concern of these organisations from input into decision-making to implementation of the decisions taken.

Participation has also been defended as a political concept in terms of psychological need. Classical theorists of democracy from the ancient Greeks to Rousseau, Marx to Cole had addressed the question of participation in terms of its normative and educative value – participation in the public sphere is a *need* of individuals which, if unfulfilled, leads to the alienation of the citizens from the civic authority. While people can learn to become active political agents, it is only through political practice that they can do so – as the individual participates in decision-making she begins to distinguish between private and public interest. This leads to a vigilant, informed public who are *better* citizens and are able to become effective political agents by linking their experiences in local democratic participation to the national political context. While a need-based explanation is vulnerable to the charge of non-contextuality in face of the empirical studies revealing patterns of public apathy (see Dews, 1986: 18), it does point to the issues of efficacy and legitimacy, and thus a structural need of any socio-political system. The question that is posed is not so much whether public participation is inherently *good* but whether it is a value that helps legitimise and therefore stabilise political systems. At a structural level, while an increased civic responsibility could lead to greater stability, the opportunity to participate in decision-making at the local level, and holding authority-holders responsible at the higher level, could provide the political structures with greater legitimacy. The opportunities available, or seen to be available, for political participation and hence for empowerment translate into levels of political stability and legitimacy.

Finally, increased participation can also lead to greater efficiency. It avoids bottle-necks that could hinder the projects by establishing open lines of feedback/communication, and, by giving people more responsibility, they disperse both reward and blame, thus motivating those involved in implementing policies, or fulfilling targets, to give their best to their projects. Many studies of industrial enterprises and workers' participation have gone to show this (Blumberg, 1968; Pateman, 1970). Thus, while the evidence of the 'apathy theorists' of the élitist model of democracy seems to deny the need for participation among the citizens, political history does not bear this out.

Putting together the concepts of autonomous and political participation we can now formulate a working definition that will be used in this book while examining the political processes of policy implementation in the sphere of higher education in post-Mao China. First, autonomous political participation takes place in the 'public sphere'; it is crucially linked to the activity of the state. Political participation would, therefore, include attempts at influencing policy-making processes, the decisions that result from these processes, and/or an involvement in the implementation of the policy decision. Second, political participation involves an awareness of 'public' issues; it is a reflective process. This is important when we consider the question of 'action'. Political participation can be either an affirmation of support or a statement of opposition involving individual or group activity, or it can be a bid to influence decisions or implementation of decisions through non-action. In either case it is purposive behaviour. Finally, political participation, as defined here, does not involve mobilisation by élites. The question of organisations and institutions is important here. While political participation can be individual it can also be organised in groups. However, the organisations representing differentiated interests would have to be able to function autonomously, without interference from state agencies, to be called politically participative. Political participation is thus integral to the concept of empowerment, 'the reabsorption of the state power by society as its own living forces instead of as forces controlling and subduing it, by the popular masses themselves' (Marx, 1976: 153). In the context of China where political and administrative power have been interlocked into a party/state system, the concept of political participation can help both in understanding the debates within the political system, and in analysing the policy options and decisions of the regime in power.

Political participation: the Chinese context

'People's participation' has been a running thread in the Chinese political discourse; the 'masses' have figured large in the rhetoric of the Chinese communist leadership. The Chinese political system has experienced the practice of political participation in at least two of the three ways sketched out above: mobilisation, and licensed participation. The Maoist period epitomised the first, the post-Mao regime took up the latter theme through calling for decentralisation of decision-making and rationalisation of bureaucratic structures. However, the reforms introduced by the Deng Xiaoping leadership have repeatedly and explicitly fallen short of any re-assessment of the actual distribution of power. Decentralisation has not led to any significant increase in autonomy; rationalisation has not raised levels of autonomous political participation.

While autonomous participation has been denied to the people in post-revolution China, the masses have not been allowed to retreat from the public sphere either: they were repeatedly mobilised in political campaigns during much of the Maoist period and there have been continuous, if only partially successful, attempts at control by the post-Mao regime. Such a system has in turn affected the relationship between individuals, groups and the political authority, and between the civil society and the state. The imposition of policies of mobilisation and control by the party/state has resulted in strategies of subversion by the 'masses', often through non-action. The lack of opportunity of open participation has led to this subversion taking 'hidden paths' – the legitimacy of available organisations and institutions has been largely eroded leading to a breakdown of the system of feedback to the state. This in turn has led to problems of efficiency both in implementing policies, and in exercising control. A distance has developed between the goals espoused by the leadership and the unarticulated and/or unrecognised demands of the population. A growing alienation of the civic population from the state authority has resulted in an exacerbation of these problems; the Tian'anmen massacre points to the danger of disregard of these issues. Political participation thus seems at the heart of not only the democratic concern, but also the political critique of 'bureaucratic socialist' systems.

'Mass line' politics and people's participation

Mao addressed the theme of political participation through his concept of 'mass line'. An analysis of this concept is important for various reasons: first, because the construction of the definition of this concept has implications for the nature of political participation conceived by Mao for the Chinese political system; second, because the *practice* of the theory of 'mass line' politics reveals the problems resulting from conflating the various forms of participation. Finally, a study of the Maoist conception of political participation can help us understand the post-Mao political reforms. While denying the Maoist political practice, the post-Mao leadership has not broken free from the Maoist definitional framework; it continues to be limited by the categories used by Mao.

Defining the concept of 'mass line' Mao wrote:

> all correct leadership is necessarily from the masses, to the masses. This means: take the ideas of the masses (scattered and unsystematic ideas) and concentrate them (through study turn them into concentrated and systematic ideas), then go to the masses and propagate and explain these ideas until the masses embrace them as their own, hold fast to them and translate them into action. (Mao, in Schram, 1985: 316–17)

Two unreconciled elements of Mao's analysis of praxis are revealed here. First, the creativity of the masses (the ideas of the masses), and second, the question of the relationship between the 'leaders' and the 'masses' (the leaders systematise the ideas of the masses). While remaining consistently suspicious of the 'leaders', Mao could also never completely trust the 'masses'. Because of this, Mao's theory of political practice remained linked to the issue of the relationship between the leaders and the led.

The linking of the theory of 'mass line' political practice to that of leadership presents its own problems. First, by linking political practice to the leader–led relationship Mao seems to be circumscribing the area of debate. The question of the autonomy of mass political action seems neglected in favour of one regarding the appropriate style of functioning of the leadership. In an attempt to subvert the stigmatisation of the Chinese people as backward and illiterate and therefore incapable of self-rule, Mao had embraced the idea: 'the outstanding thing about China's 600 million people is that they are "poor and blank" . . . on a blank sheet of paper free from any mark, the freshest and most beautiful characters can be written' (Mao, 1972: 36). While this subverted imperialist political discourse, it also redefined the relationship between the Party and the people: the masses represent the 'blank canvas' upon which the Communist Party would draw beautiful pictures of a socialist alternative in China. This position echoes the Leninist position on the question of working-class consciousness:

> Class political consciousness can be brought to the workers *only from without*, that is, only from outside the economic struggle, from the outside sphere of relations between workers and employers. (Lenin, 1969: 78)

Second, in the above definition of 'mass line' politics, there is no hint of any other organisation participating in the task of collecting and collating information and opinion from the 'mass' except the local Communist Party branches, the cadres of which Mao was referring to. There is little recognition of various interests among the masses that might require different voices to articulate their demands through various organisations, and that a legal political status for these organisations was a prerequisite for such an enterprise to be successful. This lack of differentiated institutions is, however, built into the description of the 'masses' as homogeneous category represented by the CPC. In his article 'On Correct Handling of Contradictions Among the People' (1957) Mao wrote:

> we must first be clear on what is meant by 'the people' and what is meant by 'the enemy' . . . At the present state, the period of building socialism, the classes, strata and social groups which favour, support and work for the cause of socialist construction all come within the category of the people, while the social forces and groups which resist the socialist revolution and are hostile to or sabotage socialist construction are all enemies of the people. (Mao, 1979: 36)

Thus, once those groups that represent antagonistic contradictions

– in the Maoist terms, the comprador bourgeoisie, the landlord class and the criminal elements – have been expropriated and suppressed, the rest of the groups all fall into a general undifferentiated category of 'masses'; there is no identification of specificity of interests that must exist among the various groups that compose that category. It is important to remember the context in which this description is rooted: the requirement of anti-imperialist struggle against Japan that had led to the formation of a 'united front' of all classes based on common feelings of nationalism rather than socialist transformation (Mao, 1967b). The immediate post-revolutionary period of economic reconstruction also required the minimising of contradictions between sections of the population, hence Mao's definition of that stage as 'New Democracy' (Mao, 1967b) rather than socialism. The logic of New Democracy was adopted by the post-Mao leadership in the first phase of the reforms. While the economic changes have greatly outpaced Mao's proposals set out in the New Democracy article, the political rhetoric still echoes those proposals.

However, it is also significant that Mao did not choose to redefine his position on the composition of the 'masses' even at a later stage of radical politics – for example during the Cultural Revolution. While the very logic of Mao's theory of contradictions (Mao, 1967a: 311–47) made a differentiation of contending interests *necessary*, Mao never was able to recognise the political implication of his theory in his discourse. It was in actual political practice that particular distinctions were drawn, and positions redefined. For example, the intellectuals were 'defined out' of the category of the 'masses' through the smear campaigns launched against them as the 'ninth stinking category' but no theoretical explanations were given that would redefine their inclusion into the category of the masses.

Further, the element of policy formulation and implementation is also linked to that of 'mass line':

> We should go to the masses and learn from them, synthesise their experience into better, articulated principles and methods, then do propaganda among the masses, and call upon them to put these principles and methods into practice so as to solve their problems and help them achieve liberation and happiness. (Mao, 1967c: 158)

The roots of the CPC cadres in the masses must not be shaken and must be constantly strengthened, as through them party/state policies are to be transmitted and authority delegated down the CPC's line of command to mobilise mass 'enthusiasm' in order to implement the particular policy. This was important in the period of economic reconstruction for efficient goal achievement. The CPC's revolutionary experience in guerrilla warfare buttressed the Maoist conviction that the support and mobilisation of the 'masses' was the best guarantee against failure of transformative politics. The revolutionary military principle that the communist guerrillas had put into effect during the wars against Japan and the Guomindang, of giving up territorial 'space' to gain 'time' which was to be used to create a mass political 'will', was also reflected in the way socio-economic policies were sought to be implemented, viz. the Great Leap Forward (GLF) campaign and the Cultural Revolution. Objective economic difficulties were to be overcome by the mobilised political will of the masses. When criticised by his more cautious colleagues, Mao responded impatiently during the GLF:

> During this trip, I have witnessed the tremendous energy of the masses. On this foundation, it is possible to accomplish any task whatsoever . . . There are still a few comrades who are unwilling to undertake large-scale mass movement in the industrial sphere. They call the mass movement on the industrial front 'irregular' and disparage it as 'rural style of work' and a 'guerrilla habit'. This is obviously incorrect. (Mao, in Schram, 1969: 352–3)

The essential element in Mao's strategy of development was the mobilisation of mass enthusiasm and effort, for which good relations between cadres and the people were crucial:

> It is on these cadres and leaders that the Party relies for its links with the membership and the masses, and it is by relying on their firm leadership of the masses that the Party can succeed in defeating the enemy. Such cadres and leaders must be free from selfishness, from individualistic heroism, ostentation, sloth, passivity, and arrogant sectarianism, and they must be selfless national and class heroes. (Mao, 1967a: 291)

Thus, the emphasis was on the personal qualities of cadres' style of leadership rather than institutional organisations and processes. The potential for personalisation of politics becomes much more evident in such a construction of the leader–led relationship when the position of leadership is legitimised through personal moral qualities rather than the organisational position held by it:

> Both the revolutionary and counter-revolutionary fronts must have someone to act as their leader, someone to serve as their commander . . . Comrade Stalin is the leader of the world revolution. Because he is there, it is easier to get things done. As you know, Marx is dead, and Engels and Lenin too are dead. *If we did not have a Stalin, who would give the orders?* (Mao, in Schram, 1970: 172 (Schram's italics)

The organisation thus fades in significance in comparison to the leader; the Party disappears in the face of the tremendous emphasis on the role of the individual leader's construction of policy ('orders'), which are implemented through mobilising the masses. Another implication of this is the emphasis on direct contact between cadres and the people rather than contact through representative institutions, which further tends to support the pattern of personalised politics.

Thus, three elements can be separated out of Mao's definition of the 'mass line': first, a description of the 'masses' that remains, despite Mao's emphasis on class struggle under socialism, an undifferentiated, conflated one. Second, a definition of the leader–led relationship that tends to devalue institutions, organisations, and processes in favour of exceptional individuals and loyal cadres. Finally there is an emphasis on a strategy for mobilisation of mass enthusiasm towards implementation of policy, as opposed to autonomous participation of the people through independent organisations in both decision-making and implementation.

'There will always be heads'

The lack of institutionalised pluralist politics in China also affected the relationship between mass organisations and the Party. The mass organisations that were formed during the post-revolution period functioned primarily as channels for transmitting party/state policies rather than as interest group lobbies. Their function was to mobilise their membership for the execution of the Party policies. Broadly, these organisations were established on the basis either of common professional or ideological interests – the Educational Union in the universities, for example – or of shared production or residential units – residents' committees, production teams. In both cases membership was automatic and involuntary. Such an organisational pattern reflected an artificial homogenisation of interests of various sections of the population. Further, involuntary, mass membership led to a lack of enthusiasm and participation, affecting the efficiency and legitimacy of the organisation itself. Individual members tried to realise their interests through personal contacts (*guanxi*) with the local leadership. Given the 'mass line' emphasis on personal contact between the leaders and the general membership of any organisation, this pattern of interest representation became more easily acceptable.

This pattern of organisational functioning was changed during points of political crisis, for example during the Cultural Revolution, when mass organisations were used to mobilise support for competing factions of political leadership. During these periods, however, groups were also identified as espousing 'counter-revolutionary', 'revisionist' or 'adventurist', 'ultra-leftist' politics in order to attain their particular interests. Mao's attack on the party/state bureaucracy and the intelligentsia was an acknowledgement of groups that had interests distinct from that of his own, which he described as the majority interest – 'proletarian politics'. This acknowledgement of different interests, however, did not find an institutional reflection. Organisations continued to be organised around broad socio-economic categories; it was the individuals within these organisations who came to be targeted for 'criticism' or 'reform' as well as for praise and recommendation.

Mao's analysis of the Party was also made on the same lines. On the one hand, his criticism of 'capitalist roaders' taking the rightist road in the Party mounted:

> In many localities there is a practice prevalent almost to the point of being universal: right opportunists within the Party, working hand in glove with the forces of capitalism in society, are preventing the broad masses of poor and lower middle peasants from taking the road to the formation of cooperatives. (Mao, in Schram, 1970: 184)

On the other hand, he was also concerned to reiterate that the Party was still the only available instrument, and indeed the only conceivable instrument for leading the revolution:

> Whether or not socialist transformation of our agriculture can keep

pace with the rate of advance of industrialisation in our country,
whether or not the co-operative movement can develop in a healthy
fashion . . . depends on whether or not the local party committees at
all levels can quickly and correctly shift the emphasis to this task . . .
A change of this kind depends first and foremost on the secretaries of
the Party Committees at various levels. (Lewis, 1970: 185)

The authority of the party/state and sections of Party leadership
was to be challenged in political practice but the notion of
authority and hierarchy which was crucial to the Party's power and
functioning was not questioned:

> The slogan of 'doubt everything and overthrow everything' is
> reactionary. The Shanghai People's Council demanded that Premier
> of the State Council should do away with all heads. This is extreme
> anarchism, it is most reactionary . . . In reality there will still always
> be 'heads'. (Mao, Schram, 1973: 95)

The struggle between the different political factions in the Party
did not find any institutional reflection. Within the Party the
principle of 'democratic centralism' continued to be central to
maintaining discipline. The recognition of fundamental disagree-
ments within the Party did not lead to any discussion about their
independent articulation in the political sphere. On the contrary,
Khrushchev's attempt at a preliminary formalisation of different
economic interests represented within the Soviet Communist Party
by dividing it into an 'industrial Party' and an 'agricultural Party'
was repudiated by the Chinese leadership under Mao (CPC CC
1965).

The Maoist approach to political participation was, thus, influenced by various factors: first, his belief in the masses as a
transformative force in China's history; second, a recognition of
the need of a responsive leadership to mobilise this force that was
especially important in the context of the mass-based military
strategy of guerrilla warfare that he favoured in China's national
liberation struggle; finally, the Leninist position on the structure
and functioning of a revolutionary organisation that Mao endorsed
and stood by. The primacy of the political sphere and the primacy
of the CPC in the political sphere led to a strengthening of the
position of the Party after the dust had settled on the highly
mobilisational period of the Cultural Revolution.

Post-Mao political practice: from mobilisation to control?

The present leadership in China has attempted a fundamental break with the Maoist political practice. It has rejected the mobilisational and personalised politics of the Maoist period in favour of one more geared towards institutionalised control. However, such an attempt has led to an expansion of the public political sphere in ways unintended by the leadership. As direct, oppressive political control loosened to complement economic reform, more radical demands were mounted for greater expansion of participation in decision-making and policy implementation both inside and outside the party/state structure. There was much confusion and debate among those making demands about the nature and direction of the reforms. However, we can distinguish three different responses to the Maoist political model.

The first is that proposed by Deng Xiaoping – a controlled loosening of Party control at the local level to complement the marketisation of the economy, while retaining central control over decision-making apparatuses. As an analysis of its programme for limited political change will show, it is still confined within the political framework established during the Maoist years. It is, however, close to a theoretical model that has resurrected a reconstructed version of Samuel Huntington's theories of destabilisation because of a 'lag' between political institutionalisation and socio-political participation. The 'new authoritarian' theorists in China take the view that Chinese people are not yet ready for an increased role in political life because of their 'backwardness', because of a lack of democratic tradition in China, and the imperatives of economic growth facing the country. We find echoes of the consumer-rights model of 'democracy' of the New Right in this approach. Second, there are those intellectuals who are fired by the ideals of western liberal democracy; their discourse is one of individual rights and liberty, and they reject the socialist framework. Finally, there are those who would call themselves 'marxist humanists' who would like to see the dismantling of the state socialist political structure, to replace it with an autonomous participative socialist public sphere. This last group, however, remains on the fringes of the political debate.

Licensed participation: the Party remains in charge

Deng Xiaoping, like his mentor Liu Shaoqi, is a good 'Party-man'. As such, an essential part of his critique of the Maoist period has included the importance of cadres in the process of political change in China. This echoes Liu's belief that 'to consolidate over 95% of the cadres is a prerequisite to consolidation of over 95% of the masses' (Schram, 1973: 77). The role of the Party cadres was crucial to the task of reconstruction. Differences emerged between the two leaders regarding the nature of the Party. Mao gave importance to representation of the peasantry in the Party which he sought to make part of the working class by emphasising its subjective, revolutionary political character. Deng, on the other hand, was concerned with minimising the importance of objective class origins altogether:

> The distinction that was hitherto made in the procedure of admitting new members has been removed because the former classification of social status has lost or is losing its original meaning . . . The difference between workers and office employees is now only a matter of division of labour within the same class . . . The vast majority of our intellectuals have now come over politically to the side of the working class, and a rapid change is taking place in their family background . . . What is the point then, of classifying these social strata into two different categories? (Deng, in CPC CC 1956: 200)

This was a different political perspective from that of Mao's stand on the 'masses' discussed above, but the result was similar – the collapsing of boundaries of distinct interests into one organisational body. That this organisation was the Party assumes greater political significance as it could then become the sole legitimate representative organisation for 'the whole people' rather than the revolutionary class, which was a more radical position than that of Mao. This was given theoretical form when the post-Mao leadership declared that China was still in its 'primary stage of socialism' at the 13th Congress of the CPC (see SWB/FE/8709/C1/6). Second, while this position pointed towards subjective conditions as the determining factor in classifying the class of an individual, it appeared in Deng's speech as an accomplished stage – it was not an ongoing process. What *was* in the process of changing was the 'family background', that is, the economic condition of the family; this was necessarily linked to Deng's concern with the rate of China's development.

The pattern of political practice which followed from these concerns was, therefore, very different from that of Mao's; the emphasis was on the role of the cadres to guide and control the process of political and economic development, rather than directly to mobilise the 'masses' to achieve that purpose:

> what is more important is whether the rank-and-file Party members, and *primarily* the high ranking cadres, can, in the various periods, apply the Marxist–Leninist stand, view point and method to sum up experience in the struggle, hold fast to the truth and correct mistakes. (*ibid.*: 98)

The political initiative was thus placed squarely in the hands of the cadres, rather than the individual leader or the mobilised masses.

When Deng came to power after a political eclipse that had lasted through much of the Cultural Revolution decade, a process of depoliticisation had set in as a reaction to the highly mobilisational period of the 1960s and '70s. It complemented the concern of the post-Mao leadership for stability in the political sphere that would allow for the movement towards a regulated and controlled pattern of economic growth and modernisation. As Zhao Ziyang said at the 13th Party Congress in October 1987:

> Whatever is conducive to the growth [of productive forces] is in keeping with the fundamental interests of the people and is therefore needed by socialism and allowed to exist. Conversely, whatever is detrimental to this growth goes against scientific socialism and is not allowed to exist. (BR no. 45, 1987: xxvi (inset))

To achieve economic growth there was required a change in controlling mechanisms, in the pattern of established political practice and in the role and position of the party/state.

'Political restructuring': dynamics of limited reform

The party/state had two options in order to achieve the goal of 'four modernisations' – of agriculture, industry, science and technology, and defence – that it set for China (Deng, 1984: 172).

First, to improve the economic situation through a better, more efficient use of technological/scientific expertise – to better utilise its existing corps of technicians and to rapidly expand their input into decision-making and implementation of policies. The second option was that of economic decentralisation – to slowly, but clearly withdraw the party-state from the economic sphere, thus releasing the forces of competition, incentives and rationalisation of production and distribution through the market, that was increasingly impossible to achieve through centralized planning. While the first option had the appeal of a lower potential of political destabilisation of the 'organisational principle' of a socialist state, the second option seemed to promise a quicker pace of change, and – more attractively – a lowering of the need for legitimising the party-state through the criteria of economic success. The Deng regime seemed to oscillate between these two strategies. The first step it took was in the political sphere.

It attempted to redefine certain key concepts which had been in circulation in the Chinese public sphere for a long time – politics, ideology, class, class struggle, egalitarianism, mass line, and Mao Zedong Thought. This was essential if the new policies were to be politically legitimised; it was also central to salvaging the prestige of the Party which had been severely damaged during the Cultural Revolution. Correct politics was defined in terms of 'seeking the truth from facts' – the overwhelming 'facts' of China's economic backwardness and political instability presenting what the leadership described as the major contradictions to be resolved through the policy of economic modernisation. However, by 1986 it seemed that the regime was looking increasingly to the second option of decentralisation of the economy. The adoption of this strategy could have two alternative results: first, it could result in a 'reconstitution of the civil society'. Various economic interests would emerge, demanding legal, economic and individual rights on the one hand, and wanting to organise independent interest groups to conduct bargaining with each other and the party/state on the other. This would then lead to a demand for political pluralism at the level of decision-making. The second alternative could be a risk-minimising strategy: that of 'uncoupling' the Party and the state. This could have a further consequence: as the bargaining interest groups became active, and the party/state decentralised, the organisation of the 'uncoupled' Party would become more vulnerable to intrusion from the civil society. The 'possibility spaces' for the subversion of dominant organisational discourse would expand in such a context. Deng tried to adopt the second option of separation of powers without addressing the question of its impact upon the position of the Party. The administrative and the political institutions were to separate as part of a programme of 'political restructuring' that was put on the political agenda by Deng in 1986. Deng identified the problems facing the post-Mao Chinese political system in terms of 'bureaucracy, over-concentration of power, patriarchal methods, life tenure in leading posts and privileges of various kinds' (Deng, 1984: 309).

Deng tried to redefine the role of the Party at two different levels. First, between the central Party leadership whose decision-making authority was to be unchallenged, and the local Party branches which were to be opened to criticism and supervision in their tasks of policy implementation. '[In]appropriate and indiscriminate concentration of all power in [local] Party Committees in the name of strengthening centralised Party leadership' was criticised (*ibid.*). Local leaders were accused of concentrating too much power in their hands which was 'incompatible with the development of our socialist cause' (*ibid.*). This attempt at bifurcating responsibility and power was to create major dysfunctions within the party system as the patron–client relations between national and provincial leaders were disturbed (see Chapter 4).

A second redefinition that Deng proposed was that of the party/ state relationship. Separation of executive and political powers and functions was made the centre-piece of China's political restructuring. It was regarded as a prerequisite for efficient implementation of the new economic policies:

> it is time for us to distinguish between the responsibility of the Party and those of the government and to stop substituting the former for the latter. [Party members should] concentrate their energies on our Party work, on matters concerning the Party's line, guiding principles and policies. This will help strengthen and improve the unified leadership of the Central Committee, facilitate the establishment of an effective work system at the various levels of government . . . and promote a better exercise of governmental functions and powers.
> (*ibid.*: 303)

Economic modernisation was the goal that required for its efficient achievement a political system conducive to its needs, especially once the decision was taken to introduce market forces to right the imbalances of the Maoist period. An infrastructure was needed for this that the leadership felt it lacked. As Vice-Premier Wan Li said:

> we have not yet established a rigorous system and procedure for policy decision-making, nor have we had an adequate support system, consultancy system, appraisal system, supervision system, feedback system for that purpose. (SWB/FE/BII, 2 August 1986)

This concern with efficiency and rationality in the economic sphere led to a shift from the mobilisational practice of the Maoist period to one of organisation and control:

> Historical experience has shown that no problem of mass ideological education was ever solved by launching a mass movement instead of organising exhaustive persuasion and calm discussion, and that no currently functioning systems were ever reformed or new ones established by substituting a mass movement for solid, systematic measures. (Deng, 1984: 319)

Here the question was posed not in terms of learning from the masses to refine their ideas into a theoretical political 'line' but to 'educate' and 'persuade' them of the leadership's policies.

Further, this process was to be carried out by first acknowledging the existence of differentiated interests and, second, regulating the various organisations that represented these. It is interesting to note here that though some professional groups were allowed to form associations, these were built around the area of expertise shared by these groups and not their position *vis-à-vis* the production of goods or services they were involved in. Thus, for example in the academic sphere, 'salons' around various subject areas were established, and already-established 'think-tanks' and research organisations like the Chinese Academy of Social Sciences (CASS) were reactivated. These, however, do not represent the group material interests of their membership, which continue to be represented by the mass organisations like the Educational Union (see Chapter 3). The character of these organisations continues to be the same: they are undifferentiated organisations in which all interests of a particular professional unit are collapsed; they retain their monopoly of representing all the various interests in one unit, and continue to function under the 'leadership of the Party'.

However, while the post-Mao emphasis on organisational reforms did not lead to a significant structural change in this sphere, these organisations were encouraged to follow functional procedures more rigorously:

> congresses or conferences of representatives of workers and office staff will be introduced in all enterprises and institutions. That was decided long ago. The question now is how to popularise and perfect the system. These congresses or conferences have the right to discuss and take decisions on major questions of concern to their representative units, to propose to the higher organisations the recall of incompetent administrators, and to introduce – gradually and within appropriate limits – the practice of electing their leaders. (*ibid.*: 323)

Collective decision-making, division of labour, and individual responsibility were emphasised as means of better management of time and resources and more efficient functioning of these organisations.

The question of the relationship of these mass interest organisations to the party/state remains crucial, however, and has remained unaddressed. While it is significant that an attempt was made to make the distinction between the central Party leadership and the local Party committees, it is also true that the traditional role of these organisations as party/state-supporting bodies was not questioned; they continued to be looked upon as transmission belts of state policies. These associations were thus given the licence to participate in the public sphere without redefining their institutional relations with the party/state. Thus, for example, the 'tasks' of the Chinese Women's Federation, at its annual conference in 1978, were defined as:

> [to] resolutely implement the Party's general and specific policies and fully arouse enthusiasm among the broad masses of women, and to mobilise the women to carry out the general tasks for the women's movement. (Croll, 1983: 3)

As Croll commented, this would imply that

> the new line of the Party was to be the fundamental line of the women's movement and that the central task of the Party was also the central task of the women's movement. (*ibid.*: 123)

The interests of the party/state and the 'masses' were, therefore, once again conflated. Hence, any opposition to its decisions by these mass organisations would involve questioning the primary position of the Party in the political process. However, the leadership made it clear that

> [the] purpose of reforming the system of Party and state leadership is precisely to maintain and further strengthen Party leadership and discipline and not to weaken or relax them. In a big country like ours, it is inconceivable that unity of thinking could be achieved among our several hundred million people or that their efforts could be pooled to build socialism in the absence of a Party whose members have a spirit of sacrifice and a high level of political awareness and discipline, a Party that truly represents and unites masses of people and exercises unified leadership. (Deng, 1984: 324)

The purpose of reform, thus, was to better employ the organisational network that the Party commanded in order that efforts of the masses could be harnessed to achieve efficient and economical modernisation. Whereas the 'four modernisations' encapsulated the general direction of economic development envisaged by the leadership, the 'four cardinal principles' set out the framework within the boundaries of which this development is to be achieved:

> The Central Committee maintains that to carry out China's four modernisations, we must uphold the four cardinal principles ideologically and politically. The four principles are
>   1. We must keep to the socialist road.
>   2. We must uphold the dictatorship of the proletariat.
>   3. We must uphold the leadership of the Communist Party.
>   4. We must uphold Marxism, Leninism, and Mao Zedong Thought. (*ibid*.: 264–5)

Addressing the activists of the 'Democracy Wall Movement' of 1977–9, Deng warned:

> If, like some of the people who put up big character posters on the 'xidan wall', a person emancipates his mind by departing from the four cardinal principles, he is actually placing himself in opposition to the Party and the people. (Deng, 1987: 106)

While there was an attempt at formalising the reforms through activating the legal system, this stopped short of addressing the question of the Party. Thus, the implications of distinctions that were drawn between various levels of Party authority, or the importance being given to newly emerging interest organisations as representative bodies, were worked out in actual practice, not through any institutional change. This made these officially licensed organisations vulnerable to attack by the party-state in situations of political reaction as witnessed during and after the Tian'anmen demonstrations.

Thus, the pattern of political practice being espoused by the post-Mao leadership, while distinguishing itself sharply from the Maoist model on questions of importance of organisation, of regulated and repeated political participation, of a non-mobilisational approach to politics, continued to reflect many of the traditional Leninist and Maoist concerns regarding the position of the Communist Party in a socialist state.

Such an approach to political reform had implications for the process of policy implementation: confusion as to the real position of the leadership on the question of autonomous participation; cynicism and withdrawal of the individual citizens from active participation in the public sphere on the one hand, and working around the sanctioned participative organisations on the other. This has made policy implementation an unpredictable, unchartered business and hence inefficient. It has also left unanswered the questions of participation and democracy it seemed to address in the period before the current political retreat.

The response to limited reform

The economic reforms introduced by the Deng regime, based as they were on reconciling the party/state with the intelligentsia, elicited an élitist response from a section of China's higher intelligentsia. The licensed participation offered by the state was not only acceptable to this group, but it was also welcomed by it. It was sought to be legitimised in political discourse as 'New Authoritarianism' which was first articulated by some intellectuals in 1986. Representatives of this group are Zhang Bingjiu of Beijing University, Xiao Gongqing and Wang Juntao. While the new élitist model of democracy actually echoed the Deng model, in conceptualising it as such it lost the support of the ruling group: 'To the politician new authoritarianism is something that can be done but not talked about'.

New authoritarianism drew its theoretical inspiration from the work of Samuel Huntington, and empirical evidence from the experience of the 'four little dragons' (Singapore, Hong Kong, Taiwan, and South Korea). The intellectuals who used and developed this concept saw new authoritarianism as a stage in the development of China's economic and political life. It was a 'transition to democracy', a 'midwife of modern democratic politics' (JPRS-CAR-89-080, 31 July 1989: 9). New authoritarianism was an attack on those democratic critics who 'ignored the facts' that China 'does not have a tradition in the rule of law, is economically backward, has an undereducated populace, and lacks the prerequisites for entry into the developmental stage where economic freedom and political autocracy achieve a balance' (JPRS-CAR-89-070, 6 July 1989: 11). What was called for was not authoritarianism of the old kind that denied a participative role to all sections of the population. What was encouraged was what Huntington called 'vulgar politics' (1968), an élitist democratic model where there 'is autocracy based not on depriving individual freedom; rather, authority is used to smash obstacles that block the development of individual freedom in order to protect individual freedom' (*ibid.*).

Two distinctions were thus made – between economic and political freedom, and between individual freedom and democracy. Like the leadership, this group of intellectuals gave primacy to economic modernisation, and to individual freedom which was equated with the freedom of economic entrepreneurship. What was being advocated here was a postponement of the project of democracy in favour of economic development: 'commodity economy is not opposed to all forms of centralisation' (*ibid.*). A case was made for a strong state which would be advised in its project of economic modernisation by a section of the advanced intelligentsia. This section would be able to bargain with the state for better facilities for work and living, and thus slowly introduce the elements of democratic practice to the political system. Economic modernisation, fuelled by this co-operation, would lay the basis for increased resource investment in education which in turn would make the transition to full democracy feasible. In this way China's traditional political culture, that was fundamentally authoritarian, would be slowly transformed into a modern democratic system. There was in this analysis an implicit rejection of class politics in looking at economic modernisation as an 'objective' goal to be achieved by a coming together of a strong state/

authority and the technological intelligentsia. The question of the role of the CPC in China's political system was thus examined through the prism of the modernisation theory – support the sections within the Party that support modernisation. This again leaves unaddressed the issue of the nature of the Party authority in favour of personality-led factions. Party authority is also seen as a necessary arbiter between groups of the 'theoretical community' who cannot reach a consensus on the direction that economic reform must take (Ding, *op. cit.*). The question of political participation is taken up by these intellectuals but decided in their own favour – it is a limited, licensed participation that they demand, élitist in nature, authoritarian in structure. These new élitists, while rejected by the state they looked to for support, were also attacked by the more radical democrats.

Autonomous participation or limited representation?

Among the radical democrats we again find fundamental differences. There are the 'political modernisers' like Yan Jiaqi, Fang Lizhi, Wang Ruowang, Sun Liping who looked upon the course of Chinese politics as a failure of individual authority. Leaders were fallible, and therefore structures and conventions, rules and regulations were needed to keep their power in check and ensure that a change in leadership could be brought about if and when desired by the people (JPRS-CAR-89-088, 21 August 1989: 8). Rule of law was thus the protection needed against a malfunctioning authority: 'democracy is a mechanism for correcting errors in a timely or relatively timely way. Democratic politics are the politics of correcting mistakes in accordance with established procedures.' (*ibid.*: 9) This authority could be an individual like Mao, or it could be an organisation like the Communist Party of China. Wang Ruoshui argued that alienation was not just a feature of capitalism but also of the socialist system where the untrammelled authority of the party was unbounded by accountability to the people in whose name it ruled. The Western liberal categories of representative democracy are evident here. The literary critic Liu Xiaobo put the case of the democrats this way: 'The substitution of democracy for despotism is not the substitution of an enlightened ruler for a muddleheaded one, but the substitution of laws for rule of man and the substitution of separation of powers for dictatorship.' (JPRS-CAR-89-088, 21 August 1989: 10) The democrats also took issue with the good cadre/bad cadre element of the communist political practice in China: 'the substitution of a virtuous personality for a good system has a most fatal weakness. When a regime is on the decline, putting the blame on moral degeneration can only conceal the corruption of the system itself.' (*ibid.*) A 'political responsibility system' was the corrective to this Maoist tendency of 'perfect-man politics' on the one hand (JPRS-CAR-89-078, 27 July 1989: 2) and the new authoritarian faith in an 'enlightened despotism' on the other (JPRS-CAR-89-078, 27 July 1989: 53). Mobilised and licensed participation were both under attack; the alternative was 'constitution writing' and 'direct election' (*ibid.*: 3).

However, these intellectuals seemed unable to get away from an inherently instrumentalist approach to democracy. Increased participation continued to be a corrective for the existing political ills, not a value in itself: 'When the issue in question has well-defined objectives and generates no differences in values, we must look to science, to think tanks, and to brain trusts. On scientific issues, therefore, we should not submit to the majority, but always to the truth', advised Yan Jiaqi (Yan, *op. cit.*: 9). The intellectual positivism and élitism evident here formed part of the democratic theory espoused by this group. It was also unable to address the question of how to reconcile economic pluralism that the state seemed to be offering and social equality that seemed to get eclipsed in the drive for modernisation.

Traditional Chinese concerns with centralised authority of the state were also not fully addressed. On the one hand there was the espousal of a multi-party political system, on the other a refusal to take on the implications of such a system in a country where the provinces and nationalities are as varied as they are in China. The advantage of a democratic structure, writes Zhang Weiguo, is that its 'administrative power should be centralized, but it should also be subject to constitutional and legal limits. The fragmentation of state power is the product of the absence of a system of political responsibility.' (Zhang, *op. cit.*: 3) While in recent pronouncements Yan Jiaqi has come out in favour of a 'federation with confederated characteristics', how much this is in response to the situation of exile and the need for support from overseas Chinese and Taiwan is not clear. The student movement of 1989, which drew its inspiration from this strand of democratic theory in China, reveals the contradictions that this theory is unable to resolve. There was a persistent attempt by the students, and not simply for strategic and tactical reasons, to keep the broader sections of the people away from joining their movement. Certainly, there was a tactical consideration of retaining control over the movement, but there was also an inherent élitism of the intellectuals and a suspicion of the 'masses'; their support was welcome but not their participation.

Political participation has also been the concern of another section of the radical democratic Chinese intelligentsia – those who retain their belief in Marxism, but reject the Stalinist variant of the 'existing socialist states'. Su Shaozhi, Wang Ruoshui, Su Ming could be regarded as representative of this section. Su Shaozhi's critique of the reforms introduced by the post-Mao leadership stems from two concerns. First, that modernisation is a broader concept than the Four Modernisations of the Deng regime: 'Modernization should include modernization of the political structure, social and cultural modernization and ideological modernization . . . China needs modernization, but not only the "four modernizations".' (Su, 1988: 161) Second, that China needs a socialist system but one which is 'humanistic' in character; that there is a need to 'reunderstand socialism'. In this context he looks to Western Marxism that developed out of the Frankfurt School and takes as his starting-point the freedom of the individual: 'under the influence of Stalinism, the progress of "humanization" was converted into the progress of "mechanization"'. (*ibid.*: 180) Wang Ruoshui also took up this theme in 1983 with his analysis of the concept of alienation under existing socialist societies:

> In Marx, proletarian dictatorship was only a means to an end, human freedom . . . Yet in China, not only hasn't it been propagated; some people have even labeled it erroneous . . . Some people [read leaders] used the idea of the collective to force individuals to sacrifice their own individuality to the interests of a small group who claim to represent the collective. This is what I call an alienated collective. (Nathan, 1990: 7)

However, while this critique of the existing socialism in China is from the left, the programme for political reform largely limits itself to that proposed by the liberal democrats (*ibid.*: 166). While these critics urge a re-evaluation of Marxism, they are unable to bring together the socialist concern with equality and the political impulse towards greater participation. They remain suspicious of 'peasant socialism', but offer no alternative but to develop commodity production. Further, they give little indication about the alternative political strategy that would help resolve the contradictions between the 'long-term interests of the whole people' and the 'immediate and specific interests of the different groups' which arise as a result of the introduction of a market economy.

The economic reforms introduced by the post-Mao leadership have loosened the controls by the party/state over the civil society in China. With this has also arisen the question of the representation of the differentiated interests that had been denied any recognition until now. It is in this context that the debate about political participation has become crucial. An engagement with this demand for increased participation was critical for the regime for reasons both of legitimacy and of efficacy. The suppression of the protest movement was also a refusal by the dominant section within the Party to do so. Today the alienation of various sections of the Chinese population from the regime is evident. Though the student movement has been suppressed, this has not wiped the question of political participation from the Chinese political slate. That question will have to be readdressed if Chinese modernisation and development is to become a reality. On the part of the critical intellectual élite of China, this concept poses different questions. An analysis of democratic élitism, especially in the Chinese cultural context, is essential here. One lesson that we must draw from the Chinese student movements of the past decade concerns the limitations that such a narrow base of social protest imposes. The threat of suppression or of expropriation remains greater in a movement that involves only a minute section of the population, however active. An analysis of the reforms introduced in the sphere of higher education since 1978 provides a concrete illustration of the nature of the contradictions facing the Chinese political system.

2

Modernising education: the post-Mao reforms

The old order changeth

The political context in which the reforms in the system of higher education were introduced in China was highly charged. The year 1976 had dawned heralding tremendous changes in the life of the Chinese nation. On 8 January Zhou Enlai, the charming, astute and moderate premier of the State Council of China died at the age of 78. His death was to be the first signpost of the coming U-turn from Maoist radicalism to the pragmatism of Deng Xiaoping. It also sparked off what came to be known as the 'Tian'anmen Incident' – the first open defiance of the party/state authority by the people after the Cultural Revolution. In early April, thousands of people in Beijing took advantage of the Qing Ming festival (an occasion to pay respect to the dead ancestors) to lay wreaths at the martyrs' column (which was to be the focus of the congregation of the student demonstrators in April–June 1989), to read poems in praise of Zhou as the symbol of moderation and rationality during the period of blinded chaos of the Cultural Revolution. These poems and wreaths were suddenly removed at the behest of the Maoist radicals then in power who, led by Mao's wife Jiang Qing, felt threatened at this public expression of grief for a moderate leader they regarded as unreliable and critical of their politics. Public outrage at this suppression led to demonstrations not only in Beijing but across the country which were forcibly put down. As the situation deteriorated, the wrath of an ailing Mao and his radical coterie fell on Deng Xiaoping who was regarded as a protégé of Zhou. Deng was dismissed from all his posts inside and outside the party on 7 April. Already in November 1975 Mao had given the call to 'criticise Deng and counter right deviationist trend to reverse correct verdicts' of the Cultural Revolution. This had been a response to the initial attempts by a dazed and battered bureaucracy under Zhou and Deng to begin to pick up the threads of administrative order after the storms of the Cultural Revolution.

The next blow to the party in disarray came on 6 July with the death of Zhu De, the founder of the Red Army and the hero of the Long March. The old order was passing; age laid to rest the spirits that had created and destroyed so much in the hope and frenzy to build a new China. As if he could not survive bereft of the support of these two long-standing, one suspects also long-suffering, comrades-in-arms by his side, Mao himself passed away on 9 September 1976. With him came an end to an era in Chinese politics. However, in February of that year he had, in a manner reminiscent of ancient Chinese emperors, nominated his successor in Hua Guofeng, a Hunanese party bureaucrat with little base in the Party. Mao wrote to Hua, 'With you in charge, I am at ease'; these words subsequently represented Hua's power base in the Party! Hua was made the acting premier of the State Council and on 7 April 1976 the first vice-chairman of the Party Central Committee and the premier of the State Council. For a second time, however, Mao was to prove unsuccessful in choosing the right successor. Lin Biao, Marshal of the PLA and Mao's first chosen successor, had betrayed his trust, and history overtook Hua Guofeng. At the third plenum of the Eleventh Party Congress in 1982 Deng Xiaoping effectively took over the levers of power.

But even before Hua slid into obscurity the footfalls of change could be heard – Maoist orthodoxy was cautiously, but clearly, challenged. This was made possible because of a pragmatic coming together of moderate Maoists like Ye Jianying, and the 'capitalist roaders' of the Cultural Revolution under Deng to 'reverse the verdict' of the radicalism of the later years of Mao's rule. There was a sense of urgency to restore 'normalcy' to China's socio-economic life on all sides – among those who had suffered and those who had escaped the scarring of the 'ten years of turmoil'. The Chinese government now claimed that there was an increase of only 1.7 per cent in industrial and agricultural output value in

1976; the financial deficit had reached 2.96 billion yuan (BR, 1989). Reconstruction was the only agenda. The threat to this agenda came from the 'gang of four' – Jiang Qing, Yao Wenyuan, Zhang Chunqiao and Wang Hongwen – which was expelled from the Party by this new alliance.

While the party/state realigned themselves, the social order was also experiencing change. The 'Tian'anmen Incident' of 1976 was the spark that lit the little fires of dissent that were to become the big blaze in 1989. A 'Democracy Wall Movement' emerged that was a rejection of the mobilisational politics of the Cultural Revolution and an affirmation of the right of citizen participation in politics. It was organised primarily by workers and university students of the Cultural Revolution generation who put out a whole series of journals and bulletins to express their views and demand the attention of the new, emerging leadership. This movement was to play a crucial part in the now accelerating struggle for power between Hua and Deng.

Deng had consolidated his already significant hold on the Party bureaucracy by this time and now wanted to experiment without the constraints of Maoist orthodoxy restricting him; Hua was desperately trying to balance Mao's rhetoric of 'proletarian hegemony' in politics and Deng's attempt to put the 'expert' in command of the drive for economic modernisation. The break became inevitable when Deng openly declared that the '"Two whatever" Do Not Accord With Marxism' (Deng, 1984). This was an answer to the statement that 'we will resolutely uphold whatever policy decisions Chairman Mao made, and unswervingly follow whatever instructions Chairman Mao gave' which appeared in RMRB on 7 February 1977 in an editorial and which generally reflected the position of Hua and his group. In November 1978 the Tian'anmen Incident was declared by the Beijing Party Committee to be a revolutionary act of the masses. This was the time when Deng's popularity was soaring, as he came to be regarded as the moderniser of China's economy and a leader who had the courage to admit the mistakes the Party had made and begin anew. This was also the time, as the horrors of the Cultural Revolution were allowed public airing, that the Party's legitimacy first came to be challenged. It was no longer the representative of a single, unified Truth reflecting the Chinese civil society, which now began the painful process of breaking away from the control of the party/

state. On the contrary, in its untrammelled power it had shown itself to be weak, corrupt, brutal and divorced from the reality of the people it sought to speak for. The Pandora's Box that was opened by the criticism of the Cultural Revolution – a necessity of power for the pragmatic faction – led to the first open questioning of its right to rule, though in as yet a tentative, conciliatory, reformist way. This is what made the Democracy Wall movement of 1978–9 important.

The first wall poster (*dazibao*) criticising Mao appeared on a wall near Zhongnanhai, the official residence of the Chinese leadership in central Beijing on 19 November 1978. In a period of political vacuum at the top, the grassroots movement flourished and thousands gathered in Tian'anmen Square to read the increasingly frequent wall posters, recite poems, hear and give speeches (see Munro, 1984). Unofficial journals like *April 5th Forum*, *Peking Spring*, *Exploration*, *Science Democracy and Legal System*, became the intellectual backbone of the movement. On the whole these journals reflected variations of Marxist analyses of the reality in China. The groups producing these considered themselves not as 'dissidents' but as supporters and allies of the new leadership. They saw a leadership committed to a policy of 'socialist democracy and legality', against the Maoist practice of social labelling that had made millions of innocents suffer so terribly, and to an economic recovery that promised an end to the irrationality of 'egalitarianism' in a poverty-stricken country like China. Most of the activists cast themselves in the role of 'remonstrators rather than opponents, pressing the party to reform in its own interests and in keeping with its own ideals'. (Nathan, 1990: 172)

However, early in 1979, after the third plenary session of the Eleventh Party Congress in December 1978 during which the Dengist faction consolidated its position in the Party, the Democracy Wall movement came under attack in the name of 'stability and unity'. A movement had been launched to criticise the 'gang of four' in 1977–8, but as the criticism of the 'gang' led to increasing analysis of the political system which had spawned them, and which they had been allowed to manipulate, the CPC closed ranks; the 'General Political Department's [of the PLA] decision to end the mass movement to expose and criticize the gang of four [was] . . . approved by the Military Commission of the CPC Central Committee' (SWB/FE/5993/i, 13 December 1978). The post-Cultural

Revolution importance of the army is quite evident here, and was again demonstrated in the events to come in 1989.

The political agenda that was set was one that was geared towards ensuring mechanisms of control – the weeding out of the members of the radical faction, and the demarcation of limits of popular participation in the political life. The Party was to be protected from public criticism even if the critics were supporters of the ruling faction. There was a further incentive in this exercise of control: some posters on the democracy wall criticised not only the Party but also the modernisation programme launched by Deng Xiaoping. A railway worker enquired 'whether the planned modernisation is a modernisation of Soviet-style, American-and-Japanese-style, or a Yugoslav style. The Chinese general public has not been informed about what type.' (SWB/FE/6000/BII/4, 21 December 1978) Others criticised the growing gap in wages and the insecurity in jobs being faced by middle-aged and elderly workers as a result of the policy introducing market forces in the economy, and the tendency of such a system to give 'priority to the strong'. This revealed to the party/state that the 'Democracy Wall Movement' had expanded the constituency of critics: they came not just from among the intellectuals but also from among the working class. The movement no longer seemed led and supported only by those who had suffered directly from the ultra-radicalism of the Cultural Revolution; the 'bourgeois individualism' of the intellectuals could no longer be shown to be the basis of this movement. Lenin was quoted in the political texts of the Party to speak against 'spontaneity'. Another way the Party tried to control the growing movement was by attempting to expropriate it for its own:

> Although the April 5th Movement was not a mass movement led directly by the party, all the comrades who participated in the movement had undergone many years of training by our party, and many of the key forces were communist party members and party cadres. (Nanfang Ribao, 1 June 1979; JPRS 73857, 18 July 1979: 19)

On 30 March 1979 Deng Xiaoping had enumerated the 'four cardinal principles' – socialist road, proletarian dictatorship, leadership of the Communist Party and adherence to Marxism–Leninism, Mao Zedong Thought – that ensured the monopoly of power by the CPC, and made unacceptable any challenge of political pluralism to the hegemony of the Party. These 'principles' were then tied to the project of economic modernisation, as the instruments for securing 'stability and unity' that were made prerequisites for economic growth. We can see here the narrow confines within which 'democracy' was placed: for Deng democracy was 'an instrument of mobilization whose function is to strengthen the links of citizens to the state, rather than a set of procedures for limiting state power to protect individual rights' (Nathan, 1990: 175).

As the Democracy Wall Movement became more radical it became increasingly important for the leadership to label it as deviant. This was done by criminalising the more radical element of the movement:

> We must continue to strike resolutely at various kinds of criminals, so as to ensure and consolidate a sound, secure public order . . . It is absolutely impermissible to propagate freedom of speech, of the press, of assembly and of association in ways implying that counter-revolutionaries may also enjoy them, and it is absolutely impermissible to make contacts with counter-revolutionaries and other criminals unbeknownst to the Party organisation. (Deng, 1984: 238)

However, for those who chose to operate within the parameters set by the Party, there was the licence to participate in criticism of the political system. This was regarded as necessary incentive for securing their continued support for the modernisation drive. Intellectuals were to be made the favoured category:

> We have stated there should be no arbitrary intervention concerning what to write about and how to write it. We will adhere to the policy of 'letting a hundred flowers bloom, a hundred schools of thought contend' . . . and we will drop the slogan that literature and art are subordinate to politics, because it is too easily used as a theoretical pretext for arbitrary intervention in literary and art work. (Deng, 1984: 240)

This official consent to criticise was further widened in 1986 with 'political restructuring' put on the agenda and the administrative role of the Party reviewed and attacked (Deng, 1987). In this attempt the regime was fairly successful as the majority of the intellectuals were till then unwilling to associate themselves with the more radical elements of the Democracy Wall Movement whom they considered to be premature and even irresponsible.

However, for those who were by now demanding an end to the Communist Party's monopoly of power and were rejecting Deng's attempts at reforms as irreconcilable with China's political reality (see Chen, 1984: 120–40), retribution came soon. The leadership was either arrested or driven underground; Wei Jingsheng who was sentenced to 15 years' imprisonment in October 1979 became the new regime's most famous victim. The Democracy Wall was closed down later that month. While the unofficial journals were banned, the activists kept the movement alive until 1981 through participating in the People's Congress election which the Electoral Law of 1980 had thrown open to individuals and China's eight, toothless, 'democratic parties'. Individuals like Hu Shi won hard-fought elections and paid for their success with enforced unemployment. In 1981 the first campaign against 'bourgeois liberalisation' was launched and the Democracy Wall Movement was labelled 'anti-Party and anti-socialist'. By April 1981 almost 30 of the leaders of the movement were in prison; Wei Jingsheng became the most famous prisoner of conscience of post-Mao China (see Benton, 1982). Most other activists disbanded. The grassroots movement for political reform in China came to a temporary rest.

When it re-emerged first in 1985 and more openly in 1986–7 it took on a different character than the Democracy Wall Movement of 1979. This was primarily due to two reasons. First, during this period the economic reforms of the Deng leadership had taken off. The early to mid-1980s were a time of growth and optimism. Chinese economy was thriving after the restrictions on 'commodity production' were lifted, foreign investment invited in, land de-collectivised, and individual enterprise not only accepted but encouraged. The introduction of 'material incentives' and immediate, if temporary, rise in living standards meant that the working-class support for the Deng regime strengthened. Unemployment and inflation were still in the future. Second, the agenda of economic modernisation that the leadership had set itself had led to a radical restructuring of China's education policy. This was done both to reconcile the Chinese intelligentsia with the state, and to improve scientific and technological standards of the Chinese people which had so fallen behind during the 'ten years of chaos' of the Cultural Revolution. The new education policy as it unfolded achieved in part both the above objectives, but also produced some unintended consequences of which the student movement was one. As the Chinese universities opened out to the world, as new ideas came in with new technology, and the domestic situation changed radically, the dilemma that has confronted the Chinese state and its reformers from the period of Qing dynasty onwards, re-emerged. The attempted separation of '*ti*' and '*yong*', the moral and the technical/scientific dimension of knowledge, was attempted yet again by the Chinese leadership and yet again it failed in this purpose. Their appetites whetted by the partial reforms initiated by the leadership, the intelligentsia asked for more. Starting from a position of remonstrators, the intellectuals slowly moved to a more radical position.

There were more immediate reasons for discontent. By this time the students had begun to feel uneasy about government plans to cut their grants, and the continued activity of the Party cadres on university campuses, especially their involvement with job allocation for students and promotion of lecturers. Rising prices had led to a demand by the lecturers for increased salaries which could not be met by a government trying to keep the money supply in check. The way the education policy had been introduced and implemented in the universities had resulted in many unfulfilled expectations that had been raised by the post-Mao leadership itself. The ensuing frustration was an important cause for the students to take the lead in calling for democratic reform. Thus, while the unemployed, and exiled youth of the Cultural Revolution generation had formed the vanguard of the 1979 movement, by 1989 it was university students, one of the most privileged sections of the Chinese population, who carried the banners. It is this importance of students and intellectuals in the democratic movement that makes it necessary to understand the nature of the educational reforms formulated and implemented by the post-Mao leadership.

Educational reforms: the interregnum

The educational reforms began as cautiously as had the political. At the Eleventh Party Congress of the CPC held in 1977 the 'gang's' line of 'Two Estimates' in the field of education was criticised. The first 'estimate' was that in the 17 years between the founding of socialist China in 1949 and the start of the Cultural Revolution in 1966, 'Chairman Mao's proletarian line "was in the

main not implemented", that the bourgeoisie exercised its dictatorship over the proletariat' on the educational front. The second
'estimate' was that 'the majority of the teachers and the students
in those 17 years were "basically bourgeois in their world outlook,"
that they were "bourgeois intellectuals and belonged to the
stinking ninth category of class enemies" (BR vol. 21, no. 5, 1978:
16).

While still keeping the Maoist rhetoric in education alive,
important changes were introduced in the educational structure as
early as 1978 – criteria for admissions, curricula, teaching and
examining methods – soon after the Party Congress when the
change in leadership was formalised. The denunciation of Cultural
Revolution was yet to come; this was a period when the attack
was concentrated on the ultra-left opposition, symbolised by the
'gang', to the Hua–Deng alliance within the Party:

> With the toppling of the 'Gang of Four' we have completely eliminated
> the scourge which had done so much to wreck the 'Two Hundreds'
> policy [Hundred Flowers Bloom, Hundred Schools of Thought
> Contend] and Chinese science and culture . . . With the promotion of
> socialist democracy and the strengthening of the socialist legal system,
> Chinese academic circles are stirring into life again, with different
> viewpoints contending in a normal manner. (BR, vol. 22, no. 14, 1979: 9)

Politics was still to be a prominent part of educational training:
'To help the young people correctly sum up their experience a firm
belief in Marxism–Leninism–Mao Zedong Thought must first be
instilled into them' (BR, vol. 21, no. 46, 1978: 8). However, there
was also a re-emphasis on formal education which had been
repudiated during the Cultural Revolution:

> One important criterion for judging whether a youth today is really
> red is to see if he or she delves into his or her own field of work and
> diligently studies to master science and culture for the revolution. (*ibid.*)

As part of the new policy towards the intellectuals their social
status was to be raised; they were no longer to be considered part
of the 'stinking ninth category' with other 'enemies of the revolution'. There was a recognition of the need for intellectuals to
contribute to the task of economic modernisation. Hua, in his
speech to the Eleventh National Party Congress of the CPC held
in 1977, said:

> To build socialism, the working class must have its own army of
> technical cadres and of professors, teachers, scientists, journalists,
> writers, artists, and Marxist theorists. It must be a vast army; a small
> number of people will not suffice. (CPC CC 1977: 94)

The scarcity of people capable of contributing to China's scientific
and technical advancement at the level reached by the end of the
Maoist period can be seen from the following figures: in China in
1982 among youths aged 15 years or more 79.1 per cent of males
and 51.1 per cent of females had had primary schooling, 42.9 per
cent and 26 per cent lower secondary schooling, 13.3 per cent and
8.3 per cent upper secondary schooling and only 1.0 per cent and
0.3 per cent post-secondary education. The corresponding figures
for India in 1971 were 37.2 per cent and 14.7 per cent, 21.3 per
cent and 7.1 per cent, 10.3 per cent and 3.0 per cent, and 1.6 per
cent and 0.4 per cent. Even a poor country like Colombia could,
as early as 1973, boast of 4.1 per cent of its male and 1.6 per cent
of its female population over 15 years old having completed post-
secondary education. In South Korea the statistics for post-
secondary education were as high as 6.2 per cent and 1.6 per cent
for the same year (World Bank, 1983: 124).

In 'Outline Program for National Education from 1978 to 1985'
the State Council set out the main areas of reorganisation and
reform of educational structure. Maoist concerns with 'proletarian
politics', and 'walking on two legs', i.e. running schools of various
forms and organisational patterns so as to most fully tap the
potential talent at every level, were incorporated into the text, but
the emphasis was on restructuring education for the goal of
modernising the economy.

In a sharp contrast to the Maoist policies of emphasising
secondary education, the draft noted that:

> [it] is imperative to bring into full play the important role of higher
> education in raising quality and training qualified persons, while laying
> a good foundation through attending in earnest to middle and primary
> school education. (BR, vol. 21, no. 46, 1978: 16)

Encouragement was given to postgraduate study, enlargement of
college enrolment and to establishing new institutes of higher
learning and technical training and paying attention to improving
the standards of the Communist Labour Universities, 'July 21'

Workers' Colleges and 'May 7' Colleges that were established during the Cultural Revolution (see Unger, 1982). The Maoist policy of sending urban youth to the countryside (*xiafang*) was also to be continued. However, the explanatory rhetoric was no longer purely ideological. For example, 'objective conditions' of an underdeveloped China were given as the reason for the policy of 'sending educated young people up to the mountains and down to the villages': decollectivisation and the 'family responsibility' system (Nolan, 1983) meant that greater technological input would be needed for agriculture to be profitable. The pressure of population growth, resulting in the state's incapacity to ensure employment in the cities, also meant that an ordered expulsion of youth from the cities to small towns and the countryside continued to make sense (HQ CE, no. 3–4, 1980–1: 85–93).

In 1977 national-level entrance examinations for institutions of higher education were reintroduced. While in deference to the Maoist critique of Soviet-style education (see Unger, 1982; Seybolt, 1973b; Price, 1970, 1977) rural–urban, and regional differences in the standards of education and levels of resources were conceded, it was claimed that bridging of this gap could 'only be realised by gradual, protracted effort'. In the rural areas, emphasis was to be given to popularising the eight-year schooling system (as opposed to a ten-year course in the cities), establishing agriculture high schools, technical secondary schools and part-work/part-study schools.

An important break with the educational pattern of the Cultural Revolution was the re-opening of key-point schools that had been condemned as citadels of 'bourgeois' thinking and 'seedbeds of capitalist consciousness'. These schools were targeted by the party/state for high resource funding at every academic and administrative level, better-than-average cohort of pupils, and higher achievement rates. Key schools were considered necessary because of an urgent need for raising educational standards. However, at this time the schools that were designated as 'national key schools' included both the most academically famous of the pre-Cultural Revolution key-point schools and schools linked to model units associated with radical Maoist educational reforms. This compromise reflected the ongoing debate between the factions of Deng and Hua in the sphere of education. On the one hand, Deng maintained that economic modernisation required raising educational standards for which he prescribed the concentration of resources and outstanding students chosen through the examination criterion in these key secondary schools and universities. On the other, Hua, echoing the Maoist line, insisted that the 'most powerful base and inexhaustible source of strength for the modernisation of science and technology in our country are the masses of the people in their hundreds of millions' (CE, 1984: 6). The uneasiness about these key institutions felt by the Maoist old guard was made evident in repeated exhortations to strengthen the hold of Party committees in these schools:

> The key schools attached to the Ministry of Education and other ministries and commissions should also be the key schools under the party committees and education departments of various regions. These organisations should strengthen, not weaken their leadership of these schools. (Liu, *ibid*.: 22)

That the opposition to these élite institutions came not just from the top ranking Party cadres who felt threatened by the rapid changes in policy was made evident by Fang Yi, Politburo member and vice-president of the Academy of Sciences:

> the leadership ranks of key point scientific research institutions and higher learning institutions need to be overhauled . . . We must select comrades who understand the Party's policy, who are enthusiastic about science and education affairs, who have good party sense, and who are competent as Party Committee secretaries. (*ibid*.: 45)

Four Modernisations and education

With the removal of Hua the pace and direction of the reforms in education went into high gear. The Four Modernisations programme was gathering steam, and needed a continuing input from the scientific intelligentsia. Deng made the supervision of the new education policy his own responsibility. His priorities were clearly determined by the needs of the economy. He believed that the educational system must cater to the growing demand for skilled scientific personnel generated by the programme of 'four modernisations':

> The key to achieving modernisation is the development of science and technology. And unless we pay special attention to education, it will be impossible to develop science and technology. (Deng, 1984: 53)

The 'Proposal of the CPC Central Committee for the Seventh Five Year Plan (1986–1990)' also underlined this approach of linking economic and educational development:

> Economic construction, social development and scientific and technical progress all depend on the intellectual development of the Chinese nation, as increased number of trained personnel, and further growth of education is based on economic development. (NCNA, SWB/FE/C1–23, 28 September 1985)

Deng came out unambiguously against the ultra-left slogans of the Cultural Revolution like 'Learn a speciality and you'll forget the dictatorship', 'With knowledge in hand the person is gone' and 'Once the satellite is in the sky, the red flag falls to the ground' (CE, 1979: 57). The Maoist concern with linking theoretical research with productive labour was not a priority with the new leadership:

> 'Time must be guaranteed so that researchers can put maximum energy into research . . . I think people should be permitted to bury themselves in scientific research. If someone works day and night, seven days a week on a research project, what's wrong with that?' Deng asked (Deng, 1984: 67)

It was recognised that in a situation where the intellectuals had been made into social pariahs because of their claim to theoretical knowledge, restoring the prestige of both education and the educated was a priority for the success of educational reforms. Deng went much further than Hua when he declared that 'all those who engage in mental work are also workers'. With a political sleight of hand Deng made intellectuals part of the 'working class' and hence part of the vanguard of revolutionary China. Intellectuals, he said, 'differ from the manual workers only insofar as they perform different roles in the social division of labour. Everyone who works, whether with his hands or with his brain, is part of the working people in a socialist society.' (Deng, 1984: 105) Hu Yaobang, later the general secretary of the CPC, who was particularly popular among the intellectuals for his receptiveness to their suggestions, speaking at the meeting in commemoration of the centenary of the death of Karl Marx on 13 March 1983 said: 'it is imperative that we oppose the erroneous tendency of separating intellectuals from the working class, counterposing them to the workers and regarding them as an "alien force"' (BR, 23 March 1983: ix). Thus, the restoration of the intelligentsia to political grace became once again dependent on the political considerations of the leadership in power, just as their fall had been. It was even accepted that:

> for a fairly long time to come, scientific and cultural knowledge and mental works will continue to be relatively concentrated among one section of the population – the intellectuals. (Zhao, *ibid*.: x)

The break with the Maoist policy of creating conditions wherein workers and peasants would be able to take on the role of the 'experts' was clear; the rationality of efficient production demanded specialisation and differentiation.

In its urgency for enlarging its corps of trained personnel the regime was prepared to let its potential talent go abroad for further study of the most advanced techniques, especially in the fields of science and technology. Between 1977 and 1979 alone 2,230 Chinese students were sent to various countries for higher studies (BR, 23 November 1979, see also Chapter 3); in 1984–5 the number jumped to 8,218. This contrasted sharply with the numbers studying abroad in the three decades after the revolution: 675 in 1953, and a mere 36 students in 1972, reflecting the Maoist emphasis on self-reliance, and China's general isolation from the world during this period (SEC, 1984: 126). The argument for opening the educational sphere to the West was again constructed in terms of economic rationality: that science and technology, like land, labour and capital, are part of the productive forces and that 'these things as such have no class character' and can thus be acquired from any system to suit the needs of a socialist society.

As education became crucial to the 'four modernisations' drive greater need for investment in it was recognised:

> Education cannot be promoted without increased funds. For the foreseeable future, central and local government appropriations for educational purposes will increase at a rate faster than the increase in the state's regular revenue and the average expenditure on education per student will also increase steadily. (CPC CC 1985: 5).

China's record in educational investment had not been very good. China's spending on education, as a percentage of its total budget, was one of the lowest in the world. The figures for 1979 showed

Table 2.1 Public expenditure on education (in RMB 100 million)

Year	Total budget	Total expenditure	Higher education	General education	As percentage of national budget
1976	806.20	50.49	8.03	42.46	6.26
1977	843.53	53.04	8.26	44.78	6.29
1978	1,110.95	65.60	11.63	53.97	5.90
1979	1,273.94	76.96	16.40	60.56	6.05
1980	1,212.73	94.18	19.13	75.05	7.77
1981	1,114.97	102.48	22.28	80.20	9.19
1982	1,153.31	115.68	23.86	91.82	10.03
1983	1,292.5	127.85	–	–	9.9
1984	1,546.4	148.16	–	–	10.0
1985	1,844.8	184.16	–	–	10.0

Source: SEC, 1984 and 1986a.

that the total public expenditure on education in China as a percentage of GNP was estimated at 3.1 per cent. This meant that China spent less on education than the median percentage – 3.9 per cent – of 82 developing countries for which the World Bank had information (World Bank, 1983). In the developed countries the percentage was 5.7 per cent. The central government expenditure on education as a percentage of its total expenditure was also low: 6.6 per cent as compared to 15.1 per cent in other developing countries, and 15.6 per cent in developed countries (*ibid.*). 'In 1982, the percentage of the state budget going to education rose to 10.03%, a figure still two thirds below typical expenditure in other developing countries' (Cleverley, 1985: 252).

Because of its emphasis on education as part of the modernisation programme, the World Bank estimated that between 1982 and 2000 China's recurrent expenditure on education would increase from 13.5 billion Renmenbi (RMB) to 37.5 billion RMB at 1982 prices. The party/state decided that it alone could not foot this bill; that local governments, individual contributors, and other economic institutions would have to be mobilised for raising resources. To involve the local bodies in this responsibility for securing increased finances for education, the State Council issued a circular in April 1986 which stipulated that urban areas should start collecting supporting funds for education on 1 July 1986. These would 'be based on the products tax, appreciation tax and business tax that are turned in by enterprises and individuals' (SEC, 1986a: 27).

In May 1985 the CPC Central Committee and State Council held a national education conference at the end of which, on 27 May, a document delineating the second state educational reforms after the eclipse of Hua Gofeng was issued. This included devolving responsibility to local governments for developing elementary education, a gradual introduction of a nine-year compulsory schooling programme, an increasing emphasis on vocational and technical training in secondary schools, and changes in enrolment to higher education institutions, and in the system of job allocation for graduates. It was also decided that universities and colleges would be given greater autonomy in administration of policy. In May 1985 the Central Committee of the CPC formalised many of these changes through a policy document, 'Reform of China's Education Structure'. This document was an important landmark in the ongoing process of change in the education policy in post-Mao China. It not only detailed particular reforms, it also provided the perspective, the rationale, and the direction that the post-Mao leadership had on education. It made it clear that '[the] fundamental aim of restructuring education is to improve the quality of the nation and produce as many skilled people as possible' (CPC CC 1985: 1). An early 'streaming' between those wanting to pursue higher education and those joining the ranks of 'intermediate and junior technicians' was recommended because '[without] a huge contingent of such workers and engineers, advanced sciences and sophisticated equipment cannot be translated into productive forces' (*ibid.*: 10). In the sphere of higher education the 'strategic goal' was to ensure that by the end of the century

> the institutions of higher education will contribute substantially to China's independent scientific and technological development and to solving major theoretical and practical problems that crop up in the course of socialist modernisation. (*ibid.* 13)

As a result of the recommendations of the conference, a law for compulsory nine-year education was introduced in order to raise the general educational standard of the people, and to increase the pool from which China would choose its experts. This took effect in April 1986 after approval at the Fourth Session of the

Sixth NPC. The participation of the local educational authorities in its implementation was emphasised.

Restructuring higher education

In order to implement these reforms, institutional changes were introduced. The Ministry of Education was replaced by the State Commission of Education (SEC) by the decision of the Central Committee of the CPC in May 1985. 'Provisional Regulations on Responsibilities for the Administration of Higher Education' were passed by the State Council on 12 March 1986, setting out the powers and functions of this new body (JPRS, July 1986). The SEC, like the Ministry of Education, was made responsible for drawing up a national plan that set out the national demand for professionals on the basis of which it could draw up the enrolment and job allocation plans for graduates of higher education institutions. The SEC also had an advisory function: it was to help the Ministry of Finance draw up 'the allocation proposals for investment in capital construction, education and scientific research funds, special expenses, foreign exchange, and the centralised allocation of supplies and equipment for higher education at the central level' (*ibid.*). An important function of the SEC was to run directly some universities; these were the national key-point universities (see Chapter 3).

The SEC was given few resources to disburse, most of which came from the Ministry of Finance and Planning. As the lack of financial resources was a pressing problem, other agencies were to be encouraged by the party/state to contribute to investment in education:

> [Local authorities] should encourage state-owned enterprises, public organisations and individuals to run schools and provide them with guidance. Also, they can encourage units, collective undertakings and individuals to make financial donations to help develop education, but of their own accord, not by exaction. (CPC CC 1985: 9)

This lack of financial power is felt as a real threat by the SEC: 'There is less pressure for funds on the SEC but this implies less power as well, and is a big problem before us', said the director in charge of the planning and finance department at the SEC in an interview in 1987. As compared with the erstwhile Ministry of Education the SEC has less power *vis-à-vis* the local authorities, who have set up their own financial networks, and these fears about its weakening authority have led the SEC to approach the reforms more cautiously, and perhaps less enthusiastically than it might have otherwise.

An area where the SEC has benefited from the reforms is that of overseeing curricula. In 1979 the Central Committee reaffirmed the 1963 system of a unified system of management in higher education and gave to the Ministry of Education (after 1986 to the SEC) the task of regulating nationally standardised teaching plans, teaching outlines and textbooks (see Hayhoe, CQ June 1987). This broke with the Cultural Revolution experiments with localised educational patterns and decentralised management of education. The SEC brings together experts in particular fields of research to write textbooks which are nationally recommended. Universities, however, are not obliged to prescribe these textbooks; they can set their own booklists so long as they conform to the curricula made by the SEC. Many university teachers write textbooks, now that publications have become professionally important, and materially profitable for them (see Chapter 5).

The SEC heads a network of educational ministries and management bodies. The most important of the second-level ministries is the Provincial Education Commission (PEC). It is the transmission belt for the central policy directives and for their implementation at the provincial level. It is also responsible for allocating finances to the provincial universities. This leads to disparities between provincial budgets for higher education. Shandong Province, for example, is a prosperous province, and spends more than RMB 2000 per student per year at the university level, while Zhejiang can only afford to spend RMB 1500. Both the resources of a province and its priorities thus affect the investment in education. There are central regulations to guard against neglect of education: an SEC regulation makes it mandatory for the PEC to increase the budget allocation by 12.8 per cent annually. However, as I was told by the director of the higher education division of the Zhejiang PEC, this increase fell short of the increase in the percentage of enrolment, especially in the years immediately after the reforms in education were introduced. In 1979–80, for example, the enrolment rate in Zhejiang was as high as 20.8 per cent which led to a great dispersion of scarce resources which was still to be made up in 1987, even though the enrolment rates had been brought down gradually as per central policy, to 3.6 per cent in 1986. Apart from giving a standard grant to universities, the PEC also gives financial assistance for opening new courses, funds for capital construction, and a sum for unspecified expenditures. In Zhejiang the provincial government spends RMB 100,000,000 per year on higher education.

As in the case of the SEC, the PEC is also directly responsible for the provincial key-point universities, and has supervisory powers over other universities. The Commission is responsible for personnel recruitment and promotion, and the supervision of teaching courses at the key-point universities. It recommends the number of lecturers, and their professional level, needed by each course; personnel planning is thus the 'dual responsibility' of both the university and the PEC. While the salary of the teachers is regulated by the central authorities, the applications for promotions are scrutinised by the Commission.

Great attention was paid by the leadership to higher education in an effort to push forward its expansion and development. In 1982 the 'Sixth Five-Year Plan of Economic and Social Development (1981–1984)' was published and the following projections made for an increase in the number of entrants to universities and colleges: in 1985 the number

> should be around 400,000, the number of enrolled undergraduate students around 1,300,000, the number of newly enrolled research students around 20,000 and the total number of enrolled research students around 50,000. (Henze, 1984: 133)

Further, a special plan for the development of higher education was discussed and approved in 1983 according to which the number of undergraduates would increase by 53 per cent over the number in 1982, and the number of entrants by 75 per cent, over the same period.

As a result of the policy of expansion of higher education a large number of institutions for tertiary education were established. These included universities, colleges, professional training schools and vocational institutions. The rate of expansion can be seen from the following figures: in 1983 there were 805 'regular' higher education institutions; in 1985 the number increased to 1,016 (see

Table 2.2 Expansion of higher education

Year	Regular institutions	Enrolment
1976	392	564,715
1977	404	625,319
1978	598	856,322
1979	633	1,019,950
1980	675	1,143,712
1981	704	1,279,472
1982	715	1,153,954
1983	805	1,206,823
1984	–	–
1985	1,016	1,703,100

Source: SEC, 1984, 1986a.

Table 2.2). This compares with much lower figures for the Maoist period: 434 in 1970 and 387 in 1975 ('regular' institutions include all full-time state-run educational institutions) (SEC, 1984, 1986a).

It was estimated that China will need 50 million graduates and specialists by the year 2000, but its state universities, colleges and further education classes will turn out only 15 million graduates. This led to the consideration of institutional diversification in order to expand the educational network through various patterns of financing and recruitment.

Supplementing the regular state-run universities, four different types of institutions of higher learning have emerged: first, private universities (*sili daxue/xueyuan*). These had made up for 29 per cent of the total in 1950, but had faced closure soon after the educational policy had been drawn up. They were reactivated in 1979 as part of the effort to expand the higher education system. These institutions could charge a considerable annual fee, set up their own curricula, organise their own entrance and final examinations and were to be self-financed. The State Education Commission did not allow these universities to grant degrees as their students are not enrolled on the basis of the national entrance examination (NCNA, FBIS, no. 29, 1988: 24). Beijing Language Self-Education University and Xinghua College in Beijing are examples. Second, there were the short-term vocational universities (*duanqi zhiye daxue*). These were public institutions but differed considerably from other state-run universities and colleges: students had to pay tuition; they paid their own transportation and medical expenses; the colleges did not provide living accommodation and, therefore, most students commuted daily; their students were not allocated jobs after graduation; the faculty of such institutions drew upon other institutions of higher education in the area; curricula were adapted to regional needs, and the courses lasted no more than two to three years. By 1982 the number of students enrolled in these institutions was 20,460 (Henze, *op. cit.*: 124). Third, there were the semi-private universities. There were only two of these, in Beijing and in Shantou: the Central Socialist Academy, run by the National Committee of the Chinese Peoples' Political Consultative Conference (CPPCC) – this was originally opened in Beijing in 1956 but was closed down during the Cultural Revolution. The University of Shantou was built with the donation of a Hong Kong Chinese, indicating the government's willingness to solicit sponsorship of education by overseas Chinese. Finally, there were the city-level universities. These came up largely as a consequence of the economic reforms: the reforms in both rural and urban areas created a localised economy and a great demand for skilled manpower at the local level. Provincial universities, however, were not meant to serve the specific needs of the cities or counties (Cheng, CE, vol. 22, no. 3, 1986: 263).

As a part of this programme of expansion through diversification, the Radio and Television Universities were reopened in February 1979 (see McCormick, 1986). They had been closed during the Cultural Revolution after a trial run in the early sixties. The Central Radio and TV University was founded in Beijing in 1979. Administratively, it is under the jurisdiction of the SEC and the Ministry of Radio and Television. By 1986 China had 29 radio and TV universities, including the one run by the central government, about 600 branch institutes, or groups at the municipal (or prefectural) level and in various trades and industries, as well as 11,000 small groups at the county level. The total enrolment of students reached 600,000. These are mainly workers, staff members and educated youth wanting professional training. Students of the Central Radio and TV University either enter through examinations, studying in classes full-time, part-time or during their spare time, or study by themselves from radio and TV without sitting the entrance examinations. Examinations are set in Beijing by the SEC to cover all Radio and TV Universities (SEC, 1986c). Vocational education at the tertiary level was also encouraged. 'Advanced vocational schools' were set up to admit senior middle-school graduates. These offered a two- to three-year programme of training. The students at such schools were usually self-financed and non-resident, and were not placed within the job allocation plan. In 1985, there were 118 such schools, with a total enrolment of 63,900. These institutions, apart from expanding further the network of higher education, were seen as important in training a competent work force for the country's economic programme (SEC, 1986a: 45–51). A system of higher education self-study examinations was also set up in 1983 to increase tertiary enrolment under the National Higher Education Self-Study Examination Guidance Committee. Nearly one million people registered for these examinations (SEC, 1986b).

Thus, higher education in post-Mao China diversified greatly, leading to the construction of a pyramidal structure. At the top were those key universities and colleges which stress teaching, research and postgraduate study. The second level of universities and colleges developed their research facilities but were to be predominantly teaching institutions. Beneath them were the two- to three-year colleges, offering training in specific fields. 'Last in the ranking are the TV, Correspondence, spare-time and staff and workers colleges' (Cleverley, 1985: 242).

In July 1986 Li Peng, then Minister in charge of the SEC, made further suggestions on the reform of the higher education system. He suggested the universities and colleges should be divided into three categories: first, a few with greater teaching and research potential should train students for master's and doctorates as well as undergraduate courses. They should gradually develop into educational and scientific research centres. Second, the majority of institutions should concentrate on undergraduate teaching. They should also promote research in applied science and provide scientific and technical services. Third, the remaining should be professional training colleges (SWB/FE/BII: 1–2).

However, after an initial expansion of higher education institutions to right the balance of Maoist neglect, the leadership soon began to discourage the mass of secondary-school graduates from competing for university seats. This was done because, even with

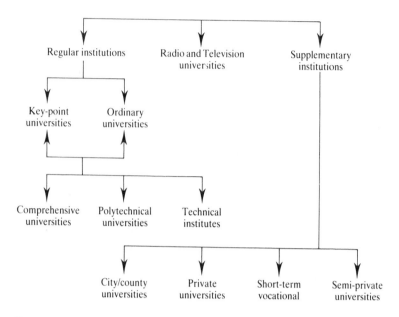

Figure 2.1   Structure of higher education in post-Mao China

the expansion of higher education institutions, the demand for seats in these far outstripped availability, which caused disaffection among the disappointed, and a great administrative burden on those involved in supervising the examination procedure. Thus, while in 1978 six million students sat for the entrance examination, by 1984 the number had declined to 1.64 million (Rosen, MC, July 1985: 311).

This diversification in higher-level education institutions, while adding to the pool of China's specialists, also created problems for the educational administrators. The SEC complained that a new university was opening every three days, and that some secondary polytechnics started called themselves universities. It also noticed that some private universities employed only visiting professors, used other institutions' teaching materials, enrolled students and even graduated them without giving examinations. This led the SEC to take a cautious approach towards these varied types of higher education institutions. On the other hand, as a Beijing survey showed, 85 per cent of graduates from private institutions found jobs and did not have to wait long. This made these institutions an attractive option for city youth seeking educational qualifications; it also led to resentment among these private institutions against SEC policies that are regarded as discriminatory. Private institutions continue to pose difficult questions regarding the controlling power of the SEC. Their exclusion from the national examination, enrolment and job allocation plan gives them a measure of autonomy that cannot be enjoyed by the state-supported institutions.

An attempt was made to right the balance between levels of higher education and proportions of specialities. Since 1978 there had been an increased enrolment of postgraduate students. Thus, the number of postgraduates enrolled increased rapidly from 10,934 in 1978 to 37,166 in 1983 (SEC, 1984: 112). In 1985 'the graduates accounted for 5% of the total enrolment in higher education institutions' (SEC, 1986a: 64). By the end of 1985 22 institutions of higher learning had set up postgraduate institutes, mostly found in key universities and colleges. However, during the same period 425 institutions started granting master's degrees and 196 granted doctorates (SEC, 1986d). Students in special professional training and students specialising in areas hitherto neglected like finance, economics, political science, law, management, liberal arts, etc., also increased (see SEC, 1984: 76).

Changes in the system of enrolment evoked the greatest interest among the students. National-level college entrance examinations were instituted in 1977 as qualifiers for places at universities and colleges. Initially the party/state controlled the distribution of students over the various areas of study. However, over the years since 1978 this system of centralised, controlled enrolment also underwent change. The universities and colleges began to enrol students through any/all of the following ways: first, in accordance with the plan drawn up by the SEC and the State Council, taking into account the personnel needs of the country. Second, the universities started 'contracting students': individual enterprises could enter into an agreement with the universities to train their employees, or to finance the study of a number of students who would join the enterprise on graduation. These numbers remain quite small, but the practice indicates the potential for expansion. Finally, a small number of students were self-supported. All these categories, however, have to pass the entrance examination, though the students in the latter two tend to have much lower marks than those in the first. In 1986 it was decided that a small number of students with 'excellent academic records or rare intelligence' be exempt from the examination and get direct admission to universities.

As the party/state felt the need for rapid expansion of higher education, it was confronted by problems both of financial constraints, and of incentives for improving students' academic performance. As a result there was a review of the student support system for higher education. With the new economic policies leading to a rise in incomes, albeit uneven, the policy-makers felt that some sections of the population should invest in the educational system. This would take some pressure off the provincial and national governments to financially underwrite all expansion. Further, it was seen as a way of creating a popular stake in the educational system which, the leadership argued, has been abused and taken for granted:

> the system takes too much care of college students and has caused the tendency of students depending on the state for everything. Also, it has caused some waste and equalitarianism as the grant is decided . . . regardless of students' performance in schools. (SEC, 1986a: 68)

The government thus decided to do away with the system of 'grant-in-aid' that supports all students in their higher studies. In July 1986, the State Council approved 'The Report on Reforming the Current State Grant-in-Aid System in General Institutions of Higher Learning'. It was decided that 85 universities and colleges would try out the proposed changes and, on the basis of the results emerging from this experiment, further reforms would be carried out, leading to the introduction of the new system nation-wide in 1987. The system that is being tried out provides for both merit- and need-based scholarships. These are of three types: first, merit scholarships. These will be of three different grades: RMB 350, RMB 250, and RMB 150 per annum. About 25 per cent of the total enrolled students will benefit from these in a ratio of 5:10:10. Second, scholarships for students in priority subject areas in specialised colleges and institutes like those of forestry, agriculture, teacher training, etc. These scholarships, of values ranging from RMB 400 to RMB 300 a year, will be provided to all students at these institutions. Finally, scholarships for students who pledge to work in border areas, economically backward areas and in professions with poor work conditions after their graduation. Those who fail to qualify for any of the above scholarships will have to finance their study by taking out loans. The loans will be released by China Industrial and Commercial Bank annually at low interest rates. These will be paid back by the employing unit (*danwei*) of the student after his/her graduation. However, this system has yet to be comprehensively introduced. The party/state itself seems to feel cautious about loosening its hold in this crucial area even while recognising the material benefits of such a policy. As a result the government stipulated that 'the money borrowing students should be limited to 30% of the total college enrolment' (SEC, 1986a: 71). This has caused resentment and dissatisfaction among the students (see Chapter 6).

Given that the scholarships at regular universities can cover only 25 per cent of the students this figure does not correspond to the stated goals of the reforms. Further, this policy could have serious implications for the composition of student enrolment in higher education. Self-financing of education would mean that only those having the means and/or the will to do so would enrol; presumably the city-based intelligentsia will predominate. This was confirmed by a Beijing student who felt that those being made to pay for their children's education were the least able to afford it – 'most of the parents of students in my class are professionals, and earn very little; the peasants are rich but they don't send their children to the university'. This was one reason that fed the anger of the students during the demonstrations in 1989. 'My parents together earn RMB 270 a month. They give me RMB 60 to live off at the university. I have another brother and sister. If they go to the university, how could my parents afford to support them?' said a student who had taken part in the 1989 demonstrations and is now in Paris.

One of the most important reforms at the university level was that in management procedures. This was done in line with a general policy of decentralising administrative authority. This also led to lively debate in higher education circles and revealed the uneasiness felt by many at the nature and the speed with which their professional world was changing. Shanghai's Jiaotong University's management reforms became a case in point. The reforms at Jiaotong included investing the university authorities with responsibility for personnel reallocation after fixing, on a two-yearly basis, the number of staff required; nearly 'six hundred people were transferred to other universities' (Liu, CE, *op. cit.*: 11). Further, a consultation company was set up in Hong Kong under the auspices of the university – the Siyuan Computer Corporation Ltd – which, it was claimed, 'is helpful in raising the level of teaching and scientific research' (*ibid.*: 21). The Dean was given the power to

> make whatever assignment in his (sic) department he or she sees fit. In case of staff shortages or work overload, he can engage from outside temporary teachers or workers without having to place them on the staff. He or she also has the final say and is authorised to pay wages to those hired. (*ibid.*: 15)

The president could also dismiss those s/he considered incompetent.

These wide-ranging managerial reforms caused unease among many academics who criticised Jiaotong for concentrating primarily on making money and for being unconcerned with teaching or theoretical research:

> Critics protested that the university emphasised the teaching of practical subjects; sought quick results and rapid profits from its research . . . and had a faculty, student body and even a contingent of foreign professors driven one-sidedly by the profit motive. (Rosen, MC, *op. cit.*: 4)

Even this critique, however, concentrated on the non-political aspect; it was the neglect of pure sciences research, of humanities, and the relatively stricter work schedules that were its focus, not the élitist nature of the reconstructed system of education. Despite the criticism, the central leadership stood by the university and 'vindicated the Jiaotong model' (*ibid.*: 5). Some other reforms were introduced in the system of higher education and will be dealt with elsewhere in this book. These included expanding the decision-making powers of the university administration and linking higher education institutions to industrial units in a bid to spread the economic costs of supporting universities and to encourage education to directly serve the needs of modernisation (Chapter 3), a contract and promotion system for university teachers (Chapter 5), and changes in the job allocation system for the students (Chapter 6).

While the changes in general educational policy and setting of goals have taken identifiable shape and form, the translation of these broad goals into specific reforms has been a more fraught project. More problematic still has been the implementation of the reforms. While the primary reason for this has been considerations of political control, there have been others too. At many points the goals of economic modernisation have come into conflict with broader educational needs, and the latter have tended to lose out. An example of this is the targeting of higher education for resource allocation – both national and international (see Hayhoe, 1989). Another case is that of implementing the policy of decentralising educational authority to the local governments. The working of the nine-year compulsory education law of 1986 was made the responsibility of local governments. However, in an environment where collective responsibility was being devalued, resources were scarce and the local governments demanding social taxes were vulnerable to being attacked as 'ultra-left', the enforcing of the law became a very difficult task. This was especially true in the rural areas. Drop-out rates have increased and graduation rates at various levels of the educational ladder have fallen sharply. 'The transition from lower to upper secondary [school] has dropped from 83 percent to 55.5 percent in cities and towns, and 33.5 percent to 11.9 percent in rural areas', notes Hayhoe (1989: 184). Together with increasing the gap in educational standards between the countryside and the cities, this policy of decentralisation has also resulted in an increased educational differential between boys and girls, especially in the countryside. 'To educate a daughter is to water another man's garden' is an old Chinese proverb and still affects parents in rural China. The SEC estimated that in 1985 three million girls stopped studying, or 7 per cent of all children (JPRS-CAR-89-090: 57). Neglect of schools has also led to a spate of accidents involving classroom collapses in which many children have been killed or injured. 'In 1987 the shortage of classroom space nationwide was 75 million square metres and there were 45 million square metres of unsafe buildings' (*ibid.*: 58). These figures show clearly that despite the leadership's support for enhancing educational levels and expanding the educational network, the measures taken to translate these goals into reality have not been successful. While the denial of individualism by a collectivising Maoist state had led to educational stagnation, unbridled individual competition encouraged by the post-Mao leadership has resulted in severe strains and unintended contradictions in the sphere of education. However, the political institutions that could manage these tensions and attempt to resolve these contradictions are still not in place. A non-representative party/state apparatus does not have the moral or political authority to counter the prejudices of a traditional civil society, and the impact of the economic reforms, and its own commitment to withdrawing from mobilisational politics, makes it more difficult for it to use coercion to do so. Further, there are old established interests within the system which the party/state does not want, or cannot afford, to hurt. It is also wary of creating new interests that might conflict with the established practices of the educational bureaucracy and lead to instability within the system, as indeed has already happened. Then there is simply a lack of management skills, and a scarcity of funds available for education. All these factors have combined to produce an effect of a patchy, *ad hoc* policy on higher education. Many new opportunities were created for the universities and for students and lecturers, but these have not been fully realised because of the leadership's concern to control the process of educational reform as carefully as that of the political. Initial excitement and expectations could not be sustained in such narrow confines. It was in the working of these reforms that the cracks began to appear. The university became a site for a tussle between the various interests, old and new.

3

Reorganising higher education: the politics of university reform

A new setting for old institutions

If the university became the site for bargain and struggle around the education policy in post-Mao China, it was for various reasons. First, simply because it was the institution where most of the Chinese intellectuals worked and lived. The intellectuals, being crucial to the success of the 'four modernisations', have become one of the most privileged sections in post-Mao China. Second, they have been used by China's new leaders in their own factional struggles. While this is not a new phenomenon (Mao had mobilised the students for the Cultural Revolution), its character is radically different. Because of their importance in the economic calculations of the post-Mao leadership, they have not simply been mobilised by that leadership. Licensed participative opportunities have been given to them to go with their new status. However, what is common in the new policy with the Maoist one is the dependence of the intelligentsia on the leadership's goodwill for their present position. While making the intellectuals vulnerable to the changes of fortune of the political bureaucrats at the top of the party/state structure, this linking of fortunes has also given them at times a greater bargaining strength, making the process of the implementation of educational reform a complex exercise. This has had its impact on the university's political life. Third, the post-Mao leadership has applied the market model that it introduced into the economy to the university system as well. This has resulted in certain important areas of the university's life – its financial arrangements, for example – to partially slip out of the control of the party/state. However limited this reclaiming of the administrative space by the university authorities, it has added a new dimension to university politics and has affected the expectations, aspirations, and frustrations of students, teachers and cadres at the local level. Finally, the university has also been the site for the introduction of the most concentrated impact of foreign, especially Western, ideas into China. It is into the university that the first foreign language and scientific academics and students were invited, from here that the Chinese young people first went abroad, and to these institutions that they returned. All these factors made the university a unique institution to reflect the new tensions and interests that gave rise to the various opposition movements that have shaken China in recent years.

Changing perceptions of the university

The present leadership differs radically from the Maoist regime in its views of educational institutions. Education was regarded in the Maoist rhetoric primarily, if not exclusively, as an instrument and a weapon: an instrument to fashion a new socialist consciousness, and a weapon with which to fight 'bourgeois ideology' and influences. The educational process therefore had to be redefined in terms that would divest it of the traditional liberal meaning of education: as a concern for individual self-improvement based upon individual choice. The Maoist strategy for economic development, based as it was on mobilisation of human resources and medium-level technology, also supported such a view of education. The university could not be central to the Maoist scheme of things in the field of education; the middle school occupied the centre stage.

In post-Mao China there was a radical shift in emphasis. Universities came to symbolise modernisation of Chinese education and became crucial to producing a highly skilled population needed for rapid scientific and economic growth. Just as the general postulates of the reforms in education were in terms of the needs of the economy, the reorganisation of the universities also followed this pattern: 'the scale of higher education will develop comparable to economic development', explained an official of the SEC in Beijing. The aim of education was to 'create wealth for society and build material and cultural civilisation through the development of intellectual resources' (Ye, CE, Winter 1986: 8). The university had always been equated with a production unit in post-revolutionary China; *danwei* (unit) is the term applied both to a factory and to a university. With efficiency and rationalisation as the slogans of the new regime, the accounting of costs and rationalising of expenditure per 'unit' produced was important:

> Since investment in education has been acknowledged as a type of investment, it is necessary to pay attention to 'output', and the output of investment in higher education is the training of qualified graduates. (*ibid.*: 9)

An increase in 'output' demanded certain changes in the functioning of the 'unit'. At the level of the university changes were introduced in the organisation and the management of the university, its financing, financial relations and financial responsibility, and its links with the outside world.

The reform of the structure of the universities and their spheres of functioning tend to reflect the continued centralised nature of planning and decision-making in China. At no stage were universities made part of the consultation process that preceded decision-making – no interests or interest organisations at the level of the educational institution itself were consulted. Those from the universities who were consulted were the well-known professors who count in their own right as individuals of outstanding abilities in the fields of education, economics, politics or related areas. Many such academics are, in any case, not in universities but work directly under the supervision of the State Council in specialised institutes such as the Chinese Academy of Social Sciences (CASS), and the Chinese Academy of Sciences (CAS), etc. The university became important at the level of implementation of the policies decided at the central level. This occurred as local cadres interpreted policy in order to implement it in their area, and controlled the flow of information resulting from its implementation. As Grindle writes, 'the process of implementing public policies is a focus of political participation and competition' (McCormick, 1987: 384). However, this lack of inclusion of the universities in formulating policy that affects them has to be seen in context. First, China is politically still a Leninist state where the 'statisation' of popular organisations and mobilisation of their membership is thorough; the formulation of policy is not a participative project and implementation involves mobilisation. Second, participation in policy implementation can be better understood in the context of the Maoist insistence upon the self-sufficiency of each unit (*danwei*) of production, which continues to be a guiding administrative principle. This has led to a 'siege mentality' among individual institutions and production units resulting in a reluctance to change routines and procedures, and a tendency of guarding its own assets and its deficiencies. As resources are few, there is a trend to minimise risk-taking. Lampton comments:

> When various networks are mobilised by opposing elements of a fragmented elite, or by local authorities bent on resisting policy, effective implementation can become impossible and corruption almost inevitable. (Lampton, 1987a: 16)

These centrifugal tendencies have been overcome in China by enforcing Party discipline, ideological propaganda, and a strict surveillance system. All these methods tend to reinforce the power of the Party organisation at the local level, and have come in conflict with post-Mao reforms and the expectations they raised.

While the post-Mao leadership tried to promote consensus-building and negotiation, coercive state and Party power remained intact as a means of enforcing policy decisions. Thus a very few key universities in cities like Guangzhou and Shenzhen Special Economic Zone have introduced the more radical reforms in the administrative and financial patterns governing them. The rest of the universities have marked time, waiting for the results of experiments to be established in practice with the approval of the party/state leadership before introducing them in their own institutions. This allowed some of these reforms to be withdrawn in the wake of the 1989 movement:

> except for a few colleges and universities that have achieved marked results in the trial implementation [of the presidential responsibility system] are thus allowed to continue the system; institutions of higher learning, in general, should implement the system . . . under the leadership of the party committees for a long time to come. (GMRB, JPRS-CAR-89-102: 11)

Further, these experiments were launched within the broad policy framework endorsed by the party/state and were not in any way a departure from the educational line set by the central government.

The pyramid of higher education

The universities in China are administered at four different levels: national, provincial, prefectural and municipal, and county (see Figure 3.1). These reflect not just varying levels of academic standards but also different financial allocation patterns and status. At the top of the list are the state universities. However, there are further subdivisions within this category: between those run by the SEC and those by the Provincial Education Commission

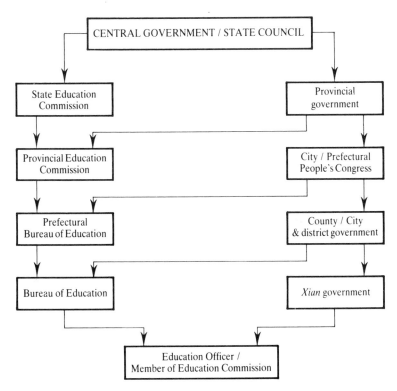

Figure 3.1 Administrative structure of higher education

(PEC), and between those run by the SEC directly and those run by various national ministries such as the Ministry of Commerce and some state-run enterprises like the China General Silk Company. The universities run by the SEC directly are the 'national key point' (NKP) universities. There are 35 such institutions in China and these are the most prestigious. Out of these 35, 9 are in Zhejiang Province alone, indicating the regional imbalances in educational facilities. The NKP universities have privileges that are not enjoyed by the ordinary institutions. First, when the distribution of resources is considered their demands and needs get priority over those of the others. This includes funds set aside for sending teachers and students abroad for further study, which is becoming a highly competitive area in education, and funds for research projects. Second, the promotional avenues in the NKP institutions are better; there are a higher number of professorial and associate professor posts available there. Finally, because of the prestige and the higher academic standard of these institutions the students of these universities are greatly advantaged in the state-controlled system of job allocations.

The universities run by the various ministries are not key-point universities. Their role is quite specific – to meet the particular personnel needs of the ministry that funds them. For example, the Ministry of Commerce is funding the Hangzhou College of Business and Commerce in order to meet its personnel needs. This has been one of the reforms introduced in the post-1978 period which has resulted in the linking of the external economic environment to the academic institutions. It was hoped that such a system would motivate both the ministries and the students to improve the educational standards and expand its network. The ministry gets a steady supply of educated personnel, the students the security of a job. It also relieves the pressure from an over-worked and under-funded SEC, and allows alternative surplus funds in other areas like that of industry to be used for education. There are, however, problems with these universities. First, they are too specialised and narrow in their educational base: the Ministry for Nuclear Energy, for example, has a university funded by it that offers courses serving only its specific needs. Such universities cannot provide the country with the much-needed administrative and research cadres who might be able to work across different areas. However, the financial constraints under which these institutions are working preclude curricular expansion. SEC officials hoped that inter-university and inter-ministerial co-operation might be the answer but this has yet to be worked out. These universities are then, in a sense, 'owned' by the various ministries and, therefore, have very different curricula, enrolment and development patterns. The economic health of these universities is also therefore dependent on the health of the ministry funding it. About 15 per cent of all university students attend these ministry-run colleges and universities.

At the provincial level the structure of higher education is again a differentiated one. The PEC is responsible for higher education in the provinces. There are glaring regional disparities among the various provinces of China in the sphere of higher education. For example, while Beijing alone boasts of 53 institutions of higher education, Sichuan has 47, Gangdong 35, Zhejiang 22, Fujian 19, Shanxi 17, Inner Mongolia 14, and Tibet only 3 (SEC, 1984: 374–91). In Zhejiang province there are three provincial key-point universities – Zhejiang Agricultural University, Zhejiang Medical University and Hangzhou University. These enjoy the same advantages in comparison with ordinary provincial universities as the NKPs do. However, the resources available to the provincial key-point universities fall far short of the national key-point institutions, as education is a provincial responsibility and therefore dependent on the financial position and policy priorities of each province. The rest are non-key, ordinary institutions but with certain exceptions. The Teachers' College (*shifan daxue*), for example, is under the 'dual leadership' of the PEC and the municipal government and occupies a unique place in the educational framework. Hangzhou University is the only comprehensive key-point university in Zhejiang Province.

The organisation of the university

The status of and the resources available to the university obviously affect the ethos and the work culture of a university. Provincial and local culture too have a varied impact on different institutions. However, when we examine the university microcosm we can still isolate certain common features and characteristics which are symptomatic of a centralised and standardised pattern of administration of these institutions which has not been entirely diluted by the post-Mao reforms.

An important reform introduced in 1985 has been the separation of powers and functions of the university administration. This has made the internal organisation of a university in post-Mao China a complex network of dual responsibility. The president of the university and the secretary of the Party committee both co-operate and compete in the performance of their respective functions, which though supposedly distinct overlap at many points, as we shall see below. The reform was concerned with defining distinct jurisdictions of the two power centres in the university – the administration and the Party. However, the pace of the implementation of the reforms tended to differ widely and their institutionalisation still remains to be completed. The in-built pressures of the Party bureaucracy which refuses to let go of its monopoly of decision-making power is an important factor in this delay, as is the vacillations of a central Party afraid of destabilisation and loss of control. These fears have been exacerbated by the 1989 student movement and there are signs of retrenchment on the question of giving greater autonomy to universities.

As we will see below, the definition of what is considered 'political' is largely responsible for this confusion. From a position of primacy in every sphere of the university's activities, the Party committee began to confront the issue of separation of powers as part of Deng Xiaoping's 'political restructuring' programme. In the 1985 'Decision' of the Central Committee on the reform of education, the management pattern of the university was reviewed and reforms introduced under what has come to be known as the 'President Responsibility System'. The document stated:

> The system under which the principal [of a school] or president [of a university] assumes full responsibility should be gradually applied. Where conditions permit, an administrative committee or senate headed by the principal or the president and composed of a small number of teachers and other employees, with teachers as the core, should be established and strengthened in order to ensure more democratic management and supervision. (CPC CC 1985: 20)

Under this system the secretary of the Party committee is in charge of the ideological work, and the president of academic affairs and general administration in the university. The latter include teaching, scientific research, personnel, finance, adult education programme

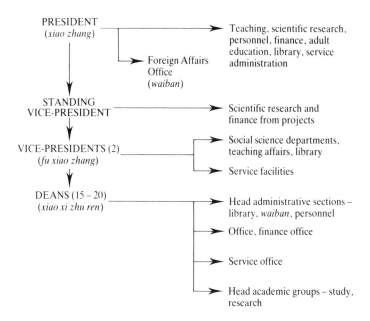

Figure 3.2 The structure of the university

in the university, the library and 'service administration'. The president is assisted by a 'director' or secretary of his office and several 'vice-directors'. The 'director' is the liaison between the office of the president and that of the Party secretary. The president is helped in administering departments by vice-presidents and deans and vice-deans of academic groups (see Figure 3.2).

Given the Maoist legacy of 'politics in command' on the one hand, however strongly repudiated by the present leadership, and the unsettled questions regarding the nature and role of the Communist Party in China's political system on the other, this reform has proved contentious to implement. The Party committees have attempted to 'stretch' the 'political' to cover nearly all areas of the university's activities. The administrators have countered with their own elastic interpretation of ideological work: 'ideological work' was also the responsibility of the president, as 'After all,' said the director of the president's office at Hangzhou University, 'to raise teaching quality is also ideological work.' The Party office has, however, continued to be involved in decisions on the

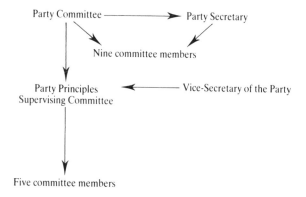

Figure 3.3   Structure of the Party in the university

promotions and recruitment of teachers, together with the president and the Academic Promotion Committee of the personnel office. This is because 'the teacher's ideological thought is also very important'; politics, represented by the Party office, remains a criterion in academic decision-making. The system of 'dual leadership lines' thus defies a clear demarcation of functions and roles;

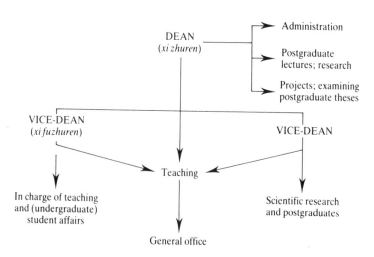

Figure 3.4   The structure of the department

such overlapping of decision-making practices can be found at every level of the university structure. This tussle between the two interests in the university has affected the attempts to separate powers between the Party and the administration.

At the departmental level, we see reflected all these authority structures of the university in a similar complexity. There is the formal academic administrative structure headed by the dean (or the head) of the department who is assisted by one or more vice-deans all looking after different areas of academic life in the department (see Figure 3.4). The reforms gave the dean the responsibility for the academic affairs in the departments under the system of 'dean responsibility', to parallel the president's position at the university level.

At the non-academic level there is the Party branch at the departmental level, with its own Party committee and its secretary; the branches of the Communist Youth League headed by a 'political director'; a branch of the Workers' Union with representatives chosen to attend the Teachers' Congress; and, at the very bottom of the scale, a class teacher (*banzhuren*) who has the general function of looking after the students' problems – academic and otherwise (see Figure 3.5). This structure duplicates the uni-

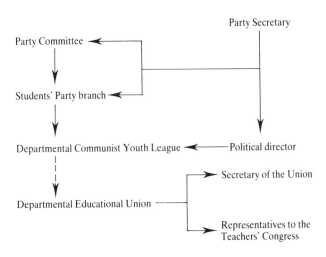

Figure 3.5 Organisational structure of the department

versity organisational structure. The class teachers have their own scale of promotion; in fact, they are the informal, departmental cadres. Many students in Hangzhou felt they take on this job to get a quicker promotion than would be their due through the normal channels. There is also a strong feeling among the students that the *banzhuren* are important cogs in the surveillance machine. Few students told me that they discussed any problems bothering them with their class teachers.

The university and its external environment

One of the most important reforms in the university administration of universities that was introduced by the post-Mao leadership has been opening them to external economic forces. This has had profound influence on the character of the universities.

Before 1978 the university came in contact only with the government and the party/state that controlled all aspects of its daily life; there were few bonds tying it to the socio-economic base of the society. The controls applied by party/state on the university were also, therefore, more direct and more predictable. This began to change in 1978, and by 1987 the university formally came in contact with the economic agencies with which hitherto it had had no connection. In June 1986 the State Council's 'Provisional Regulations of Responsibility in Administering Higher Education' laid down certain guidelines through which the universities were to be given more responsibility for economic functioning. The 'iron rice bowl' that had symbolised the Maoist state-subsidised security for universities was to be broken. It was pointed out that 'it is impossible to raise money from other sectors to invest in education' (FBIS/114, 4 June 1986: K4). As we have seen in Chapter 2, the problem of investment in higher education has been a persistent one in China.

Added to this is the tremendous pressure the Chinese education system is under, rapidly to increase its enrolment. Trained graduates are in great demand in every sphere of the economy as it takes off on its modernisation drive. The universities are in a significantly better financial position as compared to the primary and secondary sectors. For every RMB 1 spent on a primary or secondary student, RMB 72 are spent on a university student. Thus, for primary schools, per capita expenditure is RMB 30–40, for middle schools RMB 100 and for universities RMB 1500–2200. Despite this favourable position, because of the legacy of the Maoist period lack of any financial accountability by the universities and general mismanagement of resources – universities ran up enormous budgetary deficits. These were covered by taking out loans from the Ministry of Education. There is still an outstanding loan of RMB 150,000,000 against various universities.

Financial pressures have led the leadership to decide to decentralise the mobilisation of resources – material and human – and to relieve the political structure of the responsibility of serving overall social interest by introducing individual economic incentives in education as in industry. The 'Regulations' of 1986 mentioned some of the means to implement this new financial system:

> Colleges and Universities may apply the principle of 'sharing' responsibility in the use of funds, no reimbursement for overspent funds, retaining leftover funds and achieving budgetary tolerance on their own. (*ibid.*: K14)

The sources of external finance available to the university can be seen in Figure 3.6.

The governmental source of finance has already been discussed. The role that international organisations are playing in Chinese universities will be set out in the next section. Of the rest, we find that the internal university financing is still marginal.

One source of internal university funding is private sponsorship of student fees by individual rich peasants or entrepreneurs. For example,

> in 1984, a mushroom grower in the mountainous region paid the university RMB 1,300 a year to train a non-resident biologist. He has signed a contract with him to work at his farm for 8 years after graduation. (Li, CE, no. 4, 1986–7: 30)

However, it was clear that individual funding could not cover enough of the total expenditure. The cutting back of educational subsidies that supported students in higher education was seen as essential for the much-needed economic rationalisation. That any such policy would be unpopular with both the students and their parents was obvious, so the party/state decided to move cautiously, trying it out in the more prosperous areas first. The 1985 'Decision' of the Central Committee stated:

The people's grant-in-aid system shall be reformed. For students in normal schools and those who will work in hardship [areas] after graduation, the state will bear their board and lodging expenses, and their tuition and fees for extras will be waived. (CPC CC 1985: 15)

A scholarship scheme based on academic performance was introduced to replace the old grant system, as an incentive to better performance. It was hoped that the scheme would be uniformly implemented by 1988, which has indeed been the case, though it has led to much resentment (see Chapter 6).

The loan scheme is taken from the US pattern and involves the banks extending low-interest loans to students to cover their tuition and living expenses during their education. In view of the low wages and salaries, especially in the cities and towns from where a large part of the students come, these loans taken out by students will be paid off by the units that hire them after

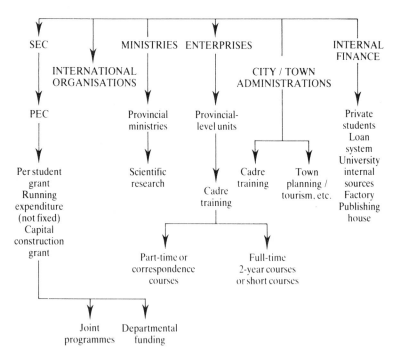

Figure 3.6   Sources of university finance

graduation. Whether this amount will be deducted from their wages/salaries, has not been made clear. If it is not, how far this will have an impact on the work and authority relations within enterprises on the one hand, and on the various disciplines being taught in the universities on the other, is yet to be seen. What was obvious from my interviews was that the financial aspect of these experiments is preoccupying the minds of the education officials at present; there was very little speculation about what the unintended consequences of these changes might be and how the university would deal with them.

Many other new schemes to better the financial position of the universities were introduced during this period. Most of these encouraged the entrepreneurial spirit in these institutions in keeping with the economic policies. In June 1986 the State Economic Commission, the SEC and the Chinese Academy of Sciences (CAS) circulated a document, 'Promoting Co-operation Among Large and Medium-sized Enterprises, the CAS and Institutions of Higher Learning' (JPRS, 18 April 1987: 30). This encouraged the universities and colleges to link up with various industries to 'focus on the development of new products, the reduction of consumption, the improvement of economic results, and the improvement of the capacity to earn foreign exchange through experts' (*ibid.*). These joint projects could be with ministries, enterprises or cities, and most were connected with applied scientific research. The form this co-operation took could differ. Teachers from universities might be invited to co-operate with these industrial and commercial units and administration on specific projects, or the university might undertake to train students for them through diploma courses. More 'advanced' universities, like Qinghua in Shanghai, could offer to establish 'scientific research and production associations' as a 'new economic entity in which technology and trade are integrated and research, development, production, application, service and sales are unified' (CE, no. 4, 1986–7: 3–6). While these latter kind of joint projects are still very few, co-operation with industrial units to research new projects or improve existing technology or management practices and to train personnel are fairly common, especially involving reputable universities in each area. Universities were also encouraged to set up their own enterprises to increase their revenues. Hangzhou University, for example, has a small paper mill on its premises and the revenue from this went to the university. Similarly, in the period 1979–86, 'the Dalian Management School earned 2–6 million yuan from its printing house, timber mill, fishing, chicken farms and computer service stations' (Cleverley, CE, no. 3, 1987: 347).

The Scientific Research Centre in every university manages these projects. Payment is made directly to the university, without the mediation of the SEC or the PEC. The Hangzhou PEC officials confirmed this when they told me that they do not have any estimate of Hangzhou University's total budget as it does not inform them about its alternative sources of income. This money does not go directly to the departments involved in the joint projects but is channelled through the university finance office, before which a certain percentage is held back for university expenses. Those who worked on the project get about 15 per cent of the sum as bonus. The units asking the university for trained graduates pay the university in different ways. 'The ministries and enterprises might either arrange to pay the university a fixed sum per student being trained, a fixed sum per project undertaken or give money towards capital construction', explained the chief accountant at Renmin Daxue in Beijing. For instance, the Ministry of Coal had undertaken to provide capital for building and equipping the Department of Computer Sciences at Hangzhou University, in return for its cadres being trained there. These projects are separate from those involving a ministry setting up an entire institution.

Due to the introduction of these new financial relations the universities have experienced a greater autonomy from the party/state, made possible by independent funding through industrial, commercial and individual enterprises. This in turn has resulted in clashes with the local governmental authorities and the Party branches which have witnessed with some alarm this growing economic clout of the universities. Further, the involvement of the economy in education has made even more marked the differentials among various universities – already significant because of the hierarchical structure of higher education – which has exacerbated strains within the educational system. Within the university, departments vie with each other for resources coming from outside the centrally allocated funds; new interests and new resentments have arisen because of this. The management of these tensions has led to the involvement of the Party to control the growing clash of interests within higher education. However, the pressing need for mobilising resources from outside the state budget has limited the party/state options in attempting to do this.

Politics of university finance

Financial reform has been one of the most important areas in restructuring the education system. It has primarily dealt with relations between the university and economic enterprises. However, the reform of financial management within the university is of growing importance. It covers the following areas: financial responsibility and accountability of the president of the university; financial relations between university administration and the SEC or the PEC; allocation of funds within the university among various departments; and the alternative sources of departmental finance and their control. Financial reforms are also seen as crucial to other areas of reform within the university: spending on student and staff welfare; the salary structure for the staff; the availability of foreign exchange and its spending by departments and the university. Tensions arising as a result of these reforms are creating new interests, tensions and contradictions as well as new possibilities for expansion of autonomy, both for the university and for the departments. These tensions have been exacerbated by the attempts made by the authorities at different levels to manage them, and so form part of an increasingly complex political story within the higher education system.

Decentralising financial responsibility

Before 1978, the structure of financial planning and allocation of resources to the universities was highly centralised. The Ministry of Education – backed by the Planning Ministry – gave the university a fixed amount that covered the basic expenditures of the university and the expenditure for development and expansion. The Ministry stipulated how many undergraduates were to be enrolled. This, of course, implied that the scope for expanding enrolment numbers in a university was minimal as any such move could lead to deficit financing. This did actually happen in the case of most universities, with the increasing pressure of the swelling ranks of high-school graduates wanting admission on the basis of '*dan wei*' (work unit) recommendations rather than entrance examination results. The university was fully accountable to the Ministry for all its expenditures, including its daily and recurrent expenditures.

Since 1978, however, this system has changed radically. Financial allocations made by the SEC are based upon the number of students enrolled in a university. Any rise in the number of students is accompanied by a corresponding rise in the grant to the university. However, this possibility of state-sponsored expansion in enrolment is counterbalanced by a greater accountability of the university to its funding body. The new system has its implications for departmental financing too. The offer of course options within a department becomes dependent on a fixed sum of money determined by the number of students. It seems more cost-efficient to restrict the options. The amount that each university gets per student varies. The figures range from RMB 1500 to RMB 2200 per student per year depending on the financial health of the province, the increase in prices for materials, and the courses being funded. Thus, for example, the Renmin Daxue accountant told me: 'industrial and scientific courses get more funding – RMB 2000–2200 per student per year; economics and finance students get RMB 1900; social sciences get RMB 1800 per student; and teacher training RMB 1900'. Distinction is also made between the levels being funded. While the above figures hold good for undergraduate students, the allocations made for each research student are RMB 4000–4200; each graduate student gets RMB 6300. These are average amounts.

Until 1978 the Ministry of Education could demand the return of any amount of allocated grant that might be left over at the end of the year. However, as already pointed out, the problem in many universities was not surplus funding but huge deficits leading to the necessity for loans from the state; the above stipulation under such circumstances then becomes superfluous. Moreover, such an arrangement gave no incentive to the university to save on costs. The reform of this system has allowed the university to retain any surplus funds as an incentive to save. Such a system was also seen to be in line with the market-oriented reforms that the party/state had introduced in education. As the universities increasingly came to be regarded as 'production units' and as economic units were increasingly placed in a market situation, the results of 'cost accounting' became more attractive as solutions to the problem of financial allocation and expenditure in universities in China:

> In initiating economic accounting in institutions of higher learning, we must first assess the results of educational investment through cost accounting. We should also take into consideration the uniqueness of the programs and areas of specialization offered by the different schools to obtain the cost index of students 'produced' by each specialty. (Ye, 1986–7: 9)

Decentralisation of financial responsibility has also proved important for other reasons. First, this has meant an increased independence for the university. While it is true that 90 per cent of the students of most universities are still financed by the SEC/PEC, the nature of the financial relations between these organisations and the university has altered enough to give the university a greater autonomy in matters relating to expenditure. One aspect of the 'presidential responsibility system' was that the president of each university was responsible for the profits and the losses of the university. However, the increased financial independence of the university has also meant that the university has become the immediate focus of discontent for competing interests vying for more funds. The university has become the focus for the pinning of expectations, of resentments, and the target of confrontation. The university, therefore, has today become a more open site for bargaining, competing and even agitating interests and groups.

Another dimension of intra-university politics introduced by the decentralisation of financial relations has been competition between departments for external resources. The various departments have different skills to sell, some more in demand than others, which means great variations in the resources that departments command. This, in turn, means that the facilities made available for the staff of each department also differ. The richer departments can offer greater material incentives to their staff while the poorer ones have had to introduce cut-backs, job losses and reduced funding for new academic research projects. The resentments caused by all this are easily imagined, and are exacerbated by the favourable attitude of the university authorities towards high-earning departments. The poorer departments feel their interests are being neglected by the university and, therefore, they are doubly disadvantaged. The rich departments, on the contrary, feel they are 'carrying' 'non-productive' departments who should be grateful to them rather than resentful. The implications that all this has for the direction of general academic orientation of the higher education system are also considerable. The importance of academic disciplines is now increasingly dependent upon the financial resources at the command of each department. Disciplines like computer research, management, industrial psychology, Chinese language have a much higher status in universities than subject areas like mathematics, philosophy, political science or history.

The universities open their doors

Like Ming dynasty China, Maoist China too had shunned the world. It was 'red', pure and unsullied by the winds of capitalism and later of 'social imperialism'. Its closed doors protected it from the contagion of revisionism that had spread from its erstwhile 'elder brother', the Soviet Union, to the rest of the socialist world. Economically, Maoist China was proud to be poor but self-sufficient. The Great Proletarian Cultural Revolution was a further exercise in self-purification and 'self-strengthening' away from the eyes of the world. With the death of Mao the lid came off the hidden frustrations and anger at the poverty and hardship that Mao had represented as cleansing. The Chinese people were no longer content to be 'poor and blank'; they wanted the material comforts denied them for so long. As the gates began to open little by little, there was a sense of shock at how far behind China had been left in the race of economic development. Even countries like India seemed to be doing better in industrial production, to the Chinese eyes, than China. And the developed West was much further ahead. 'We must recognise our backwardness', said Deng Xiaoping, 'because only such recognition offers hope. Now it appears that China is fully 20 years behind the developed countries in science, technology and education.' (Deng, 1984: 53) Foreign help was no longer unwelcome: 'Of course, in order to raise China's scientific and technological level we must rely on our own efforts . . . But independence does not mean shutting the door on the world, nor does self-reliance mean blind opposition to everything foreign.' (*ibid.*: 106–7) So China opened its doors to the world – to foreign investment in both the economy and education. This was called China's 'three orientations' – towards modernisation, the world, and the future. The impact of this opening up was profound, as can be expected. It was also destabilising. Historical parallel can be easily found in the post-Ming opening of imperial China. Deng's China was undergoing fundamental changes not only in its economic sphere with decollectivisation of agriculture and the introduction of market forces into the economy more generally, but also in its value system. The Maoist values of egalitarianism had been rejected; the new slogans encouraged the Chinese to 'get rich quick.' Capitalism was no longer a pejorative term; politically it was becoming accepted as a necessary stage in the development of a country, and economically it was accepted that socialist China had much to learn from its functioning. In the absence of an emphasis on aspects of distributive justice in post-Mao China, there remained an ideological vacuum. This was much more evident in the cities, where the traditional value system had survived less intact than it had in the countryside. While in the villages the penetration of the party/state and the process of expropriating traditional élites had made a break with the traditional civil society (see Siu, 1989), the lack of comprehensive mechanisation of agriculture meant that the new policies could lead to a partial but significant resurgence of pre-revolutionary values. This was much less the case in the cities, and even less so in the universities where the ideas of the capitalist, modernist West first found receptive audiences. With Maoism rejected, and Marxism suspect, Chinese intellectuals, especially university students, looked to the capitalist West for both technology and political ideas.

The post-revolution Chinese state had not always been averse to foreign aid. Indeed, perhaps it would not have survived without Soviet aid in the face of a Western blockade of socialist China. From 1950 to 1966 the Chinese state had engaged in a great variety of educational, cultural and sports agreements with other nations – mostly with those in the Soviet bloc – to facilitate exchange of scientific data, technology and training of scientific personnel. In 1958, for example, 'some 530 delegates travelled abroad to represent the PRC in nearly 100 cultural and educational missions' (Fraser, 1965: 67). However, the scale of Western aid to post-Mao China exceeds any previous experience of foreign co-operation. 'Since 1978 China has sent some 80,000 people to about 70 countries and regions: over 60,000 went under official government sponsorship (40,000 as visiting scholars or research fellows, 20,000 as graduate students and 1,000 as undergraduates)' (China Today, June 1990: 28). Between 1978 and 1984 5,388 foreign students came to study in China for various courses, and between 1978 and 1986 1,479 foreign teachers were invited to Chinese institutions (Huang, 1987: 231, 233). By 1985 151 Chinese higher education institutions had established links with 320 foreign institutions (*ibid.*: 236). International aid organisations like UNESCO, UNDP, UNICEF, WHO and the World Bank have played, and continue to play, a significant role in this transference of technology and culture (see Hayhoe, 1989, and Hayhoe and Bastid, 1987). By 1991 the World Bank alone will have loaned China 803.4 million US dollars to expand its educational facilities and improve its technological base (Huang, *op. cit.*: 241). Private Western foundations like the Ford Foundation, and overseas Chinese business people have also contributed to this exchange programme. Between 1978 and 1984 8,000 self-sponsored students went abroad, mainly to the United States (*ibid.*: 230). The impact of this massive educational exchange programme was profound. While bringing in new ideas and values, this opening up also alerted the Chinese leadership to the old dilemma faced by the Chinese rulers through the ages – the contradiction between the need for modern technology by the country, and for continued control of the process by the state. As the Vice-Chairperson of the Zhejiang PEC said to me, their purpose in opening Chinese academic institutions to the world and seeking exchanges with them was to 'introduce Chinese language and culture to the world and learn high technology from other countries'. It was not to engage in a battle of ideas, or a tussle between different value systems. Even at his liberal best Deng called Western ideas 'flies' that would necessarily come in when China's windows were opened to the world: they were a necessary evil to be managed and controlled. The young university intellectuals thought differently, and a consequent clash with the state became almost inevitable.

Exchanges with foreign educational agencies take place at

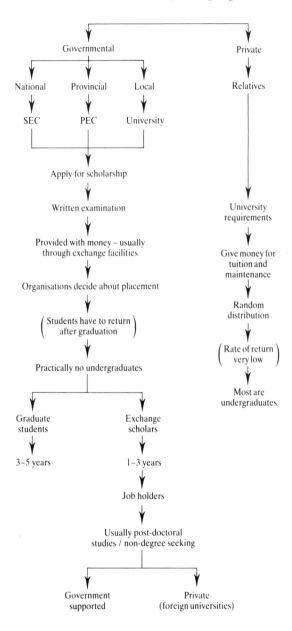

Figure 3.7 Pattern of exchanges with foreign universities

various levels – national, provincial and unit levels on the one hand, and governmental or private levels on the other. The politics of these exchanges makes a fascinating study at both an institutional and a personal level. '*Guanxi*', the network of personal relationships, shows up very clearly in this sphere as the personal connections needed here have to be very strategically placed in order to be maximised by individuals or institutions (see Figure 3.7).

Most of these exchanges are barters of educational facilities as the SEC has very little money in foreign exchange to spare, and the position gets even worse at the provincial level. However, whatever resources are available with the party/state for sending scholars abroad are allocated by the SEC through fixing quotas. This system has resulted in a 'hierarchy of quotas' developing, which feeds competition and resentment among the various institutions involved. For example, national key-point universities corner 30 to 40 places a year, Chinese Academy of Sciences (CAS) around 150 for all its institutes, Chinese Academy of Social Sciences 20 to 30, the various ministries 50 to 150 depending upon current priorities within the economic plan, the provinces between 5 to 20 to be divided among all institutions, usually numbering around 25 to 50 (Hayhoe, 1989: 54). The PEC thus has no money of its own to send students abroad. If the scholarship of the student is less than $450 per month, then the PEC might help out or give partial help towards travel. At the university level every student going abroad gets RMB 150 for acquiring an appropriate new wardrobe before leaving China. The complaint of many students is that this amount is too little and should be increased.

The problem of these students and scholars staying in their host countries is a serious one and is losing the Chinese government prospective experts sorely needed for the modernisation effort. This has been particularly true since 1986–7 when the Chinese students abroad, especially in the United States, organised to support student movements inside China. The fear of discrimination and even punishment for those who participated in these protests, on the one hand, and a professional opportunism on the part of others has meant that thousands of trained personnel have been lost to China in a 'brain drain'. This resulted in the state employing various strategies for controlling scholars abroad. The 'Provisional Regulations of the State Education Commission Concerning the

Work of Sending Scholars Abroad', which became effective in December 1986, stipulates that students sent to a particular university in a chosen country cannot apply from there to go to another university, course or country once their studies are finished. It also requires that the students sign an 'Agreement on Studying Abroad' which states the aim, content and length of study, 'the return date of such students as required by the government or unit concerned, regulations concerning the funding of such students, and other rights, responsibilities and obligations of each side' (CE, Spring 1988: 40–1). Political screening of students going abroad has increased since the student demonstrations of 1986–7. Pressure to return is also brought to bear upon students studying abroad through their families. These deterrents, however, are not enough. In conditions such as those pertaining after June 1989, foreign governments have been more sympathetic to the demands for visas by the Chinese students who do not want to return. The Chinese government has, therefore, provided incentives to those who are willing to return. First, they have assured the Chinese students at home that the policy of sending scholars abroad for study will not stop (BR, 21–7 May 1990: 29). This was done to alleviate suspicions that those inside China would be trapped and unable to go abroad, and therefore to stay out of the country if at all possible. Second, returning to China has been made attractive by setting up job placement centres like the China Service Centre for Scholarly Exchange. This centre not only puts returning graduates in touch with enterprises and institutions requiring their skill, it also sends 'recruiting teams' from various enterprises to travel abroad to 'talk personally with the candidates. These people usually do the hiring for their company on the spot.' (China Today, June 1990: 29) Offers of preferential treatment in getting residential units, and other non-material incentives, are also being used by the government, including appeals to the scholars' patriotism.

The impact of the reforms

The impact of the reforms discussed above on the university life in China has been great and varied. There has been a lessening of control of the centralised authority of the SEC and the PEC.

Alternative financing, for example, has meant greater autonomy to the university administration, and correspondingly less tight control by the SEC and the PEC. Thus, while *all* expenditures by the university were earlier monitored by the SEC or PEC, now the sum granted to the universities for daily expenditure and the fixed sum per student given to them are not accounted for by the universities, which take their own decisions regarding the areas they want to spend on (CE, Spring 1988: 40–1). Similarly, the negotiations with various financial agencies are now the responsibility of the university; no permission is needed from central administrative organs for forging such 'horizontal links' with the economy (*ibid.*). This, in turn, creates the interstices in which the demands for higher levels of academic independence can begin to grow.

The reversal of Maoist egalitarian policies and the introduction of the 'key point' institutions has led to the breaking up of the monolithic education structure created during the Cultural Revolution. It has led to the emergence of new competing interest groups within the educational system. Non-key institutions are demanding greater governmental support in view of their inability to compete with key-point institutions. The material and non-material differentials among the staff of key and non-key institutions have also caused tensions. Further, the prestige attached to the key-point institutions and their ability to command finance from areas that are not under direct SEC control have meant that these universities are able to use their influence and relative independence to experiment with greater freedom and daring than other universities, leading to the opening of some other areas to internal university management that had been hitherto denied them. While these can serve as precedents for other non-key-point universities with the same demands and problems, their realisation is more difficult, underscoring the different positions that the key and non-key institutions occupy in the educational system.

The relations between departments within a university have also grown more complex; new interest groups have emerged as a result of the introduction of the reforms. The universities have been considering making some departments autonomous – i.e., separating them from their faculties and making them financially independent. This has resulted in a contradiction. While the 'rich' departments might want such independence for reasons that are obvious, the poorer ones do not. Many universities are also ambivalent on the question of departmental autonomy. While recognising the value of the high-earning departments to the university in strengthening the institution's links with the economy, and increasing the income of the university, a university would perhaps not like to see the 'rich' departments get too independent. However, it might also want to cut its losses and let the poor departments go, in which case it has to give greater independence to the stronger departments too. Hangzhou University, for instance, has been wanting to separate the Department of Physical Education from the University and transform it into an autonomous institute on an off-campus site since 'a few years back', but the Department (already under financial stress) does not want to be in a position where the University can shirk its financial responsibility towards it. The result is an impasse: the Department refuses to move in the matter. Non-action seems to be the strategy of resistance.

As interest groups form and begin to recognise themselves in opposition to other groups, the interdepartmental contradictions also emerge. For example, a complaint against the lecturers involved in external scientific, industrial projects in Hangzhou University was that they are not giving enough time to preparing and delivering their lectures and that this will result in students having to pay the price of their teachers' negligence. Those who were engaged in projects outside the department wanted a lighter teaching load to offset their project work. An important question that is being raised as a result of the financial reforms in the University is that pure science and social science research is suffering as there are no external takers for what they have to offer. At the Psychology Department at Hangzhou University (a very prestigious and rich department), for example, there are two major areas of research – a UNESCO-funded project on child psychology, and one on industrial management psychology. The latter has involved a lot of work with industrial units that want this department to advise them on the latest worker–management techniques and devise tests for worker recruitment and promotion. We have already witnessed the plight of others like the Physical Education Department.

A result of the opening of the educational institutions to the 'outside world' has been the emergence of new, or the strengthening of already existing, interest groups. Generational divisions have emerged because of competition for opportunities now available to the academic community. Foreign tours and seminars, visiting fellowships, and bidding for incoming resources create competition within departments, and also between lecturers of different generations. Thus middle-aged professors complained that the younger lecturers neglected their teaching load in favour of preparing for the GRE examination. The younger ones felt that the middle-aged professors, trained in Russia or at home, were unable to understand the importance of studying in the West, and did nothing to encourage their younger colleagues to try to improve their credentials abroad. They also complained that senior professors used their influence with the education authorities to ensure that their own children could go abroad for further study, making it very difficult for others to get their share of the very limited number of such opportunities (see Chapter 5).

At the university level, the introduction of the 'president responsibility system' has created its own possibilities for staking claims for academic and administrative autonomy *vis-à-vis* the Party. However restricted the definition of 'academic matters' might be, however limited the sphere of influence of the president, however tentative the implementation of this reform, it has created a new space, a new dimension in which the struggle over autonomy can take place. With the introduction of this reform the tussle for power and influence between the president and the Party secretary need not remain a latent one involving personality-based skirmishes, but can take on the colour of a 'fight over principles'. The fear of being branded with the wrong political and ideological label is lessened to a degree. The same can be seen at the departmental level with greater responsibility devolving on the dean. How seriously the party/state takes this change in the university can be seen in the attempted withdrawal of the 'president responsibility system' in the aftermath of the June 1989 movement (GMRB, JPRS-CAR-89-102: 11–12).

At a much broader, political level, these reforms have also resulted in ideology losing its position of high visibility. As an antidote to the Maoist dictum of 'politics in command', the Deng regime reversed the emphasis. Efficiency not ideology was to be the new keyword. The frequent political upheavals of the Maoist period had made the ground fertile for this change; there was a general political cynicism among the youth that had led to their withdrawal from the public sphere. The lowering of the prestige enjoyed by the CPC, together with the leadership's decision to use non-mobilisational strategies for achieving its goals, also led to the same result. A relaxing of the ideological rhetoric did not, however, lead to any attempts at dismantling the political structure within the academic institutions, or even its radical restructuring. What *was* attempted was the delimiting of spheres of influence and responsibility. The withdrawal of the primacy of the political was seen as a prerequisite for the success of the economic democracy so essential to the present strategy for modernisation. However, even this partial loosening of party/state control created new spaces for bargaining that the intellectuals in the university tried to maximise and the Party cadres to minimise, leading to a sometimes lively, sometimes bitter struggle. How difficult this tussle could get is indicated by the Party cadres' call in the wake of the June 1989 protests to 'pay particular attention to improving the quality of political work cadres in schools of higher learning'; '[A] top priority task is to stabilize the existing contingent while systematically replenishing it with comrades having a firm political stand', urged a Party bureaucrat (GMRB, *ibid.*: 12).

While the university has provided the stage setting for oppositional movements in China, the key actors have been the Party cadres, and the 'high' and 'low' intellectuals including researchers, lecturers at every level and, of course, the students. The next section of this book takes up these actors separately and together to analyse their roles in the struggle for expanding their participation in the public sphere.

4

The Party in the university

Introduction

If the suppression of the student movement in June 1989 was indicative of anything, it was the intractability of the party/state to reform. During the post-Mao period the programme for economic modernisation had set the agenda for the political debate. This had been evident both in the re-evaluation of the Maoist years (CC, 1981; Deng, 1984: 357; see also Chapter 1) and in the policy decisions regarding individual rights taken by the regime (Deng, *op. cit.*: 240–1, 260, 320). However, as the political reform programme caught speed these carefully constructed limitations on political reforms came to be challenged – first in practice, later in rhetoric. The party became divided in its response to this growing challenge. On the one hand, there were the 'hardliners' – such as Yang Shangkun, Chen Yun, Qiao Shi and Li Peng – who were convinced of the need for economic reform but who refused to take on board questions regarding political pluralism. On the other hand were those who acknowledged that the success of the economic reforms depended to a large extent on the legitimacy of the government, which then begged the question of political restructuring. Hu Yaobang and Zhao Ziyang were the most prominent members of this faction. The agenda they set for themselves was not, of course, to jeopardise the power of the CPC. What they wanted was to *manage* the demand for political reform most effectively. It was to be an exercise in maintaining the whole system, even if it meant compromising the interests of some sections of the Party élite. They wanted to ensure that the CPC ruled an economically strong and politically stable country – even if that led to limitations being placed on its political power.

These two positions were not fixed within the Party. Deng symbolised the changing dynamic and the complex calculations of those in power. It was Deng who had first accepted, indeed encouraged, the view that for the four modernisations to succeed China needed not only a free market, but also a 'political restructuring' (Deng, 1987: 145–8). However, he was unable to free himself from both the ideological position of the centralised monopoly of power of the Communist Party, and the faction that represented this political view. In 1987 he cautioned: 'we will not tolerate some people's opposition to socialism. The socialism we refer to is Chinese socialism with Chinese characteristics and it is impossible to build a Chinese-type socialism without the leadership of the Communist Party.' (CPC CC, Beijing, 1989: 26) The economic logic of the market, and the possessive individualism that the leadership itself had unleashed in the heady days of the early to mid-1980s, had created the genie of articulated public choice that now came to haunt the regime. New interest groups emerged with decollectivisation of land, recognition of private enterprise, and opening up of the country to foreign aid and investment. The articulation of their interests required space in the public sphere – both to influence policy, and to place demands upon the government. As the demand for this space increased, it came to challenge the premise upon which the CPC based its rule – the 'mass line' variant of 'proletarian democracy' that left no other recognised interests, no other voices in the public political sphere but that of the CPC. It was to this threat that the orthodox Leninist party-man in Deng responded.

There were other reasons for the retreat by Deng. His earlier endorsement of curtailing the Party's power, and opening up local Party branches to public criticism, while protecting the central power organs sent the morale of the lower-level Party bosses plummeting. Local Party committee secretaries felt threatened by the pressures brought to bear on them by the concept of the separation of powers popularised by Deng himself. In 1988, for example, the Sichuan Party Committee 'abolished party groups of 9 departments and bureaux and discipline inspection groups of 4

. . . Party groups of 25% of departments and bureaux [were] abolished.' (FBIS/88/096/52) The local cadres felt let down and devalued by the higher Party authorities. Their ideological and political work was made more difficult by the changing norms governing the 'socialist commodity economy'. They also felt upstaged. The higher Party bureaucrats increasingly turned to the intellectuals – the 'ninth stinking category' of the Maoist years – for ideas. In a party of more than 47 million members, those who filled the ranks of disgruntled Party bureaucrats formed a significant interest group. And they had links through the formal and informal networks to the very top of the Party hierarchy. As the unpredictable temper of the intelligentsia became evident through their increasingly impatient critique of the Party, the discipline of the Party cadre seemed more attractive to the ruling gerontocracy of which Deng himself was part.

Further, as the 1980s wore on the question of corruption within the Party became an important issue. The increasing inflationary pressures on the falling real incomes of the urban population, and the problems of agricultural infrastructural breakdowns contrasted sharply with the freewheeling lifestyles of the children of the top Party cadres. Deng's own children came in for a lot of criticism on this question, as did the children of leaders like Hu Yaobang and Zhao Ziyang. The tone of the Party bureaucracy was affected down the line as the rhetoric of individualism met with opportunities of graft. The programme for 'political restructuring' and of 'supervision of the masses' meant that these cases of corruption got an early airing. For example, in September 1988 the central Discipline Inspection Commission made public the 'guidelines on dealing with violations' in order to 'increase the "transparency" of party work so that people can see what is being done and can supervise' (China Daily, FBIS/88/175/34). No longer was the Party a sacred cow; both Mao and Deng had demystified it in their own different ways. The option of self-rectification of the Party behind closed doors was no longer present. Throughout 1988 and 1989 stories about action taken against corrupt cadres were published and the numbers involved in corruption were large indeed. According to a Renmin Ribao report, between 1982 and 1987 177,000 Party members were expelled (SWB/FE/0285/B2/8) due to mainly economic crimes – 'smuggling, bribery, embezzlement, violations concerning foreign affairs' (*Xinhua*, SWB/FE/0232/B2/ 5). Such publicity was an attempt to appease the growing public anger. It had, however, the affect of confirming for the people their negative image of the Party. It was clear that the Party was unable to supervise itself effectively. For the people to be able to do so, a much greater degree of 'opening up' was needed, and increasingly demanded, which became an ever-increasing irritant for the conservative faction within the Party. Even as early as October 1988 Qiao Shi, who was to be one of the beneficiaries of the fall of Zhao Ziyang and is the current secretary of the Party's Central Commission for Discipline Inspection, warned that

> Some comrades . . . think that the delegation of power [implies] that they can disregard central instructions and discipline. The authority of the Central Committee and the State Council must be guaranteed. (*Xinhua*, SWB/FE/0298/B2/1)

The 1980s saw an increasing erosion of the moral authority of the Party. The Party was facing significant changes in its membership. Both the generational and the educational profiles of the Party were undergoing change. As a result of the trauma of the Cultural Revolution and the cynicism of the post-Mao period, encouraged by the Party's own assessment of its history (CPC CC, 1981), the membership of young people showed a considerable drop. In 1983 the percentage of Party members aged 25 years and younger was only 3.34 per cent, in comparison with the 1950 figure of 26.6 per cent (Rosen, 1989a: 5). This fall resulted in the Party launching a recruitment drive in 1984 which proved successful. Two-thirds of the members recruited between 1978 and 1987 were below the age of 35 and had at least a senior high-school education (*ibid.*). By the end of 1988 30.4 per cent of the total Party members were educated above senior middle-school level, and illiterate members constituted only 7.27 per cent of the Party as opposed to 69 per cent in 1949 (*Xinhua*, SWB/FE/0571/B2/8). These changes were significant in that they created generational differences within the Party. In a culture where age, seniority and authority went together, this shift in the pattern of membership created new tensions. The older people felt threatened; the younger ones frustrated. As the emphasis on professionalism increased, the resulting devaluing of ideological purity symbolised by the veteran cadres became evident. The younger members were drawn to the faction led by Zhao who seemed to have donned the mantle of Hu Yaobang as the chief reformist of the Party after the latter's fall from grace in 1987. In the factional struggle that was hotting up within the Party, generational issues became significant. As Deng came to lean towards stricter controls over the burgeoning demand for 'democracy', his alignment with the geriatric élite of the Party became stronger. It was the older cadres at every level that became the support base of this élite. Li Peng seemed to confirm this position when he commented at a conference to discuss Party affairs in October 1989: 'we used to give more importance to the professional performance of personnel working state organs than to their political consciousness, and this has weakened party work' (*Xinhua*, SWB/FE/0589/B2/3). The emphasis on ideological purity was to be reaffirmed in a context of political instability.

The move of the Party from a more tolerant to a harder political position was also influenced by the events in Eastern Europe and the Soviet Union. Deng rejected Gorbachev's programme of *glasnost* as inapplicable to China. The Soviet Party Congress where the CPSU relinquished in principle its monopoly of power was not reported in the Chinese press. China's 'multi-party' system – of the eight 'democratic' political parties – was held up as proof that China was not a one-party state, and therefore not in need of a dose of Gorbachevian reforms. Party theoretician Wu Jiang rejected, for example, the suggestion of 'some' that 'a legal opposition faction and open competition should be allowed within the Party. This goes too far', he said. It 'involves splitting up the Party' (*Liaowang*, FBIS/88/135/22). The fact that the students demonstrating in Tian'anmen Square at the time of the visit of Gorbachev on 16 May 1989 – which would otherwise have been a feather in Deng's political cap – repeatedly praised the reforms of the Soviet leader and reviled Deng was a tremendous loss of face for the Chinese leadership. While the reformers within the Party responded to the challenge of Eastern Europe by attempting to reform the Party to the extent needed to avert open rebellion by the inflamed section of the intelligentsia, the hardliners instinctively closed ranks.

These political debates and detours on the way to reform had a crucial impact upon the Party's position within the university. The various initiatives by, and constraints upon, those in authority referred to above can be seen in the politics of institutions of higher education. The management of conflict with the intelligentsia took very particular and acute forms. As we have seen in Chapter 2, two major impulses had motivated higher education reform. The first was the rejection of the Maoist model of education which emphasised the primacy of the political; efficiency became the motto of the post-Mao regime. The second was the bid to reconcile the intelligentsia with the post-Mao state. These considerations placed tremendous pressure on the university-level Party committees to step back from the centre of the university administrative structure and resulted in the beginning of a process of redefining their relationship with other agencies and interest groups in institutions of higher education. As at the level of national politics, both the reforms and their implementation became a complex exercise. Opposition to the reforms gained strength from the equivocal position of the central Party leadership on the reforms. Two simultaneous projects – of encouraging the intelligentsia to contribute to the modernisation drive by giving them sufficient autonomy, and of controlling the growing demands for greater academic and political independence – led the central Party leadership to take an ambiguous position on the role and position of the local-level Party branches. Thus, after the student unrest of 1986–7, Deng said about Fang Lizhi, the leading dissident astrophysicist of China now in political exile in Britain: 'I have read Fang Lizhi's speeches. He doesn't sound like a Communist Party member at all. Why do we keep people like him in the Party? He should be expelled, not just persuaded to quit.' (Deng, 1987: 162). Fang *was* expelled very soon after this statement was made. This admonition by Deng illustrates the inability of the Party leaders to respond to criticism from the intelligentsia that did not subscribe to the officially accepted code of political debate. The definition of what constitutes critique, its scope and nature, remained dependent upon the interpretation of the central Party leadership. However, the very process of debate, the introduction of a separation of powers at the local level, the withdrawal of a mobilisational political strategy in favour of one geared to control, and the needs generated by the introduction of market forces into higher education, made the position of the Party in the university an area for renegotiation.

The Party in the university: a tussle for leadership

The Party in the university cannot simply be regarded as an instrument of surveillance and control for the party/state. Its presence is legitimised by ideological argument. Education has been an arena for the highly charged political debates and struggles for the control of ideological apparatuses in China. At his 'Talks at the Yenan Forum of Art and Literature' in 1942, Mao had clarified:

> [Our purpose is] to ensure that literature and art fit well into the whole revolutionary machine as a component part, that they operate as powerful weapons for uniting and educating the people and for attacking and destroying the enemy, and that they help the people fight the enemy with one heart and mind. (Mao, 1967c: 70)

Education under Mao was seen both as an instrument through which the correct ideological attitudes are inculcated into the 'masses', and as a weapon that is used to destroy the undergrowth of unacceptable ideas rooted in a 'feudal/capitalist' past but re-emerging constantly like weeds in the socialist present:

> It must not be assumed that the new system can be completely consolidated the moment it is established, for that is impossible . . . To achieve its ultimate consolidation, it is necessary not only to bring about the socialist industrialisation of the country and persevere in the socialist revolution on the economic front, but to carry on constant and arduous socialist revolutionary struggles and socialist education on the political and ideological fronts. (Mao, 1977: 423)

Together, these two perspectives were to form the basis for the post-revolutionary cultural and educational policy in China, and had implications for the role that the Party was to play in the field of education. As Mao's view presupposed a class basis not just for educational structures but for any literary, cultural or academic production, it also needed to define the role of those engaged in such production:

> Our literary and art workers must accomplish this task and shift their stand; they must gradually move their feet over to the side of the workers, peasants and soldiers, to the side of the proletariat, through the process of going into their very midst and into the thick of practical struggles and through the process of studying Marxism and society. (*ibid.*: 78)

Given the political nature of educational and cultural production, it was necessary that there be an organisation to oversee the process of 'studying Marxism and society', and to assess the political impact of educational practice on society. This organisation could only be the Party. The argument for supervision of educational practice by the Party was made not just on grounds of the ideological nature of education in Marxist texts. It was also essential to counteract the influence of the 'feudal', bureaucratic, and western/'imperialist' trained remnants among the intelligentsia. The last was particularly threatening to the new regime which found itself blockaded by the western powers after its victory. An ideological 'remoulding' of western trained intellectuals was thus seen as essential from both ideological and political perspectives. As Qian Chunrui, the then vice-minister for education, said in 1951:

> . . . if the teachers in institutions of higher education persist in adhering to the reactionary thought of the British and American bourgeois class, if they persist in sticking to their personal individualism, objectivism, and sectarian point of view, and fail to carry out true reform, then all phases of the reform of higher education, the reorganising of faculties and departments, curriculum-reform, the reform of teaching methods, and the like will flounder, and it will be impossible to carry out the complete reform of higher education. (Fraser, 1965: 122)

There was, however, intense debate surrounding the issue of Party presence in educational institutions throughout the 1950s. What was questioned within the Party was not so much the supervisory role of the Party in education, but the nature of the supervision. Some, like the education minister Chen Boda in 1952, felt that

> . . . The fundamental task of the Party members in the academy is to learn with modesty from the scientists to help them do their work well . . . We cannot judge scientists of the old type by merely considering the time when they accept Marxism–Leninism of their own will. The important thing is to see whether or not they are carrying on work in their respective scientific fields with a realistic attitude. It is very important for Party members to understand this (Fraser, 1965: 166).

What was at stake for the intelligentsia was a sphere of relative autonomy from the party/state control in areas of research, teaching, literary and artistic production. The 'double hundred' movement was a result of this debate. It ended unhappily for the intellectuals when an 'anti-rightist' campaign was launched in 1958 that led to the persecution of thousands of intellectuals who had spoken out in favour of freedom for academia (for details see MacFarquahar, 1960; Fraser, 1965: 209–12, see also Chapter 5).

The Cultural Revolution reopened the question of the relationship between the Party and the intelligentsia in a most contentious way. Mao had always been suspicious of the intelligentsia hijacking the communist revolution by monopolising the membership of the state bureaucracy and of the higher education system. The developments in Eastern Europe and in Brezhnev's Soviet Union seemed to confirm his worst fears about communist parties becoming self-perpetuating bureaucratic élites alienated from the 'masses'. A simmering antipathy among the sections of the party/state cadres that supported Mao in his concerns found a spark in the combustible situation of struggle for political power between Mao and Liu Shaoqi in 1966. Liu basically supported the Soviet model of economic and political development. Mao gave the call for a purification of the party/state – for bombarding the 'Headquarters' where 'capitalist-roaders' were planning a 'restoration of capitalism'. The struggle between the influence and power of the 'capitalist-roaders' and the revolutionary fervour of the Maoist radicals was not characterised as a 'struggle among the people' – it was an 'antagonistic contradiction' which could be resolved only through class struggle (see Mao, 1964). As the intellectuals were characterised in the Leninist tradition as being 'petty bourgeois individualists', their class position put them in the camp of political and ideological suspects. They became the 'ninth stinking category' to be reviled, and supervised and controlled as closely as possible. This was made possible through the forming of 'three-in-one' revolutionary committees in educational institutions composed of workers/peasants, the People's Liberation Army (PLA) and revolutionary cadres. These committees determined the policies and management of schools and universities 'including [their] curriculum, production work, intake of students and budget; [they] vetted the performance of teachers and students and organised the work of door-keepers, medical staff, office workers and cooks' (Cleverley, 1987: 183). As 'politics in command' became the dominant rhetoric of the period, these committees came to wield increasing power over the lives of the intellectuals, as their approbation and disapproval could make or break careers and lives in the university. They also thus came to symbolise the alienation of the intellectuals from the Party during the period as they were used to conduct the witch-hunts that formed the bulk of the 'political rectification' of the intelligentsia.

While the Party went through a split in its ranks during the upheavals of the Cultural Revolution, at no stage was its right to command socio-economic policy questioned. Mao had raised a crucially important question regarding the nature of a ruling party in a socialist political system, echoing Marx's question 'who will educate the educators?' Mao had pointed to the need for mechanisms to supervise the Party by the masses; organisations for the people to be able to participate in the making and implementing of policies that affected them. However, even when Mao attacked the party 'Headquarters' and declared it to be infiltrated by 'capitalist-roaders', the target of the attack was not the organisation and the position of the Party in socialist China, but those who controlled it (see discussion in Chapter 1). The concept of the Leninist party organisation was not reworked: 'If all [of these organisations] are changed into communes, what will we do with the Party?' asked Mao in February 1967 of the Shanghai radicals Zhang Qunqiao and Yao Wenyuan who had set up a commune and wanted the rest of the country to follow suit till it could be named 'People's Commune of China'. Mao admonished:

> Where will we put the Party? In the committees set up under a commune, there will be members who belong to the Party, and others who don't. Where will we put the Party committee? . . . There has to be a nucleus. It doesn't matter what it's called, it is all right to call it a Communist Party, it is all right to call it a social-democratic party, it is all right to call it a social-democratic workers' party, it is all right to call it a Guomintang, it is all right to call it the I-kuan-tao, but in any case there has to be a Party. In a commune there has to be a Party; can the commune replace the Party? (JPRS, Miscellany, 1969: 453–4)

The Cultural Revolution did lead to reaffirmation of the 'mass line' politics, but with the role of the Party as the only mobilisational organisation intact. The continued strength of the Party was evident in the way it took over the task of reordering the social and political patterns after the army withdrew from the scene, at the official withdrawal of the movement in 1969.

The debate regarding a separation of powers marked a change

in the political climate in China. Until after 1978, both the demand
for a change in the political system and the response to the demand
had been implicit: built into the process of the implementation of
policies in sectors other than political. A demand for structural
political change had been raised during the 1978–9 Democracy
Wall movement:

> from the bourgeois two- or multi-party system to the proletarian single-
> party system, and then from the latter to a proletarian two- or multi-
> party system – this alone constitutes the truly requisite path towards
> the withering away of the political parties. (Chen, 1984: 34)

However, it was never put on the political agenda for discussion by
the party/state leadership. The suppression of the movement made
it clear that political debate within the Party still centred around
the pivotal, vanguard role of the Party:

> As long as the class struggle exists at home and abroad, as long as
> imperialism and social imperialism still exist internationally, not only
> must the state machinery of the dictatorship of the proletariat not be
> weakened, it must be continuously firmed up and strengthened . . . we
> will never countenance any so-called democracy in which a minority
> violates the democratic rights of the majority. This kind of so-called
> democracy is not a social democracy but is rather anarchism. (GMRB,
> JPRS, no. 1, 18 July 1979)

It was only with the removal of Hua Guofeng and the placing
before the country by Deng Xiaoping and his team of the
programme for economic modernisation as the primary goal that
political reorganisation became a focus of debate. In his report to
the Twelfth National People's Congress of the CPC on September
1982 Hu Yaobang said:

> The party should, of course, exercise leadership over production,
> construction, and work in all other fields. Effective leadership has to be
> informed and competent. However, the party's main role is to provide
> political and ideological leadership in matters of principle and policy,
> and in the selection, assignment, assessment, and supervision of
> cadres. It should not be equated with administrative work in a
> government department nor production in an enterprise. A party
> organisation should not take everything into its own hands. (Zeng,
> 1987: 87)

What the new regime aimed at was the separation of powers of the
Party and the state in order to make administration more efficient,

and economic policy more workable. The continued interference of inexperienced Party bureaucrats in areas of economic policy-making and implementation had been identified as a major cause of the economic backwardness of the country. Deng acknowledged:

> we have placed too little emphasis on ensuring the necessary degree of decentralisation, delegating necessary decision-making power to the lower organisation and opposing the over-concentration of power in the hands of individuals. We have tried several times to divide power between the central and local authorities, but we never defined the scope of the functions and powers of the party organisations as distinct from those of the government and of economic and mass organisations. (Deng, 1984: 312)

What was needed was an efficient system of government that could take advantage of intellectual expertise, and a political system controlled by the Party that would be better able to serve both the modernisation of the economy and the political interests of the ruling élite. 'China's political reform is aimed at separating the Party and administration, decentralising political power, trimming and improving administrative staff and reinforcing democracy', explained a China Daily editorial (CD, 17 July 1978).

There was a second purpose involved in the separation of the Party from administrative organisations. It was to curtail the powers of the local-level Party committees with whom the 'masses' came into daily contact, while retaining for the central Party organs the authority to formulate and dictate policy. Deng pointed to the tendency of

> inappropriate and indiscriminate concentration of all power in Party Committees in the name of strengthening centralised Party leadership. Moreover, the power of the Party Committees are often in the hands of a few secretaries, especially first secretaries, who direct and decide everything. Thus 'centralised Party leadership' often turns into leadership by individuals. (Deng, *op. cit.*: 311)

It became important to make this distinction between the central and local committees as the pressures created by the economic reforms resulted in political disaffection. The central Party's monopoly of power remained unchallenged as long as the local Party committees drew the focus of popular frustration: '[in] the past we used to equate party leadership with leadership by the party committee. This is a one-sided view.' (Zeng, *op. cit.*: 89) As specialisation and individual responsibility in meeting targets and implementation of broad policies came to be regarded as the antidote to the inefficiency of the bureaucratic Party committees, it became essential to trim the committees' power and influence to cover less of the administrative terrain. However, this separating out, while necessary for the efficient achievement of the targets of the modernisation programme and for the image of the Party, also posed a dilemma for it. Efficiency and rationality increasingly came to be seen as contingent upon this division, and appeared invested in the functioning of the state rather than in the more subjective and arbitrary functioning of the Party. This adversely affected the legitimacy of the Party, and in turn brought into question the assumption of the overall leadership of the Party over the state.

In education the primacy of the Party was challenged on various grounds: economic, 'scientific' and political. The first attempt by the new leadership to protect the intelligentsia, whose co-operation was needed for the 'Four Modernisations', was to try and take education out of the category of 'superstructure' and hence of 'struggle':

> except for a small part, education basically is not in the realm of superstructure . . . In education many things are not built on the basis of or serve the economic basis, and they do not necessarily change whenever the economic foundation undergoes changes . . . under certain conditions, education is a productive force . . . because the labour force is the most active element of the productive forces and the cultivation, elevation and improvement of the labour forces have to be carried out through education and training. (GMRB, JPRS, no. 1, 18 July 1979)

This meant, however, that the nature of protection conceived for education effectively defined the nature of freedom allowed to the intelligentsia. The specialists were to be fitted into the economic machine and enough independence was to be granted to them as to create an unrestricted environment for scientific research. The intelligentsia itself 'seldom questioned that the purpose of demo-cracy was development' (Nathan, 1986: 84). The progress from the stigmatisation of the Maoist period to inclusion among the ruling classes – the working class – offered by the new regime was a tremendous boost to the morale of the intellectuals. The limitations of a licensed participatory practice were to emerge later.

The argument for the lessening of Party control over academic work was also made under the slogan 'No forbidden zones in scientific research!' The old Leninist dictum about discipline in the Party which Mao had endorsed – '(1) the individual is subordinate to the organisation; (2) the minority is subordinate to the majority; (3) the lower level is subordinate to the higher level; and (4) the entire membership is subordinate to the Central Committee' (Mao, 1967b: 203–4) was revised to recognise that

> [in] academic issues, the minority must not be subordinated to the majority, nor must views be unified mechanically and forcibly. As proved repeatedly by historical experience, forcible unification actually creates superficial unity. (*Beijing Zhe Xue Yanjiu*, JPRS, no. 46, January 1980)

It was further pointed out that:

> Some of our comrades are accustomed to seeking great unity in ideas and unify people's thinking by force . . . we must not place unity of action and independent thinking on opposite sides. Only when people are permitted to think independently will it become possible to concentrate the wisdom of the masses. (*Guangzhou Ribao*, JPRS, no. 165, 25 February 1981)

Finally, it was acknowledged that there was a need to institutional-ise the process of democratisation: 'Principles and policies are not enough. For example, double hundred policy should be legalised. Laws are needed to . . . safeguard their [teachers'] rights and interests . . . to safeguard the freedom of speech and guard against its abuse' (RMRB SWB/FE/BII, May 1984: 12). Two major areas were identified by the intellectuals that needed urgent reform and protection by the constitution and the law: first, the granting of substantial autonomy to academic organisations and scientific associations representing the interests of the intelligentsia and, second, reforming the teaching of political courses in universities – which led to a debate regarding the status of Marxism–Leninism–Mao Zedong Thought as the dominant ideological framework for academic research.

While this intellectual critique of education developed, pressure was also put on the Party cadres to acquire new skills of efficient management, and to improve their educational standards:

> Not being sufficiently knowledgeable or professionalised is another problem of leading bodies in need of a solution. At present, of the leading cadres of our country's schools of higher education, those who

have received a specialised university education and studied a profession, number less than half. (*Jinian Dazhong Ribao*, CR, no. 176, 1 April 1981: 1)

The head of the CPC Organisation Department, Song Renqiong, emphasised in 1980 that 'the main source [of future recruitment of CPC cadre] should be outstanding college and technical secondary school graduates, or young people with the same educational level, not from workers and peasants with low educational level' (RMRB SWB/FE/BII, 19 September 1980: 6). Even the political education of the Party cadres was rudimentary. In Hangzhou University, for example, there seemed to be little familiarity with even Marxist texts among Party members. The student members were aware of few original texts from the writings of Marx or Lenin. Most of the study of Marxism was confined to textbook interpretations of important texts or of current Party documents. As a student Party member explained,

> [We] study Marxism but not in the original; [there is] not enough time. [We] study a lot about Party organisation. There is a lot in the textbooks on Mao Zedong Thought. Usually we read a bit more [than other students], for example, the Communist Manifesto, and Liu Shaoqi's 'How to be a Good Communist'. [There is a] Party Institute Study Group organised by the Department; every student can join. Usually those who want to apply, join it.

Because of such a narrow theoretical base, the local Party cadres were unable to grapple with many of the issues arising out of the progress of the reforms, and the changing relations of various emerging interest groups.

The policy of recruiting Party members from among the better educated was a negation of the Maoist policy of giving primary importance to the class background of the potential members. As the post-Mao leadership came to include the intellectuals in the category of the working class, the need for revolutionary antecedents became less important. The emphasis on academic qualifications can be seen as an attempt to correct both the prejudice against the intellectuals within the Party and the image of the young Party members before the non-Party majority. This shift in emphasis did not go unopposed. Older Party cadres felt threatened, and feared for the Party's ideological purity: 'In the past, entrance to the CCP depended on a person's class background; now you see if a person is a specialized (sic) or [from] 10,000 yuan household. In the past, you looked at class consciousness, now you look at the ability to become rich.' (Rosen, 1989a: 7–8) Extensive and heated debate went on in the Party journals on this question throughout 1988–9. That the question of reinterpretation of class was not a settled one became evident after the June 1989 movement. As the conservatives gained political ground, there was a resurrection of the rhetoric of the 'right' and 'wrong' class background of Party members. A Beijing municipal party resolution affirmed that 'Exploiters cannot be admitted to the party and those already in the party . . . should spend their post tax profits on production and public welfare and not on private needs'. It warned that, 'If they failed to do this, they can no longer be party members' (*Xinhua*, SWB/FE/0590/B2/1). In an atmosphere of political uncertainty scores will necessarily be settled against those who pose a threat to the political élite at every level.

Through the 1980s the Party committees increasingly came under pressure to retreat from areas that were not strictly political:

> In the past all matters great and small were concentrated in the party committee. The party committee was busy grasping the concrete tasks and did not have the strength to grasp the work of the party . . . if specialists and professors took over certain leadership work, not only could they fulfil their activist role in the running of the school, but this would help improve the work of the school. (*Jiefang Ribao*, CR, no. 14, 7 September 1979)

This threat to the Party units at the local level slowly began to gain momentum. In February 1988 it was reported that

> In order to define responsibility, rationalise relations, reduce links, improve efficiency and strengthen Party building, it is proposed that the Party committees of departments under the Central Committee and the Party Committees of central state organisations be changed to work committees. (NCNA SWB/FE/BII, 27 February 1988: 1)

The functions of these committees would remain the same as those of the Party committees but the fact that enough pressure was felt by the Party for it to withdraw these committees from the public eye in state organisations indicates the kind of problems facing the local cadres. The Party units in the universities, however, were not abolished. The reforms shifted the burden of implementing Party policy in the sphere of higher education from the Party committee to the university: 'the fundamental principles, policy and tasks for running universities are set by the higher authorities and it is the duty of the university, as a grass-roots organisation, to carry them out' (Zeng, CE, no. 4, 1986–7: 89). This was an important shift in responsibility.

All these challenges to the power of the middle-level Party bureaucracy and the remnants of the old 'leftist' leadership at the top hierarchy of the Party led to a growing opposition to the reforms within the organisation. The 'anti-spiritual pollution' campaign of 1983, the 'anti-bourgeois liberalisation' campaigns of 1985 and 1987 and, of course, the more brutal suppression of the student movement in June 1989 all show the strength of the resistance of the 'hardliners'. The opposition to the erosion of their position surfaced first in resisting recruitment of Party cadres from among the intelligentsia:

> Some Party members have misgivings about recruiting Party members from intellectuals and worry that this will affect and change the nature of the Party. Others mistakenly think that intellectuals are 'merely expert but not red' . . . Still others are not willing to recruit Party members from among intellectuals who have ordinary history problems because they are afraid of committing mistakes. A small number of Party leaders have selfish ideas and are afraid of being replaced by intellectuals after they join the Party. (GMRB SWB/FE/BII, April 1984)

At the level of the university attempts at blocking decentralisation by Party cadres were made by delaying the implementation of the 'president responsibility system' (see Chapter 3: pp. 67–9); Hangzhou University, for example, had not implemented it until mid-1987. The Party organisation was consulted at all levels in the making of major policy decisions. 'In our university "president responsibility system" is not implemented as in Zhejiang University', said the director of the president's office. 'Both the party secretary and the president are responsible. The trend of development, however, is to implement this system.' In the aftermath of the 1989 student movement and the victory of the hardliners within the Party, this 'trend' has had further setbacks. The vice-governor of Heilongjiang Province made it quite clear that it was time to

> recognise the influence of rampant bourgeois liberalisation over the past few years, which resulted in ideological confusion in institutions of

higher learning . . . by slackening of efforts in the party's leadership and the ideological and political work for a period of time. (JPRS-CAR-89-121, 22 December 1989: 81)

The system was put on hold in October 1989 (see Chapter 3).

University Party organisation

The position that the Party holds in an educational institution is dependent on its organisation and functioning within the institution. As can be seen from Figure 4.1, the Party structure is independent of supervision or control by the university administration. It is responsible for its functioning not to the university administration, but to the Party committee of the city and it functions, as the spokesperson of the Hangzhou University's Party committee explained, to 'guarantee that the Party's education policy is carried out'.

However, it does more than that; it is also responsible for the maintenance of general ideological standards in the university for which purpose it is organisationally present at all levels – in the departments, in the class-rooms, and in the various mass organisations: '[We have] links with students and teachers. The political

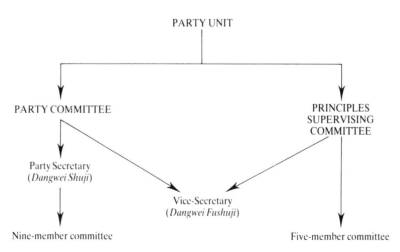

Figure 4.1   Organisation of the Hangzhou University Party unit

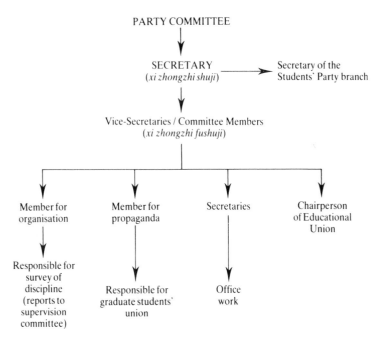

Figure 4.2 Structure of the Party unit of the Department of Political Science

staff is very alert to what's happening among students . . . some are whole time workers, [others are the] *banzhuren*; many monitors of the classes are Party members.'

The university Party committee keeps contact with the departmental units through regular meetings where 'tasks' are assigned and reports heard. The 'Principles Supervising Committee' is headed by the Vice-Secretary of the Party. It is an intra-Party disciplinary committee and is 'comparatively autonomous'. The Party secretary is not a member of this committee.

In Hangzhou University the secretary of a departmental branch of the Party is elected by the Party members of that unit after his or her name has been approved by the university Party committee. The term is for two years with a provision for re-election. Despite the increasing pressure on the office-bearers of the Party to 'improve their cultural standards' and take on a greater role in the academic life of the university, very few Party secretaries do any teaching work in the departments. The organisation of the Party at the departmental level more or less replicates the university committee. It is interesting to note (see Figure 4.2) that departmental Party committee members are also responsible for organisations like the graduate students' union and the Educational Union. The Party operates at two levels: among the students and among the staff. This is done through separate Party organisations for the two groups.

At every level the functioning of the Party revolves around the secretary of the Party unit and the Party committee. The personality of the Party secretary and the strength of his or her position in the local power network is an important factor in the organisation and the role that the Party unit plays at any level. This has been particularly the case since the administrative reforms were introduced into the universities since 1985. As the reforms have gone through periods of progress and of retreat, the personal positions of the Party secretary and the president in the university has played an important part in their implementation. In Hangzhou University it was generally conceded that the university Party secretary was too powerful to be ignored by the president who deferred to her in most important decision-making. Personalities were important at the departmental level too. An English teacher at Hangzhou University Foreign Languages Department illustrated this: 'We booked room 205 for a drama performance a week in advance', she said. 'A week before the performance we were asked to change [the venue] as it was needed for a teachers' meeting. "The Party secretary wants it", we were told. The teachers went to him to request personally, and he agreed to let us have the room.' At both the university and the departmental level, the Party secretary is generally associated with all important decision-making processes. These include recruitment and promotion of teachers, job allocations for graduating students, setting curriculum in the departments and overseeing discipline. At Hangzhou University, for example, 30 students were expelled on various charges of misdemeanour in May 1987; the decision for this was taken by the Party committee at the university level which 'took into consideration the opinion of teachers, *banzhuren* and students', explained the spokesperson of the university Party branch. It is interesting to note that no distinction was made between the private and the public spheres in which the students acted when coming to this decision. Most students were accused of 'gambling in their bedrooms', drinking and having premarital sexual relationships. The questions of personal morality and personal conduct were conflated and the Party judged both. It was also widely acknowledged that these expulsions formed part of the 'anti-bourgeois liberalisation' campaign that was unleashed after the student demonstrations of 1986–7 and the fall from grace of Hu Yaobang.

At the level of the department, the Party committee is equally involved in the administration. The Party secretary of the Politics Department told me that his opinion was sought and given on matters regarding the introduction of new courses. The reason for such consultation becomes clearer when we take into account the political importance of education – or reclaiming, rewriting, refashioning history to conform to current explanations. For example, the Party committee of the Politics Department participated in deciding whether to split the two majors – History of Chinese Revolution and Political Science – which had hitherto been taught as one. This was not just an academic decision, it was also a political statement; it was a delinking of politics as an academic discipline from the history of the Communist Party which needed close monitoring. Similarly, describing the 'dean responsibility system', the Dean of the Department of Psychology at Hangzhou University said,

> The dean is responsible for teaching, research, department-level student and faculty selection and training. The Party monitors the administration to guarantee its smooth functioning. The leadership is of the Party . . . *the two are not separate* (my italics). They co-operate. The dean will do most of the work.

The Party's intervention in the process of recruitment is justified because of the ideological level of the prospective lecturer. While the emphasis on political rhetoric has been declining in the past years, the middle Party bureaucracy still tends to hold on to political criteria for granting material and non-material 'goods' as a means of control and power in the university. As the Party secretary of the Department of Politics explained: '[We] look at their [the prospective teachers'] ideological attitude towards Party policies; if transferred from another place – that unit's report on [their] working attitude, responsibility, political work, moral character.' Such control is made easier by the system of keeping files on each individual – a file that travels with the individual wherever s/he works. Thus, in the incident of students' expulsion noted above, it was made clear that '[those expelled] have very little chance to get good jobs. [It] will be recorded on the file.' The same argument is employed to maintain the presence of the Party on the Academic Committee which decides promotions.

In the period since June 1989 there has been a renewed call for increasing Party control over the institutions of higher education. Zhao Ziyang was blamed for proposing to 'reform the party and thin out party leadership, which actually was a proposal for the elimination of that leadership', by an editorial of *Guangming Ribao* (JPRS-CAR-89-102, 12 October 1989: 11). The Party units in the universities were urged by the central committee of the CPC to 'bring into full play their role as the political nucleus (sic)' and that the 'party committee [of the university] must assume leadership over every aspect of ideological and political work' (*ibid.*).

The changing role of the Party in the university

Despite all the limitations on the nature of political reforms concerning the Party, these have led to significant shifts in the role played by the Party organisation in the lives of ordinary people. The Maoist view of the voluntarist party that derived its strength from the charisma of its leader and the fervour of its cadres has been rejected. Further, the post-Mao leadership has also modified significantly the Party's campaign-style political practice. While movements like the 'anti-bourgeois liberalisation' campaign have been initiated, these have not led to the mass witch-hunts of the Maoist period; mass mobilisation has largely been substituted by political control:

> [It is] important . . . to further change the campaign-type leadership method, lead the schools according to the law of education and correctly carry out the policies of the party . . . Due to the fact that in the past the school took launching political movements as their central task, a tendency gradually appeared for the party secretaries to take

command in all affairs, the party committees monopolised everything, and there was no distinction between the party and the administration. (*Wenhui Bao* Shanghai, Daily Report, no. 65, 5 March 1980: 45–6)

Political leaders like Peng Zhen have reiterated their long-held position that 'social and political control can be achieved best through formalised law in the form of command rules' (Hamrin and Cheek, 1986: 46). This, it was felt, would serve to alleviate distrust of the Party among the people in general and among the intellectuals who had had most cause to be wary of the independent authority of individual cadres interpreting Party policy. The role of the reforms, Deng emphasised, was to free the Party committees from daily routines so that they can concentrate on carrying out political and ideological work and performing their organisational and supervisory functions. Instead of weakening the Party leadership, the political reforms were designed to more effectively improve and strengthen the Party leadership (Zeng, 1987: 88)

The political reforms have, however, been partial. The local Party committee retained its 'organisational and supervisory' functions under the reformed system of administration. This allowed the Party committees to redefine their role more loosely and left an ambiguity in the reforms that was exploited by the Party cadres to enable them to continue taking an active part in the administrative functioning of the university. It is this situation which has allowed the rapid regrouping of the Party strength in the universities after the Tian'anmen demonstrations were suppressed. As the Party had never fully retreated from the administration of the university, it was easy for it to attempt to reclaim its lost territory.

The implementation of the education reform policy that was introduced by the post-Mao leadership led to the emergence of competing interests which were not reconciled and which exacerbated tensions within the university. On the one hand, the Party committees felt under increasing pressure to withdraw from active interference in administration, while on the other, they were repeatedly asked to ensure political discipline. The local Party cadres were denied the support of the national leadership in favour of the intellectuals and the 'experts', but were also found indispensable for securing control with the heating up of the political system. These contradictory signals left the Party committees confused, belligerent or impotent, according to their particular situation; the same went for the university administration.

An area where the Party committee was given complete responsibility was that of 'ideological education'. In the post-Mao period this was a thankless, dispiriting task. The Cultural Revolution with its iconoclasm had destroyed much and replaced little in the ideological sphere. Its repudiation by the post-Mao leadership had further aggravated the sense of loss of direction and of cynicism. 'Some disillusioned students felt that Marxist theory had no basis because "he who is in power is always right" or that they could not have confidence in Marxism because it could be "changed to suit anybody"' claimed a study conducted in early 1979 by the Communist Party propaganda department in the provinces of Hunan, Guangdong and Fujian (GMRB, CR, no. 142, 1 December 1980). The gap between rhetoric and reality in the Chinese political sphere made the task of political work more difficult for the Party committees at the grassroot level. As the emphasis on political rhetoric and mobilisation lessened, there was a sharp decline in interest in politics and its study. The fact that political study courses are compulsory, dry and dogmatic has not helped to sustain interest in them. After every student movement since 1978 there has been a renewed emphasis on the political study programme together with an acknowledgement of the need to make these more interesting to the students. In the aftermath of the 1989 movement, for example, 'A ceremony [was] organised . . . to award prizes for innovative ideological and political work . . . in Xinhua News Agency offices this afternoon', reported Xinhua (FBIS-CHI-90-145 *Xinhua*, 26 July 1990).

One of the important functions of the Party in the university was to stem this tide of disinterest by making political courses more in tune with the changing realities of the Chinese political life and making teaching methods more accessible and democratic:

> Teaching methodology should be reformed drastically in order to thoroughly improve the current situation in which theory in the political science courses is divided from reality . . . We should consider adopting the heuristic method and discussion method of teaching (GMRB, CR, no. 142, 1 December 1980)

Continuing emphasis on political education was also important to help replace the old rhetoric of class struggle with that of modernisation and 'patriotism' and support for the present leadership's policies. The break with the previously tightly controlled economic and political strategy of the Maoist years could lead to great confusion in the minds of the young people. New boundaries and ground rules had to be drawn up and explained and the people persuaded of their validity:

> What does the requirement that university students be 'socialist-minded' mean? Before the Cultural Revolution, the Qinghua University Party Committee urged students to support the leadership of the Communist party, support socialism, and accept the jobs assigned to them by the state. They still regard these requests as applicable . . . With respect to questions concerning the content and methods of political and ideological education, the Qinghua University Party Committee has proposed 'three tiers' . . . patriotic education, socialist education and communist education. (GMRB, CR, no. 93, 30 June 1980)

This 'educative role', however, needed a bolder imagination and a more open political context than was available. In a period when the Party was being held responsible for the 'lost decade' of the Cultural Revolution by both its present leadership and the people who had suffered at the hands of the radicals, it was not enough to blame those who were now discarded. The equivocation that the national leadership indulged in at the expense of the local Party units did not help matters. No one was prepared to risk losing political control, no one was ready to share power. Those who soldiered on in the 'educative' project only adjusted their rhetoric to reflect the demands of the new strategy for development and modernisation. While this interested the intellectuals for a while it also encouraged a demand for broadening the boundaries of debate. The 'myopic reform policies', however, 'stressed delegating power and allowing enterprises to keep their profits and dismantling old institutions, and ignored the creation of new institutions', said Wu Jinglian, the former executive director of the Economic, Technical and Social Research Centre, one of the many think-tanks of the reformist leadership (*Chingji Taopao*, in JPRS-CAR-89-121, 22 December, 1989: 19).

However ineffective, political propaganda is one of the important roles of the Party committee in the university. This function of education and propaganda is carried out in various ways. There is a tradition of wall newspapers that take the form of blackboard writing or putting up notices and 'big character' posters (*dazibao*).

This is done by both the departmental Students' Union and the students' Party branch. Exhortations, information and party policies are conveyed through these means. It is interesting to note, however, that the individual citizen's right to put up '*dazibao*' was taken away by the post-Mao leadership in the new constitution promulgated in 1988. However, students and intellectuals have continued to use wall posters effectively to register their protest with the party/state, and these formed an important motif in the 1989 movement.

Through organising political education the Party is also able to monitor the university population, explained the Party secretary of the Politics Department in Hangzhou University:

> Look[ing] to teachers' [and students'] ideology [and] problems regarding understanding of policy . . . [The Party tries] to unite the thought of the teachers [by holding] meetings. For example during the anti-bourgeois liberal campaign there was discussion about it . . . [it] asked the teachers about their thoughts; if [they] were not correct then [it] explained the real meaning of this term.

These meetings take place once every two weeks and usually concentrate on reading and discussing the recent policy documents of the Party or the Party newspaper. These are widely resented and are looked upon as compulsory 'body counts', as one student expressed it. As these meetings are usually held on Saturday mornings the infringement on the time of those attending is even more resented. The meetings are an important means of transmitting and explaining policies of the Party. Issues regarding local politics and individual cases are also taken up at these meetings. While the singling out of members and criticism and struggle against 'deviants' are much less in evidence now, these regular periods of interaction are important to the surveillance system of the Party in the university. Such meetings were convened, for example, during the students' demonstrations in the winter of 1986–7 as a means of accounting for members. The student Party branch also meets in a similar way. A member of the departmental students' Party branch committee at Hangzhou University explained:

> [We have] meetings twice a month [when we] read Party documents and discuss some work regarding students. In the last meeting we read documents about [an] advanced Party committee branch, and its experiences in organising meetings.

The frequency of political study classes is an important indicator of the state of the nerves of the Party. The number of hours of compulsory political study have changed in the last few years at various times, reflecting the needs of political control of the Party. We find that after every period of political activism the number of hours of these meetings is increased. For example, after the June 1989 movement, the students in Chinese universities now have to spend two hours each, two days a week for 'political study', whereas before the student protests this varied from one hour a week to two hours every other week in different institutions. This time has been used to target student activists, to ask them to make 'self-criticism', and to transmit the present political policy of the Party.

The educational function also is carried out by the Party members through 'exemplary behaviour'. This has been a tradition in the CPC which has upheld its 'model' workers as role models for the people (see discussion in Chapter 1: p. 13). At Hangzhou University a Party activist claimed: '[Party members are] model teachers. [They] teach and educate. Their teaching load is greater. They show great concern for other comrades.' Student Party members also serve to exemplify communist virtues: '[Party members are] model students. [They are] most active as organisers [and] co-ordinators. Some backward students don't want to study; we help them', said one. In the post-Mao period of emphasis on individualism and material gain, these 'virtues' are regarded sceptically. Increasing corruption within the Party and unhappiness with the Party's style of functioning have meant that the image of the Party, the exemplary behaviour which the cadres should enhance, has actually taken a knock. Various surveys point to the plummeting prestige of the Party. For example, whereas only 6.3 per cent of those polled in a sample of 1,694 felt that Party cadres had a very good image, the figure for those believing teachers to have the same was 32.7 per cent (Rosen, 1989a, Table 9).

The selection procedure for membership involves an extremely close screening of the applicant. This helps maintain the ideological purity of the Party, gives it the cohesion and discipline that is needed for a cadre-based party and an identifiable profile that maintains its exclusive position in the university environment. The whole process – from application to evaluation and acceptance/ rejection – takes over a year. The prospective members' ideological and 'moral' level is observed and judged for that time before membership is granted. Thus, in the Department of Politics at Hangzhou University, which has one of the highest membership ratios among teachers and students, there were only three Party members out of 160 undergraduates in 1987, while there was a substantial rise at the postgraduate level, with 14 out of 30 as members. The low figures of Party membership are indicative of the exclusive nature of that membership and the prestige that was attached to it. A survey published in early 1989 of various occupational groups, however, shows a sharp decline in the pride that the intellectuals take in their membership of the Party: only 51.04 per cent of the 175 polled in March 1989, felt proud to be CPC members. In another survey of 371 intellectuals on 'the public image of the Chinese Communist Party', 69.85 per cent felt that the image was not good (Rosen, 1989a). The tightly controlled organisational structure also enables surveillance of the prospective members over a relatively long period of time.

The CPC is not the only political party in the Chinese political system. It is, however, constitutionally endowed with the power and responsibility to give 'leadership' to the eight other parties and to supervise the non-party, mass organisations in the university. The preamble to the constitution states:

> Under the leadership of the Communist Party of China and the guidance of Marxism–Leninism and Mao Zedong Thought, the Chinese people of all nationalities will continue to adhere to the people's democratic dictatorship. (NPC, 1983: 5)

In the university the Party not only oversees the functioning of non-party organisations, but also provides 'leadership' which determines the substructure of power relations between various organisations in the university. The mass organisations that had been used as organs of surveillance and control by the Party were left untouched in the programme of the reform of educational institutions; the redefinition remained a matter for negotiation between those involved. As the democratic movement grew among the intellectual circles, this lack of autonomy of mass organisations from Party political control became one of the major causes for struggle. As Su Shaozhi, the erstwhile director of the Marxism–Leninism–Mao Zedong Thought Institute of CASS, now in exile, noted:

the relationship between the Party and the mass organisations is not that between the 'prime mover' and 'conveyor belts' . . . The mass organisations can only be bridges between the party and the masses, or they will become components of the party organisation . . . The relationship between the party and the mass organisations should be one of mutual co-operation, supervision, co-ordination, and promotion. (*DUSHU*, JPRS, no. 8, 18 February 1987: 28)

The reform faction led by Zhao did respond to this critique; included in the minutes of a meeting of the secretariat of the party chaired by him were the notes: '(7) There should be media supervision . . . (8) The supervisory role of democratic parties and mass organisations should be brought into full play.' (*Xinhua*, SWB/FE/0361/B2/2) However, the mechanisms through which such supervision could be exercised were not in place and the growing resistance within the Party to further liberalisation was gaining ground.

The pressures from within the Party consistently worked against loosening of Party control. Thus, after the student unrest in 1987 and the expulsion from the Party of leading intellectuals Fang Lizhi, Liu Bingyan and Wang Ruowang, China Youth Magazine wrote:

Improving party leadership never means cancelling party leadership. Instead, it is for the purpose of more effectively and firmly strengthening and adhering to the party's leadership . . . All remarks that try to weaken, shake off, deviate from and negate the party's leadership, are completely wrong. (*Zhongguo Qingnian Bao*, *ibid.*: 29)

The apprehensions of the Party cadres about loss of control and power were real. Their resentments – fed by both a political legacy of distrust of the intellectuals, and what must have seemed to be a usurpation of their rightful place in the administrative and power structure – led them to interpret the political reform policy very narrowly, thus keeping as much space open for their intervention as they possibly could. As the Party secretary of the Taiyuan Engineering Institute said:

The Party should take care of Party affairs and fundamental issues . . . It should concern itself with major issues, keep abreast of the whole situation and take care of its own affairs . . . [It] should keep in touch with the masses, gather information on teaching, research, and support services for the president, and serve as his/her councillor, offering advice and suggestion. (Ye, 1987: 79–80)

The Party bureaucrats undermined the idea of a separation of powers by arguments of primacy, importance and a non-divisibility of performance and supervision: 'The president's leadership role in university administration and the party committee's supervisory role are two aspects of the same task which have to be carried out simultaneously' (*ibid.*). What the Party cadres wanted was only to let go of the minor details of administration while retaining their right to have a say in the forming of major policies concerning the institution and to oversee their implementation. Even the initial and tentative attempts at separating out responsibilities and authorities in the universities seem under threat as in the current political climate the Party bureaucracy reasserts its power: 'Political leadership means the direction to be taken; ideological leadership is the premise; and the organisational leadership is the support. The three are organically linked and completely inseparable', asserted an editorial of the Peasants' Daily (*Nongming Ribao*, 7 March 1990, JPRS-CAR-90-31: 21).

The Party committee had the advantage of experience to back its claim. It had administered educational institutions since 1949 and had constructed the required apparatus for this task. Its information-gathering network is extensive, well knit and tightly controlled. The discipline of its organisation and the efficiency of its surveillance machinery means that it is in a more advantaged position than academic administrators. The process of decision-making itself is more familiar to it. The process of consultation, formulation, and transmission of decisions comes more easily to an organisation that has been taking responsibility for the functioning of the university since the revolution. The position of the Party bureaucrats has also been strengthened because of a reluctance on the part of the 'experts' to take major decisions. The lack of institutional structures that could protect the non-party decision-makers, and hence the high levels of risk that have been involved in taking decisions and identifying with them, have made the 'experts' insecure. Finally, despite the erosion of its good public image, the prestige of the Party and the long-standing power position of its bureaucrats has made the creation of a new base of power difficult. The network of *guanxi* (mutual obligations) established by the Party bureaucrats could be used to undermine the position of the academic administrator. The Party committees have thus remained central to the function of surveillance and control of education.

Renegotiating the Party's position: new contexts and contentions

Since the post-Mao reforms were introduced new contexts have been created in which specialised knowledge, academic contacts and professional status became more and more important and these could be traded for greater independence and distancing of the Party committee from certain key areas of administration. First, in opening China's academic institutions to the world, the old Western-trained professors played an important role. The contacts that they had made in Western universities immediately before and after the revolution were used by the government to initiate the process of interaction. Their greater familiarity with the Western system of education, however outdated, made them important links in the new chain. They have headed academic delegations and represented China on international symposia. Such activity has a prestige attached to it, especially in a country starved of contact with the 'developed' world and actively seeking such contact. That prestige had its own potential power attached to it that could be used for bargaining with the Party. Second, as already documented, the overwhelming need of intellectual expertise in the drive towards modernisation led the state to attempt to reconcile its intelligentsia. At the university level this need is no less urgent as its links with the economy could be made only with the help of the specialised knowledge of the academic staff. The emphasis on universities to become financially less dependent on the state encouraged the need of the universities to market the skills of their staff. This strengthened the position of the university intellectuals. This could be seen even more clearly at the departmental level where the mobilisation of resources through the farming out of expertise was not only more visible but also more urgent. Finally, the support of the national leadership for these reforms made it easier for the academics to argue their case. The general sympathy of the political environment is an important factor in this context. The legitimacy granted to the concept of specialisation and rationality, efficiency and economy, led the intellectuals to argue that an academic administrator would be better able to perceive the problems of the staff and resolve the questions relating to academic matters in the department. However, at Hangzhou University a Party official, while conceding this point, was quick to point out what he called the 'contradiction': 'Energy is limited,' he said, 'therefore teaching [in addition to] administrative work becomes too much.'

A question that recurs constantly when one looks at these attempts at granting autonomy to the experts and at the withdrawal of the Party from the administrative sphere is that of the construction of the Party itself. The vast majority of presidents and deans of universities and departments are also members of the Party. (Interestingly enough, though, the last vice-chancellor of Hangzhou University, Professor Chen Li, is not a Party member, but headed the Hangzhou University *Jiu San* Society, one of China's eight 'democratic parties'. It has a membership only of 'higher intellectuals'. 'Formerly only those above associate professor [could join]', Professor Chen said. 'Now lecturers are also admitted.' The present president of the University is, however, also a member of the CPC.) Thus, any meaningful debate on autonomy would also have to bring into question ideas central to the conception of the Leninist party, especially that of 'democratic centralism', and the space allowed to members of the Party to dissent. The emphasis by the Party leadership on the 'Four Cardinal Principles' has been crucial (see Chapter 1: p. 16). In December 1980, Deng Xiaoping reasserted that:

> The core of these four cardinal principles is upholding leadership by the Communist Party . . . Whether inside or outside the Party, all tendencies towards weakening, breaking away from, opposing or liquidating leadership by the Party must be criticised. (Deng, 1984: 339)

Thus, on the one hand the leadership of the Party was made non-negotiable, and on the other, the structure of the Party also remained unquestioned. The attempt since 1979 has been to refurbish the Party's damaged image, to regain the political legitimacy that the Party seemed to have lost in the aftermath of the Cultural Revolution, and to make it more efficient to better serve China's economic reforms.

Conclusions

As we have seen above, the Party committees at the local levels did not relinquish effective power during the period of radical reform in China. In the universities they continued to participate in the administration and decision-making. Though faced with increasing difficulties in the face of growing cynicism about the Party and frustration at the contrary political signals coming from Beijing, they continued to be responsible for the political education of the students and teachers. The factional struggle at the national level was reflected in the universities too. The absence of clear guidelines about the scope of political reform, and the partial enforcement of the 'presidential responsibility system' encouraged this. The actual power position of the Party secretary in a particular institution came to have greater importance for the position of the Party committee than the policy of decentralisation in its general formulation. Those universities that were more able to take advantages of their new links with the economy were generally more effective in ensuring the implementation of the policy of separation of powers. While the reforms were slow to take root, the impact of the political climate in the country, the increasing 'marketisation' of education, and the debate regarding the role of Party committees at the local level resulted in considerable movement in the positions of entrenched interests in the universities.

The suppression of the democracy movement in June 1989 has put back considerably the questions raised in debates about the role of the Party at the local levels. However, it would not be correct to assume that there has been a complete reversal of policies on many of the questions regarding the balance of power between the Party committees and the universities' administrative bodies. The Party is undergoing a systematic purge of its ranks. This is not the purge of the Maoist period, linked to mass campaigns around mobilisational politics. It is a bureaucratic, quiet, limited and bloodless purge. In October 1989 the Beijing municipal party resolved that to 'purify Party organisations, a drive will be conducted to investigate how Party members, especially officials, behaved in quelling the riot' (*Xinhua*, SWB/ FE/0590/B2/1). Thousands have been expelled from the Party, or disciplined, and all Party members will have to re-register after their records have been checked and 'self-criticisms' exhorted where necessary. 'According to a recent circular, Party members will in future be assessed annually by a combination of self-evaluation, discussions at Party group or branch meetings and opinions of non-Party people', reported Xinhua (*Xinhua*, SWB/ FE/0356/BS/1). Discipline Inspection Commissions of the Party are doing brisk business once again after the purges against the radicals in the period after Mao's death. There is a renewed emphasis on the importance of political education. All sections of the socio-economic élite have been recruited to call for greater attention to be paid to 'education in ideology, morality, culture, and discipline'. Xia Jie, chairman of the board of Beijing Kentucky Fried Chicken Corporation Ltd, asked at a forum on 'Problems in Higher Education', 'Why is it that when China trains an individual his only concern is for money?' Other businessmen at the forum 'fondly called to mind the slogan "both red and expert" current during the 1950s and 1960s . . . [and felt that] the preeminent standard by which to measure a talented individual must be his political orientation' (*Jingji Ribao*, JPRS-CAR-89-106: 50). Mao's 'Talks at the Literature Forum in Yenan' have been commemorated across the country to redefine the relationship between intellectuals and the state (see p. 94 above). Emphasis is being laid on 'patriotism and stability'. A *Renmin Ribao* editorial stressed the need for 'patriotic education, with special emphasis on the history of the Opium War, comparing this with last year's "political tempest"' (*Kyodo*, FBIS/90/104/12). Anti-West rhetoric is once again finding currency among the political leadership. Beijing students have suffered more than others in this campaign for political education: the class of 1989 has to spend the first year in the army to be politically educated and then to re-register after taking an examination in political attitudes. More significant has been the trend to reassert control over mass organisations:

> Such mass organisations as the trade unions, the Communist Youth League, students' unions and graduate students' unions are . . . a vital force the school party committee will rely on to carry out ideological and political work . . . It is even more important for party organisations on campus to strengthen leadership over these mass organisations. (GMRB, JPRS-CAR-89-102: 12)

Non-party/formal organisations like salons played an important role in organising the student movement in 1989; these are under threat of closure: 'All illegal mass organisations and "salon" activities that have not been approved must be resolutely crushed.' (*ibid.*) Elections to people's congresses at the grassroot level were postponed in February 1990 until later that year to contain political debate (*Ming Pao*, FBIS/90/038/20: 7).

The strains put upon the Party in the last decade of reforms by the re-evaluation of its position and the student opposition movements have resulted in the emergence of factions within the Party. After the 1989 Tian'anmen movement 'moderates' led by Jiang Zemin and Li Ruihuan, and the 'hardliners' represented by Li Peng and Yang Shangkun. Li Ruihuan, for example, admitted in May 1990 that the 'students should not be solely blamed for the 4 June incident . . . that the Party also had made mistakes . . . that there was something wrong with the way the students were handled' (*Ming Pao*, FBIS/90/103/33). Sections of the Party (and of the army) have been shaken by the violence used against the protestors; such suppression does not square with their self-image, or with their political rhetoric. This has resulted in an 'identity crisis' within the Party, which in turn has led to a breakdown in legitimacy and in motivation within the Party itself. This allows moderates within the Party to subvert certain policies of the present leaders through non-action; for example, 'The purging (sic) campaign of Party organisa-tions in Beijing has met with resistance from a large number of people', reported Hong Kong-based *Ming Pao*. 'A report by a party organisation . . . says that only 5000 Party members were involved in the democratic movement in Beijing. The report has made Li Ximing [Beijing Party secretary] very angry.' (FBIS/90/003/6) There are reports of rifts within the army: the Liberation Army Daily observed that 'Some make frivolous remarks about Central Committee policies and do not implement them' (FBIS/90/049/12). The Party is also witnessing this breakdown of discipline because the recruitment drive of the early 1980s (see above, p. 91) has allowed the civil society to penetrate the political organisation. The increased membership of intellectuals who were not steeped in the Leninist traditions of 'democratic centralism' – were perhaps not even convinced of the socialist ideals as defined by the Party – has created 'possibility spaces' which, while circumscribed by the narrowness of the political structures, allow a process of redefinition and reworking to develop. Further, the gradual dilution of the *political* role of the Party, especially in the post-Mao period, in favour of an administrative, bureaucratic role has resulted in the organisation losing its *élan*; it is no longer able to inspire either the people or its own membership (see Lewin, 1988).

Outside the Party opposition has taken both organisational and spontaneous forms. There are now at least three confirmed dissident cells in Beijing – Mainland Democratic Compatriots' Committee, the Social Democratic Party, and a chapter of the Paris-based Federation for Democracy (FBIS/90/088/28; FBIS/90/028/10; FBIS/90/107/31). They do not offer an alternative to the CPC, of course, but given that the risks involved in organisational opposition are great, they underline the alienation of young intellectuals from the party/state. At an informal level there have been reports of demonstrations and sit-ins by Beijing University students to mark the suppression of the movement. There have been 'frequent complaints from soldiers of waiters and shop assistants making things difficult for them and people throwing stones at them' (*Tang Tai*, 21/04/90; FBIS/90/080/21). On 4 June 1990 'despite the presence of armed police Beijing citizens are mourning the martyrs in every possible way . . . Piles of burning paper money [for symbolic burning at funerals] have continuously appeared around the square' (*Ming Pao*, 02/04/90; FBIS/90/107/26). The Party has labelled the student movement a riot. The students struggled against this at the height of the movement when they demanded that their protest be recognised as patriotic. In the aftermath of its suppression, the Beijing citizens have embraced the label to rob it of its meaning, to delegitimise the abuse by making it their own: 'A couple whose son was shot dead last summer by the PLA, but was classified as an "onlooker" because of his parents' contributions to the revolution. They insisted that he be labelled as a "rioter".' (*Ming Pao*, 16/03/90; FBIS/90/052/17)

All factions of the Party, however, seem determined to carry on the economic reforms; all sections of the post-Mao Party derive their legitimacy from association with these reforms. Thus, Deng clarified in his congratulatory speech on 9 June 1989 to Beijing army commanders who had participated in the suppression of the movement: 'The future policy should still be a marriage between the planned economy and market regulation. What is important is that we should never change China back into a closed country.' (CPC CC, 1989: 18) The leadership is also aware that the economic reforms are as dependent today on the expertise of Chinese scientists and technologists as they were in the early 1980s. There have thus been consistent attempts to conciliate the intelligentsia in the period after the suppression. Jiang insisted at a conference on higher education in July 1989 that the intellectuals 'are part of the working class and have worked hard for construction and reform. We must rely on them for the four modernisations. We must not waver on this point.' (*Xinhua (C)*, SWB/FE/0510/B2/1) What is still on offer to the intelligentsia is a form of licensed participation in the public sphere in return for their co-operation in the modernisation programme. The building of a new legitimacy is the primary task before the Party today; it is not an easy one.

There had been in Mao's time a continuous emphasis on ideology and a political morality which, while not entirely consonant with reality, had held the imagination of the Chinese people. Mao's own prestige had been a powerful lever in the hands of the Party; he had symbolised the independence and strength of the Chinese nation. Deng had inherited that mantle, and had been supported by the masses, but in rejecting the Maoist period he had opened a Pandora's Box. If Mao was associated with the revolution, and the revolution through Mao with the Cultural Revolution, the repudiation of one led to the rejection of the other (see Dirlik and Meisner, 1989: 12–13). The Party had begun to lose its hold on the people in that moment of turning its back on its own history. As Habermas points out:

> the organizations which are responsible for making and applying law are in no way legitimated by the legality of the modes of procedure (or vice versa), but likewise by general interpretation which supports the system of authority as a whole. (Habermas, 1976: 10)

The Party could only survive now on a different basis of legitimacy – as a modernising state, but not as a moral and political arbiter.

The Party thus is in a state of confusion. The suppression of the student movement and the form it took has resulted not only in delegitimising its position in the eyes of the masses it seeks to represent, but also in fracturing its link with its own past. There seems to be a sense of loss within the Party as it faces the decade ahead – a loss of confidence in itself and its relationship with the masses. The relationship most affected is that with the intellectuals of China, who have become for the party/state the genie that once let out refuses to go back into the bottle.

5

University intellectuals and the post-Mao state: dilemmas of reconciliation

Introduction

The June 1989 movement demonstrated the shift in the position of the Chinese intelligentsia from being supporters of and petitioners to the party/state to being challengers to its authority, and protesters against its policies. The relationship between the Communist Party and the intellectuals had never stabilised into one of mutual respect and co-operation. Even during the heady days of the revolution, Mao's 'Yenan Talks for the Forum on Art and Literature' indicated the Party's attempts to control the individualism of the intellectuals. The Leninist party model gave the legitimacy needed for attempting to circumscribe critique, as did the constraints of forging an effective military and political organisation to fight a bitter war. The Party spoke in the voice of the struggling 'masses', the working people, whereas the antecedents of the intelligentsia in imperial China were not spotless. The Confucian intelligentsia had served the Emperor; the gentry had been part of the exploitative structure that the communists were committed to overthrow. There had, of course, been reformers and critics among the intellectuals, but they were mostly liberal modernisers who did not speak the language of revolution, and many were monarchists. They thus needed supervision, and to be put in touch with the people. They needed to be cured of romanticism and schooled in realism. The intellectuals on their part were fiercely nationalistic and saw themselves as an important part of any project of 'self-strengthening' that the Chinese state might attempt. They had however

> no access to China's political and social resources. They could cohere only among themselves, in academic and professional congregations . . . they were themselves, in principle and by temperament, incapable of the kind of organised militancy that might have turned them from petitioners into power-brokers. (Grieder, 1981: 353)

They needed a stable China to be able to function as critics. As the country continued its decline into anarchy and annexation, the intelligentsia became increasingly convinced that the Chinese communists alone could provide the answer to their need. The nationalism that the CPC had been able to tap to such good advantage among the peasants, also affected the intellectuals. Thousands flocked to Yenan as the communists consolidated their position in national politics after the Long March, and hundreds came back to China from all over the world to participate in the project of reconstruction of the Chinese nation and culture as the People's Republic came into being in 1949.

Young socialist China had few friends. The Western blockade ensured that the Soviet influence in China during those early days of reconstruction was paramount. It also encouraged anti-Western, anti-liberal feelings among both the state and the people. The liberal, bourgeois democracies of the world chose to support the corrupt regime of Chiang Kaishek in Taiwan; vigilance against their ideas and their machinations was the only price for socialism. Those who had links with the West became suspect. Mao was particularly suspicious of the intellectuals and thought them opinionated, ill-disciplined in party work, and arrogant. They looked down upon the masses, were élitist, and unreliable. Mao's utopian egalitarianism found it difficult to find place for this group in the new scheme of things. However, the devastation of the country called for radical measures to be taken; the intellectuals were needed for their skills as the West was for its technology. In the 1860s Feng Guifen, a Suzhou scholar, had devised the formula that allowed the state to pursue its military/scientific modernisation without confronting the issue of challenge to traditional authority and culture:

> Would not the best of all possible stratagems be to retain the social relationships and the illustrious moral principles of China as the

foundation, and to reinforce them with techniques that the various countries [of the West] have used to attain wealth and power? (Grieder, 1981: 73)

New China applied the same formula to the same problem that had confronted the Qing dynasty and its reformers in the mid- and late nineteenth century – the imperative of modernisation on the one hand, and of pressures on the political structures on the other. Both tried to resolve the problem by attempted separation of '*ti*' and '*yong*', the moral and the technical/scientific dimensions of knowledge. This allowed the state to protect itself from military attack and economic competition, while at the same time to legitimise itself as the preserver of the Chinese 'Way' or 'Chinese-style socialism'. The *yong* was essential to protect the *ti*; *ti* was the 'essence', the end, and the *yong* the means. The Manchus had been unable to stem the tide of new ideas capturing the minds of the intelligentsia; the Chinese communists did not fare much better.

The contradiction presented to the post-revolutionary state by the *ti/yong* dichotomy has yet to be resolved. Several attempts were made in this regard – the Hundred Flowers Bloom campaign of 1957–8 (see MacFarquahar, 1974a), the anti-rightist campaign of 1958–9 (see Fraser, 1965) and, of course, the Cultural Revolution of 1966–9 (see MacFarquahar, 1974b). All these resulted in the alienation of the intelligentsia from the party/state. The intellectuals rejected the enforced division between cultural/moral knowledge and technical expertise. The Chinese state in its turn, while willing to give enough space to the technical intelligentsia, denied the same right to the critical social science intellectuals. It could do this because, White points out, as the

'cultural intellectuals' not engaged in directly productive activity, [they were] regarded [by the Party] as less sacrosanct than their technico-scientific counter-part, exerting greater political pressure with less fear of immediate damage to economic objectives. (White, 1981: 3)

At the same time, the intellectuals were subject to, and continue to attract, political pressure because of their crucial role in transmitting ideas and attitudes to the younger generation that legitimise (or not) state power.

In 1978, after the death of Mao and the defeat of the radical faction within the Party, another attempt was made to reconcile the intelligentsia with the state, by confronting the issue of *ti/yong* dichotomy. Deng Xiaoping tried in the early 1980s to recognise the necessity of regarding the moral/political ideas and the technical/ practical knowledge within the same framework. The question of institutionalised guarantees to the intellectuals for securing their rights as 'experts' as well as critics was examined. It seemed that the Chinese party/state was recognising the fact that economic modernisation requires an opening up of the public political sphere, together with the economic market-place. If the public sphere were to involve a critical debate with the state (public authority) through various media (Habermas in Rowe, 1990: 312), it posed fundamental problems of power, authority and legitimacy for the Chinese state. The reform faction within the Party began to move towards the view that interests and interest groups emerging as a result of the reforms needed established procedures and autonomous organisation to articulate their response to various policies of the state if the implementation of the reforms was to be efficient. This recognition was born out of the exigencies of a new economic policy, a recognition of the importance of reconcil- ing the intelligentsia to the modernising state. It prompted the party/state to advance both material and non-material incentives to the intellectuals (see below). However, considerations of the Party's power were no less important to the Party's reform section than to the 'hardliners'. At every stage of the debate regarding political reform, sharing of power was ruled out by all factions. Political reform and democratic centralism were strange bedfellows, but the need for rapid economic modernisation seemed to bind them together. The strains and tensions of the relationship, however, resulted in demands being made by each party that could only be unacceptable to the other. The intellectuals demanded that they be given a right to participate in the process of policy- making. China is a country 'in which academics are given the task of justifying a policy only after a decision has been made, and has been put into practice by a politician', complained He Xin of the Chinese Academy of Social Sciences (Barme, AJCA, January 1990: 54). The Party cadres, however, felt shocked and angered at what they saw as the arrogance of the intelligentsia that Mao had warned them against when they read the increasingly militant demands of some intellectuals. Liu Xibo, in exile after June 1989, for example, claimed: 'intellectuals' respect for the "truth of knowledge" should override good and evil in morality and the progressive and the conservative in politics' (*Chengming*, November 1989, JPRS-CAR-90-013). In a complete rejection of the Maoist emphasis on combining physical and intellectual labour, Liu wrote: 'An intellectual who used mental labour to earn a living has absolutely no need to learn how to cultivate land and make iron. This is not a shame. It is determined by the specific characteristics and independence of the intellectuals.' (*ibid.*) While the reformers within the Party had already accepted this by including the intellectuals in the ranks of the working class, the growing self-confidence of intellectuals like Liu made them wary, cautious and angry. The intellectuals were demanding 'literary pluralism' as a matter of right; the Party saw it as a gift that was not being appreciated in the spirit in which it was bestowed. In the aftermath of the repression of the Tian'anmen movement, 'literary pluralism' has been particularly attacked. An article in *Qiushi* (Seeking Truth), the CPC's ideological journal, noted: 'the idea of the "plurality of truth" cannot be substantiated . . . the proponents of "literary pluralism" used some of the literary fronts that they [held] in their own hands to allow only criticism of Marxist literature and art' (*Qiushi*, 1 February 1990, JPRS-CAR-90-032). The repression of the opposition movement in June 1989 has to be studied in the context of this growing alienation between the party/state and the intelligentsia, which began to move in the mid-1980s from the position of petitioner to that of a protester.

Defining the actors

In China anyone who can recognise 500 characters is considered literate, and all those who have secondary or higher education (BR, 23–9 July 1990: 13) are called *zheshi fenzi*, or 'knowledgeable elements', the intellectuals. Without going into the debate about defining the term 'intelligentsia', it would be pertinent to point out that the term arose first in Eastern and Central Europe around the middle of the nineteenth century. It then referred to a 'culturaliy homogeneous stratum' in Russia and Poland which was 'set apart from other educated elements . . . by a specific combination of psychological characteristics, manners, style of life, social status, and above all value systems' (Gella, in Schlesinger, 1986: 87). The element of nationalism and the relationship with the nation state formed an important part of the 'value systems' of the intelligentsia. In most socialist societies this conception of the term has been replaced by a more technocratic conception of a 'working intelligentsia' (see Churchward, 1975). A CPC handbook circulated in early 1949, for example, defined intellectuals as follows:

> Intellectuals include professors, scientists, engineers, reporters, authors, artists and students. They are not a social class. (Yeh, 1987: 87)

More recently, the journal of the Chinese Sociology Society defined intellectuals as all those

> who have acquired due knowledge of science and culture and due technical abilities and skills and can engage independently in mental work . . . [as well as] those physical workers who are mentally active, technologically or technically creative, and enthusiastically engaged in innovations. [*She Huixue Tongxun*, 1984; CE, Spring 1987: 67]

This shift can be traced, says Schlesinger, to Gramsci's writings where he ' "expanded" the conception of the intellectuals, one which focused upon the role of mental labour in the organisation of production generally, not just upon intellectuals as producers of ideologies' (Schlesinger, *op. cit.*: 85). Such a definition of the intelligentsia allows the Chinese party/state to organise this group as one in mass organisations that reflect no distinctions of educational level, professional positions, or political clout. However, the party/state, while conforming with this 'expanded', homogeneous definition, does distinguish – in practice if not in rhetoric – between 'high' and 'low' intellectuals. The high intellectuals are scholars and scientists who have made significant contributions in their fields, and who have developed a national stature that allows them access to, and the protection of, the party/state. We find this group active in Chinese politics through all its different periods, and it was extremely active in the 1989 democracy movement. All the important ideologues of the movement – Yan Jiaqi, Su Shaozhi, Liu Binyan, Liu Xibo – came from this group. The low intelligentsia is the teachers, the technicians, the job-doers, who are more easily mobilised and have less protection against the party/state. The university intellectuals straddle the two camps. While they are not part of the various institutes like the Chinese Academy of Sciences and the

Chinese Academy of Social Sciences concentrated in Beijing, or the think-tanks that have flourished in post-Mao China, some of them do have an independent status which allows them and their institutions greater bargaining leverage with the local party/state units. Together, the Chinese intellectuals comprise 2 per cent of the population (BR, 23–9 July 1990: 13).

The carrot and the stick

In May 1977, Deng Xiaoping made it clear that

> The key to modernisation is the development of science and technology. And unless we pay attention to education, it will be impossible to develop science and technology. Empty talk will get our modernisation programme nowhere; we must have knowledge and trained personnel. Without them how can we develop our science and technology? (Deng, 1984: 53)

The change in policy towards education and the intelligentsia was based upon the needs of economic development. The 'Guiding Principles of the Educational Reform' set out by the SEC in the 1985 elaborated:

> Economic construction, social development and the programme of science and technology, all depend on talent. This problem must be resolved by greatly developing the cause of education on the basis of economic development. The extreme importance of talent decides the strategic position of education in the construction of the Four Modernisations. (SEC, 1985b: 37)

Focusing on the needs of the economy as the basis for raising the status of the intelligentsia created a specific context for the reconciliation with the intellectuals. Greater academic freedom was seen as essential, primarily because it was needed for rapid growth of the corps of scientists and technicians.

The reconciliation of the state and the intelligentsia had also become important to the post-Mao leadership for reasons of legitimacy. Given the alienation of the people from the Party after the Cultural Revolution and 'the lack of a political system in which the people could express themselves directly', critical intellectuals 'assumed the role of a conduit by which the people's views could reach the political leadership, who were expected to respond to people's wishes' (Goldman *et al.*, 1987: 8–9; see also Chapter 1). When the simplistic hopes of the early 1980s that China could modernise its education and its economy by simply encouraging applied sciences gave way to a more holistic approach, the question of control still remained significant, and tied to the needs of economic development. The intelligentsia was offered a regulated, licensed space within which it was given relative freedom to discuss and to criticise, to make demands and put forward suggestions. The party/state as the licenser, however, retained the right both to take away that licence and/or to change the terms of reference for it.

The slogan and rhetoric of the 'two hundreds' policy of 1956 – Let a Hundred Flowers Bloom, a Hundred Schools of Thought Contend – was re-employed by the post-Mao leadership to create the historical situation for the opening up of the public sphere. The Chinese media drew upon the 'two hundreds' campaign quite heavily to convey a sense of freedom and autonomy, of respect for the views of the intelligentsia and a need for their critical abilities in the modernisation programme being pushed by the leadership. Indeed, the parallels are easily drawn: between the rhetoric employed, the audience addressed, the socio-economic needs of the periods, the response of the intelligentsia and, more importantly, the patterns of problem-solving. First, both the movements were launched from similar fora. Liu Tingyi made the first official statement on the movement before a gathering of scientists, social scientists, doctors, writers and others in Beijing (Liu, in Fraser, 1965: 151–63); Deng first laid the groundwork for the change in education policy in a National Science Conference (Deng, 1984) and Wan Li's detailed explanation of the Party's position was given at a Soft Science Conference (SWB/FE/BII, 19 August 1986: 1–11). Thus, the first audience addressed in both cases was the intelligentsia itself; these were not appeals to the 'masses' in general but to the educated élite for co-operation in the task of economic development. Second, the forms that the demands of the intellectuals upon the political system took also show similarity: seminars, symposia and conferences of scientists and academicians were supplemented by writing of *dazibaos* (big character posters) and articles and interviews in the media. Third, the timing of both movements is also significant: in both periods the ruling élite had come through an economic and political crisis in a more secure and confident mood. The completion of the land reforms and subsequent collectivisation by 1956, and the decollectivisation of the communes and the introduction of the 'individual responsibility system' by the early 1980s, gave the Party leadership the confidence in both instances to attempt new experiments in the political sphere. Further, at both these points in China's national history the country was poised for a period of rapid economic growth which necessitated the harnessing of the scientific and managerial skills of the intelligentsia, the expansion and growth of education, and the investing of education with a social prestige that would encourage the youth to join the ranks of the 'specialists'. Finally, the sense of political *déjà vu* is enhanced when we try to identify the issues that were taken up in 1956 and compare them with those thrown up in post-Mao China: academic freedom, greater autonomy for academic institutions, the freedom of the press, the tightening of the legal system, and greater material benefits for the intellectuals.

The re-employment of the rhetoric of the 1956 movement by the reform leadership of the post-Mao period served two purposes for the party/state. First, to point out that the agenda established during 1956, but interrupted by the anti-rightist campaign that followed in 1957–8, was being taken up again – more seriously and systematically. By criticising the broadening of the anti-rightist campaign, Deng hoped to allay fears of a sceptical intelligentsia. Second, it served to set boundaries and remind the intellectuals of the non-negotiables in the process of the extension of their participation in problem-solving. Mao, when launching the Hundred Flowers campaign, like Deng in his 'four cardinal principles', had 'proposed six political standards for differentiating fragrant flowers from poisonous weeds. The two most important of these standards are the socialist road and the leadership of the party' (*Qiushi*, 1 February 1990, JPRS-CAR-90-032). The 'Resolution on Certain Questions in the History of Our Party Since the Founding of the PRC', adopted by the Sixth Plenary Session of the Eleventh Central Committee in mid-1981 endorsed the Hundred Flowers movement. However, it also claimed that a 'handful of bourgeois rightists seized the opportunity . . . to mount wild attacks against the Party' which made necessary the anti-rightist campaign that followed in which thousands of intellectuals had been persecuted, although 'the scope of this struggle was made far too broad' (CPC CC 1981: 27).

A clearer indication of how the party/state would view dissent came after the student unrest of 1986–7 when a movement against 'bourgeois liberalism' was unleashed. While the earlier campaign style was not employed to deliver the message and mobilisation of the 'masses' was avoided, the hardliners in the Party made it clear that 'all of our party's policies must be based on the four cardinal principles', and that the 'double hundred policy was no exception' (HQ, JPRS, 13 April 1987: 23). The events in Tian'anmen Square in June 1989 illustrated the depth of resistance in the Party bureaucracy to any significant opening up of the public political sphere to the intelligentsia. The repercussions of such resistance for the relations between the party/state and the intellectuals proved far reaching.

Pinrensi – contracting intellectual labour

The incentives that the party/state offered the intellectuals in the universities were substantive. However, even as they built up crucial support for the leadership among the intelligentsia in the early to mid-1980s, these reforms also had some consequences unforeseen by the leadership. They encouraged new tensions and contradictions among the intelligentsia, especially at the university level. One important reform was part of a broader policy decision to 'break the iron rice bowl' of secure, tenured employment in every sector in order to encourage efficiency. A job contract system for university teachers was introduced in 1985. The implementation as well as the terms of the contract varied considerably from area to area, and university to university. Thus, while Hangzhou University was introducing this system in May 1987, Zhejiang University, also in Hangzhou, had initiated it the year before in 1986. Most universities have, after an experimental stage involving 'advanced' institutions, implemented this system.

The contract system was an attempt at solving two major problems confronting the Chinese university system: incentives to intellectuals for higher work efficiency on the one hand, and the over-staffing of university departments on the other. As in the larger economic setting, the rationale of market forces was employed to solve these problems. The pressure of the possible non-renewal of a contract and the incentive of a clearly defined work load are expected to raise efficiency. Thus each department can have a schedule of the total work load, together with the number of teachers required to teach it, and can limit its recruitment of staff accordingly. A contractual system, it is believed, could give a flexibility to the recruitment pattern – if either side is not satisfied, they can withdraw. Young teachers, who might like to find better-paid jobs, can take advantage of this as can the university in the case of inefficient employees. There are two sections to the contract – one is called 'the tasks', which sets out the work load of individual teachers; the other is called 'the invitation to work', which states the duration and terms of the contract. While the 'tasks' are made out for the year ahead and reviewed at the end of it, the pattern for the teaching contract is usually two years. There are some universities, however, where the contract is yearly, and others where it is reviewed after every three years.

This system of contract for labour was first introduced in the factories as part of attempts at rationalising production and was discussed in the press and in different labour organisations. The procedure which was followed before introducing this into the university system is illustrated by what happened at Hangzhou University. A lecturer in the Law Department explained:

> First, the SEC gave a draft to the PEC who changed it according to particular demands [and then] it came to the Hangda [Hangzhou University] leadership who made their own draft . . . First all the deans [of the departments] were called by the President to tell them about the regulations. They came back and talked to the department teachers . . . most teachers agreed. [It was] not discussed at the university level . . . none of the teachers' organisations discussed it . . . no vote was taken.

However, it was significant that while the leadership projected this reform as one of the key instruments in correcting the mismanagement of the universities, neither the Hangzhou University authorities, nor the lecturers themselves, seemed to share this view: 'I think it is a formality or formalism . . . all teachers will always be engaged', said a lecturer in Politics. It was looked upon more as a method of rearranging teaching work load or readjusting surplus staff: 'Geography Department has more teachers than needed . . . [they] will have to go to other departments or units', said a lecturer in the Politics Department. The teachers seemed to regard this change rather lightly. 'Theoretically speaking [it] is good, but I don't know what the results will be'; '[It is] neither too good nor too bad – just OK . . . [It is] not an important change'; '[It has] not much influence . . . [it is a] change in administration. Department office [can] take charge of how many teachers they want and what new course is to be offered'. These were some of the reactions of the lecturing staff at Hangzhou University.

However, there are indications that this system might become a spur to competition, provoking tensions between generations of lecturers: 'Today China needs modern scientific knowledge, but older teachers have served for so long. Because of the contract system's emphasis on academic excellence the promotion of middle-level teachers is very difficult', said a young lecturer at Hangzhou University. Here 'academic excellence' implies academic degrees, publications, and participation in seminars, symposia and conferences in China and abroad. This, as we shall see later, is an important source of friction that is resulting in the gradual differentiation of interests in the universities.

University lecturerships are not highly paid in China (see Table 5.1). Many young lecturers would like to look for jobs in the growing enterprise sector of the economy. The proposal to deregulate the job allocation system has increased this possibility. These lecturers resent the fact that the contract system, while giving the freedom of hiring and firing to the university, does not provide them with the opportunity to improve their careers.

The university can refuse to release them, and without a

Table 5.1 Pay scales for college teachers (Unit: RMB per month)

Rank	Basic salary	1	Graded increments						
			2	3	4	5	6	7	8
Professor	40	315[1] 260[1]	215	190	165	150	140	130	120
Associate professor	40	190[1] 165[1]	150	140	130	120	110	100	91	82
Lecturer	40	110[1]	100	91	82	73	65	57	
Teaching	40		57	49	42	36	30		

[1] This salary is only received by a limited number.

Source: Chao Ch'i-cheng (ed.), *Kan-pu jen-shih kung-tso shou-ts'e* (*Handbook on cadre personnel work*) in Li Hua-cheng, 'The Peking Regime's Policy on Intellectuals during Deng Tsiao-ping Era', *Issues and Studies*, Vol. 26, No. 7, July 1990.

reference from their *danwei* (work unit) they could not find another job. Hence, the contract system is not equally empowering for both the parties involved. A further question undermining the implementation of the contract system is the system of *fenpei*, or state allocation of jobs. Unless the job market is freed from the constraints imposed by this system, the contract system cannot function efficiently. A free movement of labour is required for the two contracting parties to make an efficient use of this device. The Chinese planners have recognised this and have loosened some controls in this area but problems of economic development and political control preclude complete decentralisation of this planned process. The student movement of 1989 and its suppression have led to greater caution among the leadership in this regard. While before June 1989, the plan was to open up the job market completely to market forces by 1993, this is no longer on the agenda. Further, the contract system has also the potential both for the tightening of political controls in the university and for the strengthening of resistance to those controls. The secretary of the Party unit in the Politics Department in Hangzhou University complained: 'Another aspect [is that the] amount of work is delimited, that is, teachers can refuse to teach . . . therefore, [it is] not good.' On the other hand, Hangzhou University had also 'reallocated' two lecturers from the Biology Department to schools in the city. It was widely believed that this was a punitive transfer because of the lecturers' links with the student movement of 1986–7.

The success of the contract system is linked to another policy. A market-based rationalisation of intellectual labour requires not just the threat of redundancy but also the promise of promotion. The party/state provided for incentives in the university by producing a promotion package that is, like the contract system, also clearly influenced by the American model.

Tishen: the politics of promotion

Academic degrees had been abolished during the Cultural Revolution. After a four-year course at the university the students were graduated but without any specific degree or diploma to indicate their academic status. Those allocated jobs as university teachers were thus an undifferentiated body, without academic qualifications marking distinctions between various levels of competence. There were salary grades based on seniority, not academic achievement. As there was no academic hierarchy, there was no sense of promotion or movement. The post-Mao leadership felt that the result of such a system was a general lack of enthusiasm for improving qualifications and the teaching methods in the universities as everyone came to 'eat from the same big pot'. The pressure of competition leading to improvement of standards was absent, as was the scheme of material incentives for those who wanted to improve themselves. The incentives that were provided were non-material ones, of public recommendation as 'model teachers' – a singling out that carried its own burden of expectations of the local Party units and envy, and even the suspicion (without monetary recompense) of colleagues.

The post-Mao leadership introduced the promotion scheme in 1985. This was made possible by introducing another reform: a retirement scheme. Until 1985, the university staff had in effect a job for life, which made most institutions top-heavy. The retirement scheme echoed Deng's call to senior Party cadres to retire from their posts and to let younger cadres take over responsibility: 'Tenure for life in leading posts is linked both to feudal influences and to the continued absence of proper regulations in the Party for the retirement and dismissal of cadres', he said (Deng, 1984: 314). Under the new regulations male staff were to retire at the age of 60 and women at 55, 'except well known professors'. The pension scheme is fairly generous to make it attractive. The chairman of the Education Department at Hangzhou explained that 'those who have worked since before 1949 [get] full salary pension . . . [others] according to the number of years they've worked'. Many teachers get re-employed after retirement and can get up to one-third of their original salary, together with the pension.

As part of the promotion scheme four grades have been introduced in the university: assistant lecturer, lecturer, associate professor and professor. The mobility between each grade is dependent upon two major factors – the length of service, and the qualifications of the applicant. These include command over a foreign language, publications and the 'teaching quality'. The latter is judged by taking into account student reactions to each applicant's teaching method and the opinion of senior teachers who attend the classes of applicants to judge the quality of the lecturers. Further, the rate of promotion of students of a particular class/course to the next grade is also taken into account at the time of considering applications. However, there is a stipulation by the SEC/PEC regarding the proportion of the staff that can be in a grade at any level, as it is a question of increases in salaries and living facilities. For example, at Hangzhou University 27 per cent of the total of associate professors could be put up for promotion to the professorial level. The procedure for promotion takes into account the application, the publication record of the candidate, and recommendations of professors. A lecturer can apply for promotion to the next grade if s/he has worked in his/her present capacity for five years with graduate qualification or two years with an MA.

The promotions are decided by a Promotions Committee: at the departmental level for associate lecturerships; at the university level for lecturerships and associate professorships; and at the provincial level for professorships. These committees are headed by the dean, the president and the chairperson of the SEC/PEC respectively. However, the head of the higher education division of the Zhejiang PEC stated that 'all applications are viewed here as well'. This system obviously draws on the American experience for inspiration – the threat of termination of contract, and the importance of academic production judged by number of publications. However, cultural, structural, and political differences have meant that the introduction of competition in institutions of higher education has been regarded warily. The head of the higher education division at the PEC said: 'We cannot get used to the American system.' This feeling of disquiet is enhanced by some of the tensions that are emerging as a result of this new scheme, even though the overall response seems to be positive.

The tensions are of two kinds. First, new contradictions are emerging between generations: the younger lecturers feel hard done by as they believe the senior lecturers are being promoted with or without requisite qualifications. Second, there is the conflict between time spent on research and publishing on the one hand, and preparing for and teaching courses on the other. Both the contract system and the promotion procedure emphasise publications and there is also the feeling that the Promotion Committee exacerbates the situation:

> [it is] not teachers' error . . . [the committee] depends on the theses and looks down on the teachers. Teachers have put forward their view, but there is no response. If it is not resolved, teaching quality will lower . . . teaching is the main purpose of a university

said a senior lecturer in the Department of Politics at Hangzhou University. Senior lecturers teach for fewer hours, and are therefore able to publish more. They also have better *guanxi* (connections) among the publishers. The younger lecturers, who are interested in new areas of research, especially in the field of science, feel neglected, deprived of funds and encouragement. This is creating a situation where the cynicism of the younger teachers is beginning to show: 'If officials in the department do the work according to regulation, the system itself is OK. But *guanxi* works', said one.

The question of control also has a bearing on the promotion scheme. On the one hand, the Party cadres fear a loss of power as ideological considerations become less important in decisions concerning promotions. On the other, the scrutiny of the authorities over the staff is intensified in judging the quality of teaching through personal observation. This further raises the levels of tension between the senior and the junior teachers. A lecturer in Chemistry in Hangzhou University complained:

> I have been teaching since 1982 and haven't been promoted. I can't do anything about it. Neither the department nor the university decides. I don't understand. It is not a question of no vacancies either. I'm so confused! . . . Very few young teachers have a chance to be promoted.

Generational politics in universities

The changes in higher education policy have resulted in formalising a distinction among university staff on the basis of criteria of professionalism rather than of political affiliation and/or patronage. This has allowed some identifiable procedures of promotion and distinction to be established as opposed to the nebulous, arbitrary and ever-shifting standards of a 'correct' political line as was the case during Mao's time. This change has also led to the separating out of the several interest groups based variously on average annual salary, overall standard of living, professional opportunity and mobility and recruitment to positions of power within the university (Davis-Friedman, 1985: 180). However, the rapidity of the change has led to a heightened sense of confusion and insecurity which, because of a non-availability of autonomous organisations for interest articulation, finds expression in a general feeling of resentment against other competing groups and the university and Party authorities.

The development of modern education in China passed through two distinct phases before it was stamped by the Maoist image – in the pre-liberation and immediately post-1949 China we can see a strong influence of the American system of education. Educational reformers, philosophers and missionaries who either took an interest in China or actually went there to set up institutions of education left a deep impact on Chinese educationists (Keenan, 1977; Borthwick, 1983; Educational Association of China, 1971; Ayers, 1971). Many Chinese scholars, for example, went to Columbia University in New York and were trained at its Institute for Education or to Christian institutions of higher education in China like the Yenching University (West, 1976: 138–41). Most of this corps of pre-revolution Chinese educational élite were from a wealthy, middle-class background. The CPC too had a policy of sending its members and sympathisers to Europe and Japan to make contact with the West and make propaganda against Western imperialist policies in those countries. Many Party supporters thus took training in the West during the period of the revolutionary movement. Most conspicuous were Zhou Enlai, Deng Xiaoping and Zhu De, all of whom spent time in France. With the establishment of the People's Republic the leadership was faced with the huge task of reconstruction for which trained human capital was a prerequisite. The CPC appealed to Chinese intellectuals all over the world to come back and join its struggle to construct a new China, and to those in China to hold national interest above political preference. Incentives, in terms of salaries, facilities and status, were provided in order to mobilise their energies. Those who came back from the West formed the backbone of the Chinese educational system.

Things changed, however, with the increasing pressure and

isolation resulting from the hostility of the USA and the West. The Chinese party/state became more dependent on the Soviet Union, and its model of economic and educational development. More and more young intellectuals were sent to Russia for training. Between 1950 and 1960, when the schism between China and the USA reached a climax resulting in the virtual breaking off of relations, the Chinese party/state sent 8,208 students to the Soviet Union while none went to the United States (SEC, 1984: 126). The pattern of educational administration was slowly restructured to conform to the Soviet model.

More than 600 Soviet experts worked in Chinese universities as advisers. By 1957, they had trained 8,285 graduate students and teachers. While many benefited from both the Soviet training and the political prestige attached to it, the old intellectuals trained in the West were not sanguine about the effect that this relationship with the Soviet Union might have on the educational framework. The Soviet polytechnical education, for example, emphasised applied science as opposed to pure research which meant the latter did not take off in the Chinese universities until the 1980s. Engineering, agriculture, forestry, and medicine and pharmacy formed the bulk of the courses established between 1955 and 1957. Engineering accounted for 501 courses out of a total of 885 that were established during this period (SEC, *op. cit.*: 56). The intellectuals also felt their own status in revolutionary China to be threatened. However, before the Soviet model could take root, the Sino–Soviet friendship itself collapsed in the face of the growing differences between Mao and Khrushchev on questions of strategies for economic and political development and the international communist movement (CPC CC 1965).

Mao's search for an educational model that would combine the qualities of the 'red' and 'expert' – of correct ideological training with a high level of skill acquisition – led to large-scale experimentation during the Cultural Revolution. As the goals of educational enterprise shifted, so did the method of training; destruction of old structures was an integral part of the building of the new. This project of destruction also included 'those individuals who had been responsible for the failure to systematically promote educational reform' (Glassman, 1974: 238). Thus, 'capitalist-roaders' and 'bourgeois elements' were identified within each institution and made the target for 'struggle'. The wave of anti-intellectualism that swept across China during this period greatly damaged the fabric of student–teacher relations (see Unger, 1982; Chan, 1985; Hinton, 1972). The wounds were deep and no serious attempt was made to heal them until 1978, even though the Maoist leadership could not but be aware of the damage that was being caused:

> The poor relationship between teachers and students was a big obstacle to the resumption of classes . . . At first, most of the teachers were unwilling to teach classes. Some of them went reluctantly to teach the classes but could not get along with the students. Some others asked to be transferred to another trade and to other posts. Some students despised their teachers and reproached them as being backward and conservative. (RMRB, SCMP, No. 4063, 20 November 1967: 16)

Many of these students are teaching as young lecturers today. They are not, however, a homogeneous group with similar political histories. There are those who were actively involved in the persecution of the intellectuals during the Cultural Revolution, but had not been purged because they probably changed sides in time. However, as a senior professor of Politics at Hangzhou University, much maligned during that period, said: 'We can never forget; this hate will go to our deaths with us.' The painful memories of the worst years of the Cultural Revolution are daily relived as the ex-tormentors rub shoulders with their victims. (For a graphic account of this phenomenon see *Stones of the Wall* (Dai, 1987.)

There are others who either suffered because of their bad class background or were not active or have genuinely reconsidered their earlier views; this group realises the value of the second chance given to them and is willing to work hard to make the most of it. The problem it faces is that of competition with the post-1978 generation of students who are now flooding the academic job market. This threat is significant. The patchy training of the Cultural Revolution generation and the long interval of virtually no education has left that generation insecure. As the numbers enrolling for taking the national examination increased, the party/ state began to discourage this group from applying by imposing age restrictions. They, in turn, have mixed feelings about the younger undergraduates. On the one hand, they despise the new generation as 'soft'; they have not been tempered in the political and social havoc that they themselves had to go through. As a young lecturer who had to serve in the army in the countryside for five years during the Cultural Revolution said, '[We] studied very hard; in the 1980s [students] do not study very hard. Why? Because [we had a] feeling of wasted time during the Cultural Revolution.' On the other hand, they are conscious of the inadequacies of their academic training and the feeling of superiority that this arouses in the post-1978 students:

> People of our generation, middle aged teachers, I mean, are supposed to be the pillars of today's society, but we don't have much to show for ourselves . . . We are more like fruit that has frozen on the vine before it's ripened; and we probably never will get a chance to ripen. In ten years of turmoil, who hasn't lost something? We lost time, energy, our dreams, our enthusiasm. (Wang and Wen, 1984: 57)

The problem is greater because of the age factor: the Cultural Revolution generation is now in its mid-thirties or older and there is a long way for people to go as members of production units – material or cultural – even with the new retirement regulations. 'Old teachers are doctoral or master's tutors; young teachers work hard; middle-aged teachers have a low level of education', said the Dean of the Psychology Department at Hangzhou University. This means that these middle-aged teachers cannot be promoted very easily. The Dean explained: '[they] can only become lecturers; they cannot become associate professors. If young teachers are promoted over the heads of the middle-aged teachers, some will oppose it . . . [We can] only rely on political education to resolve this contradiction.' The universities feel the pressure of what they see as an intellectual dead-weight but are unable to respond with correctives. As the Dean of the Psychology Department noted, 'The responsibility is not of the individual but the party's. We can look after them, but not at the expense of education.' So, most of the ex-worker/peasant/soldier students and the Red Guards, he said, 'have been transferred to other spheres. The office of our university gave them other work but not teaching. Those who continued to stay, we help them raise their level . . . give them time to study.' The resentments caused by such moves can easily be imagined. The middle-aged lecturers pose an even greater problem in this regard. Further, the process of political rehabilitation of the purged Party members in the universities has brought forth its own tensions. As White points out:

Party members who had been rightists, practically all of them intellectuals, were treated more leniently than non-Party members . . . [They] received salary reimbursements (*bufa gongci*) to cover the years of the incorrect classification. This windfall, in most cases considerable . . . allowed CCP ex-rightists and their families to live in style; and it caused resentment among many rehabilitated non-Party rightists (White, 1987: 256)

These then are the four groups that can be identified in the academic staff of the university: first, the old Western-trained professors; second, the middle-aged, Soviet-trained associate professors; third, the young lecturers educated during the GPCR period; and, finally, the post-1978 corps of assistant lecturers. While the divisions between age groups and the grades are not always that clearly marked, some such rough correspondence can still be made. At Hangzhou University, for example, there are 170 associate professors of whom only 7 are less than 40 years of age while of 20 full professors none is less than 40.

These four groups have only recently begun to emerge as identifiable categories and there is, as yet, little evidence of any articulation of their group interests at an organisational level. These interests span a whole range of problems facing these groups – general and specific – and are causing frictions and competition between them. The major areas of competition are for resources and influence: the allocation of living space and facilities; promotion and work load; and the opportunities available for visits abroad, for further study, seminars and conferences, and exchange programmes. As the resources and opportunities available in all these areas are limited, competition for these has placed a severe stress on the university system.

The tensions between interest groups are most visible in the sphere of professional competition. A senior associate professor remarked:

Senior teachers [want to] improve pedagogy and scientific research . . . their own age is great so . . . some want to open laboratories for research students or write books . . . [They want to] transfer their knowledge, not increase it . . . Younger teachers want only to increase their own knowledge. They have different aspirations . . . for example, senior teachers don't all want to go abroad. But in some courses it is necessary.

The younger lecturers, of course, feel this to be an untenable position. They *do* want to go to the US or Europe for further studies and for this they are prepared to work hard, but their complaint is that the senior teachers and cadres do not share in their ambitions and inhibit their endeavours. Bureaucratic interference is also resented. For example, the university bureaucracy at Hangzhou decided that too many students were being sent to the US for further study and too few to West Germany, a country with which they want to expand relations. So schedules and arrangements were changed for some students of particular departments. In the Politics Department five students – out of whom four do not speak any German – were asked to go to Germany after their applications to go for study in the US had already been approved. One of those going wanted to do a doctoral course on Sino–US relations, but could only do a year's course in Germany. In an attempt to prevent switching of courses, lengthening of stay or moving from one country to the other, the SEC has prohibited any transferral or change in the original programmes decided upon (see Chapter 3).

The opportunity for extra teaching and hence extra income is also bound up to a great extent with the status and age of the teacher. An assistant lecturer commented: 'only a few teachers get extra money through teaching, not most'. The fee for each extra lecture, arranged on a contractual basis, also differs. In Hangzhou University in 1987, for example, professors and associate professors got Y6, lecturers Y5 and assistant lecturers Y4 per lecture. Publishing generates income, and here too the younger lecturers feel left out in the cold. *Guanxi* is needed which they do not have. China's ageist culture also makes it more difficult for the younger lecturers to be taken seriously by publishers. 'It is very difficult for young authors [to publish]. No one trusts you . . . One associate professor of Chinese language earned Y10,000 from the royalty of a book. I got Y2,800 for one publication', admitted the head of the Comparative Education Department at the University. The academic area the teachers are involved in also affects their income and becomes a source of income inequality. A lecturer of Law at Hangzhou, for example, also worked as a lawyer at the municipal courts and earned on an average RMB 30–60 per case, depending upon the nature of the suit. 'I can earn much more than other teachers', she said.

If the younger teachers complain about lack of opportunity,

middle-aged teachers feel overburdened with work and unappreciated by the state. A survey carried out in Hubei Province in 1987 by the Research Group for Intellectuals' Problems interviewed 514 middle-aged intellectuals, most of whom described themselves as 'operating on overload'. They are the mainstay of their faculties; '35% of them assume leadership of a section, subdivision, or group and 27% hold cadre positions in the Party . . . 22% have either old folks or sick people depending on their care' and all have young children whose problems take up a lot of time and energy; '68% have to undertake household chores personally. This percentage is even higher among the women intellectuals. As many as 89% of them are involved in the housework' (*She Huixue tongxun*, 1984; CE, Spring 1987: 56–65). This, together with low wages – usually 50–60 yuan per month excluding 'bonuses' – and poor accommodation, leads to ill health; 78 per cent of those surveyed did not consider themselves healthy, and 14 per cent were chronically ill (*ibid.*).

Living conditions have always been a source of dissatisfaction among the Chinese intelligentsia. The living quarters have been cramped and facilities inadequate. The amount spent on construction of housing for the university staff has always fallen short of the demand. As, until recently, all work units were responsible for their employees' residence requirements and as there was no market of private housing available, the result has been a distressing shortage of space which has resulted in the crowding of people into very small areas:

> Our one room of twelve by thirteen feet: a big bed and a smaller bed took up over half the room, and in the space left over, after you allow for a book case, cardboard cartons, and a cupboard, there was just barely room for a desk . . . I don't have to tell you what the typical hallway in this type of mass housing is like: dark and creepy . . . and piled high on both sides with all kinds of wicker tubs and bamboo baskets, messy coal bricks and clay pots for cooking, and even pickle urns and bicycles are there. (Wang and Wen, 1984: 75–6)

Lack of housing facilities has meant great emotional stress for couples and families who are separated because their 'units' cannot find them reasonable accommodation. Competition for scarce facilities fuels generational conflict. With differentiation of grades, there has also come about a slow improvement in the living facilities. Thus, the professors have been accommodated in better housing. For example, at Beijing University a huge new complex with modern and fairly spacious accommodation has been built for the five hundred or so professors. '[It is] a problem for younger persons . . . Each year 150 new residents are added. Older teachers [professors] all have three-bedroom houses', admitted a professor. The problem is further compounded as even after retirement the professors retain the houses. Until recently the children of the staff of the university could 'inherit' the rights over the official accommodation and continue living there while the newly recruited staff suffered worsening conditions. Those young teachers whose parents are living in the same city as them do not even now get their own university accommodation as they are expected to live with their families to reduce the pressure for housing. Such distinctions in standards of living have begun to fuel feelings of resentment between various levels. There are also broader implications: '[this] is one reason why Hangda cannot employ younger teachers from other universities, as it will have to provide accommodation', said a lecturer at the Psychology Department in Hangzhou University.

There are thus increasing contradictions emerging among generations of university members. The smaller the institution, the poorer the 'unit', the more these are visible. In Hangzhou University, for example, it was easier to identify groups than in Beijing University where both greater resources, a bigger campus, and much greater numbers of lecturing staff diffused to a degree the impact of these divisions. However, in each case the articulation of these interests and resentments remains informal and hidden. There are no separate organisations representing the interests of different groups in the university. All lecturers belong to one organisation that also includes the services and administrative staff of the university (see below). This affects the enthusiasm of the various groups in the implementation of the new policies; attempts at subversion through non-action have a long history in post-revolutionary China.

Jiaoyuhui and the organised intelligentsia

There are four organisations that constitute the institutional network for the non-student population in the university – the

Party branch, the Communist Youth League (CYL), the Teachers'
Congress and the Educational Union (*Jiaoyuhui*). All these
organisations are geared towards transmitting party/state policies
to their membership and/or mobilising their membership to
implement these. None of the organisations encourages participation
of their members in policy implementation. As they all function
'under the leadership of the Communist Party', they are under
close surveillance. They represent the interests of their members
by petitioning the Party, not challenging it. The Educational
Union, sometimes called the Workers' Union (*gonghui*), is the
biggest organisation of the staff of any university. The Teachers'
Congress meets only once a year to take stock of the work done by
the Educational Union and by the university authorities. The
Party branch is representative not of teaching or administrative
interests but of the political interests of the party/state. The CYL
looks after the ideological training of those aged less than 28 years,
but is more active among the students. *Jiaoyuhui* is a mass
organisation. Together with the teaching staff, it includes in its
membership the administrative cadres of the university, as well as
the workers. The criterion for membership of the *jiaoyhui* is,
therefore, simply membership of the university in a non-student
capacity. This precludes any importance being given to the nature
of work of its members. As such, it encompasses a wide spectrum
of political opinion and distinct and competing professional and
economic interests. However, as these differences within its
membership are not officially recognised or formally articulated,
the organisation remains a vehicle for mobilising support for Party
policies.

The Educational Union was established in 1953, but during the
period of the Cultural Revolution its activities remained suspended
as 'class struggle' became the only agenda for the Chinese polity.
Special interests were divisive and therefore unacceptable. It was
reactivated only in 1978, after the death of Mao and the fall of the
'Gang of Four'. Its constitution was formalised and ratified in
October 1983 at the Tenth National People's Congress (NPC).
The *jiaoyuhui* is a national organisation with a network of local
branches (see Figure 5.1). There is little difference in the
organisational pattern of the *jiaoyuhui* at different levels.

The Hangzhou University Educational Union, for example, is
run by a 13-member Committee headed by a chairperson

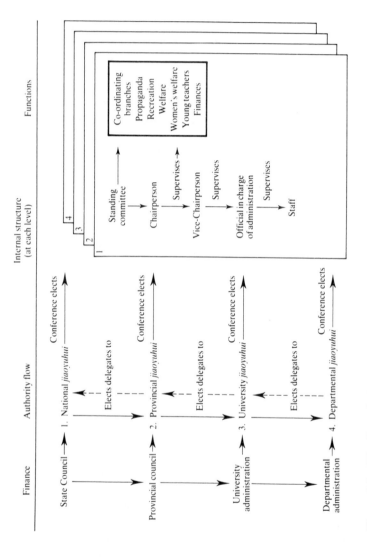

Figure 5.1 The *jiaoyuhui*

(*jiaoyuhui zhuren*) elected for two years. The Committee is chosen by a system whereby each department recommends a name, which is screened and then put up before the Teachers' Congress for election. The Teachers' Congress meets once every year to review teachers' problems. The Committee looks after propaganda work, recreation, welfare and other problems facing its members. It also oversees and co-ordinates the working of the 26 departmental branches. The Union is financed from three sources: first, the fee from its membership; second, the contribution of the University which comes from a 2 per cent cut from the salaries of all members; and third, a grant to cover unexpected expenditure by the university administration. Forty per cent of the amount collected by the 2 per cent deduction from the teachers' salaries is given over to the Provincial Educational Union.

At the departmental level in Hangzhou, the Union elects its chairperson and committee for a tenure of two years. This is done by choosing from names recommended by different teaching groups of the various 'majors' being taught in each department, after they have been 'screened' by the outgoing committee. Many young lecturers at Hangzhou University, however, did not seem to have a clear idea about these procedures. 'At the departmental level there is no list to choose from; at the university level, yes . . . the chairman is elected for several years. As far as I can remember there has been only one election during the last four years', said an assistant lecturer in the Department of Education. However, this pyramidal structure is constructed quite loosely; there is not much regular consultation or joint activity between levels: 'There is no regular meeting; if there are any activities arranged at the university level, we are asked to attend', said the chairperson of the union of the Meteorological Department.

As a result of a general policy of reactivating university organisations that had been superseded by the revolutionary committees during the Cultural Revolution, in order to stabilise the university environment under a new leadership, the status of the Union was raised in 1978: it now 'takes part in meetings at the university level in order to raise teachers' problems', said the Union chairperson in Hangzhou University. Most of the functions of the Union are welfare activities – the bringing together of the non-student population of the university in an attempt to create a unity of interests. The very nature of the organisation precludes any but the most generalised political rhetoric. It is through a sense of recreational participation and marginal material benefits that this unity is attempted. 'For example,' explained the chair of the union in the Department of Computer Sciences, 'we bought beer . . . everyone gets a crate; it is much cheaper [to get it] from the factory. Every teacher pays, but [it is still] cheaper than to buy in shops.' The contacts of the departmental union members are used to make such bulk purchases. Some department unions might get seasonal fruit, oil or vegetables to its members through making bulk purchases from farms or factories. This can best be done at the level of individual units and leads to localised activity: '[the union] does its work individually in each department, but sometimes there is interdepartmental activity, for example a volleyball tournament', said the Computer Studies union chair. The regular activities of the Union at the university level, said the chairperson of the university *jiaoyuhui*, include:

> propaganda, arranging matches, organising sightseeing tours during the summer vacation away from Hangzhou – this costs us Y7000–Y8000 a year; arranging off-work education for workers, health survey for women teachers for special diseases; sending some Educational Union cadres for further training – each year there is an election of the best cadre and we give a prize; organising recreational bodies like calligraphy society, chess society, fishing society.

The nature of such an organisation precludes any confrontation with university authorities on behalf of its members. The young teachers are especially at a loss as they do not feel that their grievances can be heard, much less righted, through intervention by this organisation. A young lecturer said, 'In China we don't demand things; we have to wait for the government to give it to us . . . If I go [to the authorities] they will notice me, and think why can't *I* wait . . . The Educational Union cannot help.' The result is a growing sense of frustration among this group of teachers. The fact that after the student demonstrations of December–January 1986–7 there was a renewed call for increased propaganda and 'ideological education' through the Union is indicative of this and of the concern of the authorities. 'The students demonstrated, and the young lecturers fanned the fire during the demonstration', said a student activist.

Similarly, there has been no attempt made by the Union to take up women's issues. While there is no separate women's organisation in the university there is a women's 'unit' of the *jiaoyuhui*. However, this was set up only in 1986 and 'therefore it has not done much work yet', said a member. The unit, also represented at the departmental level, mainly works in the field of women's welfare: propaganda work for birth control, distributing contraceptive pills, maintaining university kindergarten and crèche, and visiting its members after delivery or when ill. More contentious issues like the discrepancy of retirement ages of men and women have not been taken up by the women's wing of the Educational Union and there seems no move to do so. The Chinese Women's Federation which should deal with this at the national level (as the regulations are the same for other sectors of the economy) has not taken this up either. The result of this conflation of women's interests with general interests has meant that politically sensitive issues such as discrimination against women in employment, promotions and retirement have remained unaddressed. Indeed, among the middle-aged women staff of Hangzhou University there is a persistent insistence upon an image of the de-sexualised worker, especially among older lecturers who have lived through the radical Maoist era. A woman lawyer said, '[I] don't think very much of the fact that [I'm] a woman; [I'm] a teacher . . . most departments don't have much problems regarding women . . . [separate women's organisations] are not needed.' While it is true that many intellectual women are addressing problems specific to their own sex and seeking to separate out the woman from the woman worker, this remains confined to a small section of 'high' women intellectuals. The lack of an active women's unit at the level of the university continues to sustain the undifferentiated image of the 'worker', while allowing the traditional images to re-emerge in the context of the new economic reforms (Rai, 1988: 10–12).

By making all the non-student populations a part of an organisational structure that is functioning at various levels of the university system, it becomes possible to keep this population under surveillance. The relationship with the Party unit at every level remains strong and is one of subordination. A departmental union chair explained, 'leadership [is] with the Party . . . [we give the] major plans . . . to the Party leaders . . . [and] ask their opinion . . . Sometimes we invite them to take part in our meetings.' Further, the undifferentiated nature of the organisation precludes it focusing on demands and issues affecting specific interests. The pattern for dealing with special problems remains one of individualised intervention; the person concerned has to make him/herself visible to the authorities. Not many are prepared to do this.

It is the marginal material benefits that the *jiaoyuhui* can provide to its members that gives it a greater relevance in their daily life than it would have otherwise. This is especially true of teachers with families. The recreational activities, such as trips out of town on heavily subsidised rates, are especially popular. The *jiaoyuhui* also provides a sense of belonging to a group, a means of identifying with the work environment and with colleagues on a non-political, social level. This is important as during the Cultural Revolution the social fabric in the universities was greatly damaged, as a result of which there is very little visiting or fraternising among colleagues outside of work. The fact that there are no common areas where teachers can meet in their free hours in the departments also adds to this fragmentation. Further, the organisation does take up certain issues with the university authorities for the teachers' welfare; for example, it was suggested to the Hangzhou University authorities to start a bus service for teachers living off campus and this was accepted. However, in the words of the chairperson of the Hangzhou University union, 'We can only give suggestions. We can do nothing else.' The lack of an organisational framework within which the particular fears, frustrations and anxieties of different sections of the intellectuals could be aired, and which could provide a space for a dialogue with the authorities, became one of the factors in the cracks that appeared in the post-Mao relations between the intelligentsia and the party/state.

The intelligentsia's response to state initiatives

Given the history of its relationship with the post-revolutionary state, the initial response of the intelligentsia to the overtures of the state was remarkably positive. The rejection by the post-Mao leadership of Maoist anti-intellectualism, and the introduction of concrete measures to right the balance in favour of the intellectuals, however limited, together with a more general opening up of the public sphere and rising expectations for further improvement, led the intelligentsia to once again try and mend its fences with the state. However, problems regarding the redefinition of this relationship arose quickly. The ambiguities in the state's reform initiative led both the intelligentsia and the Party at the grassroot levels to define the official version to their best advantage, leading to a sense of confusion and uncertainty on the one hand, and opening up spaces for redefinition and subversion on the other.

Starting from a demand for greater autonomy from Party surveillance in their professional spheres, a demand soon arose among the intelligentsia for greater freedom of general political expression. Amongst the 'high' intelligentsia this was highlighted by the debate on the concepts of alienation and humanism under socialism in 1985–6 out of which arose four demands. These were spelled out in the essay 'Defence of Humanism' by Wang Ruoshui, the erstwhile editor of RMRB who was dismissed from his post and expelled from the Party in the 'anti-bourgeois liberalisation' campaign that followed the student demonstrations of 1986–7:

> (1) . . . uphold the equality of every person before the truth and the law; and uphold the sanctity of personal freedom and dignity. (2) . . . assess the individual's worth on the basis of what he is in himself and not on the basis of origins, position, or wealth. (3) Recognise man as the goal, not only of social production but of all work . . . (4) Stress the human elements of social production. (Kelly, 1987: 170)

It is this stand that brought about Wang's fall from official grace, but not before making the relations between the Party and other social institutions representing diversified individual and group interests a significant political issue. These demands were taken up by university professors like Fang Lizhi and projected on to the national political screen during the student demonstrations of 1986–7 (see Chapter 6), making the universities a focal point of attempts at reworking the relations between the Party and other mass organisations such as the people's congresses. The argument, as we have seen above, was not couched in terms of efficiency but of individual rights; it was an attempt to subvert the narrow confines of the debate as constructed by the Party leadership.

However, the majority of the university lecturers were concerned with more immediate problems – price rises, deteriorating conditions of living as fixed incomes were eroded by inflation, and most important, the difficulties arising out of the readjustment of the relationship between university administrative bodies and the university Party branches. The material hardships and the separating out of various interests as the reforms in higher education took root, required a representative organisation free of the constraints imposed by the local Party bosses. The reform introduced in the system of administration – the president responsibility system – demanded a substantial withdrawal of the Party from the day-to-day running of the university. Neither were forthcoming. Party corruption (see Chapter 4: pp. 89–90) was also provoking anger. As the Party was unable, first at the local level and then at the national, to respond creatively to the growing expectations and demands of the intellectuals, the prestige of the Party in these circles fell rapidly. In a survey of 371 intellectuals in March 1989, 69.85 per cent felt that the 'public image' of the party was 'not good' (Rosen, 1989a: Table 11).

The Party's reaction was predictably indignant (see Chapter 4). During the 'anti-bourgeois liberalisation' campaign of 1986–7 the intellectuals were reminded that

> the basic task for the university is to train qualified personnel for the modernisation cause . . . the universities cannot act as the decision making and guiding centre of the whole country . . . According to the Marxist view point, the party should exercise leadership over everything. (*Jiefangjun Bao*, JPRS, 22 April 1987: 18–19)

The tension between the party and professional roles of the intellectuals was resolved in favour of the Party:

> Party member professors and lecturers should be Party members first, then scholars. They are not allowed to make speeches on liberalisation or liberalism in the course of teaching without bearing any responsibility. (*Heilongjiang Bao*, 1986; SWB/FE/BII, 1986: 5)

The controls on the teachers were to be tightened:

> From now on necessary systems enacted in inviting people to teach and give speeches at universities should be implemented in line with teaching plans to conform to education purposes and training goals. (*ibid.*)

However, to avoid panic about the party/state once again reverting to retaliatory policies against the intellectuals on the one hand,

and to state clearly the non-negotiable rules of political discourse on the other, it was made clear that the intellectuals retained their professional independence, but within the political framework set by the Party. Those intellectuals who were dismissed from their posts were, it was clarified, disciplined not as professionals but as Party members (*Jiefang Ribao*, 1987; JPRS, 7 April 1987: 9). Further, that this action did not mean

> negating writers' freedom of creation and speech; it only means negating the freedom to oppose the Four cardinal principles and the freedom of citizens to break the law and of party members to violate the party constitution and discipline. (GMRB, 1987; *ibid.*: 7)

The terms of the intellectuals licence given by the Party to this group were thus reiterated.

However, despite Hu Yaobang being sacrificed to the 'hardliners' within the Party, and the temporary retreat of the radical intellectuals, the process of opening up the public sphere in China during this period was not an insignificant one. Major breakthroughs were made during the mid-1980s in redefining the relationship of the Party with other institutions and groups. The implementation of economic, social and educational reforms opened new spaces for resistance which were successfully exploited by the intellectuals to make demands upon the state and to participate in oppositional activity.

In 1986 at the Soft Science Conference (see Chapter 2) the policy of 'opening up' the intellectual sphere was first put forward by the political bureau member in charge of education, Wan Li. By 1989 China had seen a considerable freeing of the public sphere, and the intellectuals had particularly benefited by this. Apart from the reforms in higher education, there had been increasing exchanges between the Chinese intellectuals and their colleagues in other countries, especially in the West. These exchanges influenced the thinking of the Chinese intellectuals, and also made them known in the West, which allowed them some protection from the wrath of the state in times of crisis. Events in Eastern Europe and the Soviet Union also affected the intellectuals; they looked to the Soviet Union to provide lessons in eliminating 'the obstacles of bureaucratic and privileged stratum . . . organising the election of people's representatives . . . and giving the people's congress the right to veto laws passed by the Presidium of

USSR Supreme Soviet' (*Chengming*, JPRS-CAR-89-072). The deputy Party secretary at Beijing University noted that 'political changes in Eastern Europe had bolstered the "liberal" forces inside China, and helped form "underground" opposition and political organisations', reported the *Hong Kong Standard* (FBIS/ 90/088/28). With the privatisation of parts of the service economy, many private publishing houses and bookstores were established. Dule Bookstore, the first collective bookstore in Beijing, was opened by a young woman, Yu Yansha, in 1984. Its story illustrates the importance of such outlets for the intellectuals. It was given wholesale rights, but when in 1988 it began to distribute a magazine called *Xin Qimeng* edited by Wang Yuanhua, a scholar and former director of propaganda under the Shanghai CPC committee, to which figures like Wang Ruoshi, Yu Haocheng and others critical of the party/state contributed, Dule Bookstore began to be victimised. Its licence was cancelled twice without notifying Yu (*Chengming*, April 1989; JPRS-CAR-89-070). Many new journals appeared during this period, and some, like the now famous Shanghai-based *Shijie Jingji Daobao* (World Economic Herald), *Jingji Cankao* (Economic Information), and *Xinhua Wenchai* (China Digest) of Beijing and many provincial journals and magazines, were crucially important in giving a voice to the critical intellectuals. Through these journals intellectuals tried to get in touch with the reformers within the Party, as well as to reach out to a wider audience. In an interview published in *Shijie Jingji Daobao*, for example, Su Shaozhi said:

> The leaders should realise that many intellectuals have views and proposals but no channel of expression. If there were enough channels, the leaders would understand the masses better and regard letters from lower levels and newspaper articles as opinions for reference rather than something to be detested. (SWB/FE/0443/B2/6)

The economic reforms and the 'political restructuring' that had been advocated by Deng led to the establishment of scores of research institutes and think-tanks which also played an important part in giving intellectuals both a safe environment in which to work, and a legitimate voice with which to speak. While the luminaries of these institutes were members of the 'high' intelligentsia, their researchers tended to be young graduates with links with their alma maters. Both these groups became active in the opposition movements at different levels. For example, during the Tian'anmen demonstrations, 'three institutes and one society' played important organisational and supportive roles. These were the Institute of Restructuring of the Economic System which had Zhao Ziyang as its patron, the Institute of Development under the State Council's Rural Development Research Centre, the Institute for the Study of International Problems of the China International Trust and Investment Corporation, and the Beijing Youth Economic Society (JPRS-CAR-89-090). Seminars and conferences were organised by these institutes which gave the intellectuals platforms from which to engage in debate among themselves and with the party/state. Another factor that played a part in the increasing radicalisation of the intelligentsia was the number of surveys of public opinion carried out by the numerous survey institutes established in the 1980s with the encouragement of the reform faction within the Party. Their publications made known to the intellectuals not only what their colleagues, but also what the people, were thinking, reinforcing their view of a growing dissatisfaction with the party/state (see Rosen, 1989a).

As the intellectuals became disenchanted with Party policies, their criticism became more focused. They pointed out 'five insufficiencies' in the reform programme of the party/state. These were a lack of theoretical preparation, the lag between economic and political reform, a rigid policy-making pattern, an inability to keep up popular support for the reform, and a lack of honest self-appraisal (*Chengming*. April 1989; JPRS-CAR-89-072). As new contradictions and new ideas began to engage the minds of the intelligentsia, and the political structure responded in a halting, limited fashion, the relationship between the licenser party/state and the licensed intelligentsia began to deteriorate. 'Participation mean[s] taking part in government and social life', said an article in *Jingji Cankao*. 'It is both a demand of society upon the individual as well as the individual's bounden duty and responsibility to society.' The intelligentsia was thus demanding the right to be able to fulfil what they saw as their duty – to participate in a critical dialogue with the state, and to act as the voice of public conscience. The intellectuals began to loosen the bonds that had tied them to party/state patronage. While, in the period following the Tian'anmen massacre, the official Chinese journals are condemning Liu Binyan for coming up with the concept of 'two loyalties' (see BR, 25 June–1 July 1990: 29–31), one of which was characterised by unquestioning and therefore unhelpful loyalty to the state, and the other by critical support which could prove more useful in the long run, the more radical intellectuals like Liu Xiaobo rejected the idea of loyalty itself. 'It is exactly the faithful character of Chinese intellectuals that makes it difficult for them to break their attachment to the despotic system', he wrote. 'Intellectuals . . . should not be loyal to political power at any level. Instead they should be loyal to their own beliefs and the law.' (*Chengming*, April 1989; JPRS-CAR-89-088) The state still needed the intellectuals for its modernisation programme, but such radicalism was threatening. The dissensions within the Party, which the 'high' intelligentsia exploited – as much as their radicalism was used by opposing factions within the Party – also played their part in stalling the process of further opening up. With the changes in the fortunes of the radical patrons of the intellectuals like Hu and Zhao, cracks began to appear in the alliance that had been forged in the early stages of the reforms between the intelligentsia and the party/state. On 6 January 1989 the break came when Fang wrote to Deng asking Wei Jingsheng to be released. Thirty-three well-known Beijing intellectuals supported Fang's request on 13 February (*Ching Pao*, March 1989; JPRS-CAR-89-077), and another similar letter was signed by 43 intellectuals on 17 March (*Chiushi Nientai*, April 1989; JPRS-CAR-89-080). As Wei is the Deng regime's most famous political prisoner, this request was seen by the 'hardliners', as an open challenge to the party/state authority; Deng saw it also as a challenge to his personal authority. As the dialogue between the intellectuals and the leadership became increasingly restricted and the intellectuals felt more alienated from those in power, they began to look for alternatives for putting pressure on the government. There were some like Yan Jiaqi who looked to the National People's Congress to reverse the trend of tightening political control by appealing to it to pass a vote of no confidence against the government. Others looked to the growing student movement emerging from the campuses of China's universities to act as a pressure on the party/state. Unlike in the earlier post-Mao democratic movements, thousands of intellectuals, 'high' and 'low', openly supported the movement, marching together with the students and joining in the hunger strike that was to capture the imagination of the entire nation in May 1989.

The 1980s witnessed the making and breaking of the alliance between the critical Chinese intelligentsia and the CPC. All the factors discussed above contributed to the break – the reforms in the higher education system initiated by the Deng regime itself resulted in unforeseen contradictions emerging between various groups of intellectuals, and between the intellectuals and the local Party bosses: the expectations produced by the rhetoric of the 'political restructuring' created its own pressures; the acknowledgement by Deng and other Party leaders of the importance of the intelligentsia to economic modernisation gave this group tremendous bargaining power which it used to press its case for greater independence; and the self-perception of the intelligentsia as the educated, rational voice in the Chinese political system which needed extensive reworking. While the party/state has rejected an unlicensed opening up of the public sphere, it recognises the continued importance of the intellectuals to China's modernisation programme. It has therefore attempted to conciliate the intellectuals by stressing the difference between the majority of the nationalistic intelligentsia and the minority of those 'misled' by Western propaganda. Jiang Zemin, speaking on 4 May 1990 to mark the anniversary of May Fourth Movement of 1919, said that the Party officials at all levels 'Should listen to their [intellectuals'] opinions' (*Xinhua*, 13 May 1990; FBIS/90/093/41) and 'that young intellectuals as a whole are good and reliable, and he attributed their weakness to "errors made by the Party"' *Hong Kong Standard*, 5 May 1990; FBIS/90/088/23). The Party has released many intellectuals who were arrested during and after the June 1989 massacre, while the workers who were incarcerated have not been so fortunate. Further, the Party has stressed that its policy of sending intellectuals abroad for training and to attend conferences and seminars would not be reversed. However, these attempts seem incongruous in the context of the suppression of the student movement, and the tightened controls over the intellectuals more generally. *Guangming Ribao* stated on 17 April 1990:

> The leadership of institutions of higher learning must be firmly in the hands of cadres loyal to Marxism. It is necessary to establish a contingent with Party members as the key members as the mainstay in

running socialist universities. It is particularly necessary to strengthen the ranks of teachers with party members and they must understand that they are first and foremost party members. (FBIS/90/088/27)

Deng wants to go back to retain the policy of licensed participation of the intellectuals in the economic and political life of the country; the intelligentsia is no longer satisfied with such concessions.

6

The reforms and student activism

Introduction

The history of the relations of the students and the party/state in post-revolutionary China has been a chequered one. The Chinese communists found support among nationalist and socialist students throughout the period of the revolutionary struggle. Mao Zedong, speaking to Chinese students in Moscow in November 1957, said:

> The world is yours, as well as ours, but in the last analysis, it is yours. You young people, full of vigour and vitality, are the bloom of life, like the sun at eight or nine in the morning. Our hope is placed on you . . . The world belongs to you. China's future belongs to you. (Mao, 1972: 288)

This section of the Chinese intelligentsia has been characterised by a Confucian approach to education that required the educated élite to be socially responsible and participative, a fierce nationalism that was mobilised not diluted by the struggle for socialism under the CPC, an educational expertise that could be utilised in the service of the country, and a youthful idealism. This has led the students into involvement in China's political life at regular intervals. The tradition of political activism in movements for change that started in the context of the anti-imperialist struggles – the 1911 Revolution, the May Fourth Movement – was carried forward by the CPC into the post-revolutionary era through its mobilisation of educated youth. Students have been frequently mobilised by one and/or the other faction in the CPC to aid its victory.

The post-Mao regime tried to mobilise the students in support of its programme of 'four modernisations' through various schemes of incentives and disincentives to encourage and control students. The students responded to these in the context of the promise of broader political reforms with varying degrees of enthusiasm and scepticism, confusion and resentment, and finally, open opposition. A study of the student movements in China in the post-Mao period reveals a progressive widening of the distance between the party/state and the student intelligentsia. This has led to a progressive raising of the political stakes, and updating of the political agenda in the country. Thus, while the 1986–7 student movement could be seen as one of support for the reformers within the party/state, by 1989 it became gradually, but definitely, oppositional. On 3 June 1989 the Chinese students protesting in Tian'anmen Square took their pledge before the advancing People's Liberation Army (PLA) units:

> I pledge that for the cause of developing democracy in our motherland, for the prosperity of our country, to prevent a small group of conspirators from undermining our great motherland, to protect our one billion people from white terror, I pledge our (sic) young lives to the defence of Tian'anmen, to defend the republic. (Cai Ling, *Overseas Chinese Economic Journal*, 8 June 1989)

The leaders of the Chinese revolution and the modernisers of the country had become 'conspirators'.

The reasons for this dysfunction in the Chinese political system were many. Some related directly to the unintended consequences of the economic and educational reforms introduced by the post-Mao regime – higher prices, less state subsidies, job insecurity, lowering living standards together with higher expectations. Others were particular issues affecting the student community – living conditions within the universities, uninspiring teaching methods and texts, changing patterns of financial support and of employment, and a lack of institutional means of reflecting their concerns in the public sphere. Together these raised explicitly political demands for representative institutions, for more open government, against government corruption, and for freedom of expression and association. These demands posed, or were seen to pose by the Chinese regime, a threat to the political position of the Party. The question it faced was how to deal with the threat: its immediate response was repression. Around this response is now being attempted an exercise in ideological 'consensus building' which is artificial and wholly inadequate, and is contributing to the crisis of confidence in the CPC.

Students in the university: surveillance and control

In China under Mao education was regarded as an instrument of the revolutionary class, to be used to create a 'new socialist man' (see Mao, 1967b: 382). It was a process of moulding and remoulding ideas and attitudes, of inculcating revolutionary enthusiasm, and weeding out erroneous tendencies – a constant surveillance of not just academic quality but (and more importantly) of personal morality. The organisation of Chinese universities reflects this concern. The surveillance of students (and lecturers) in the university remains high. It is surveillance through 'making visible':

> There is no need for arms, physical violence, material constraints. Just a gaze. An inspecting gaze, a gaze which each individual under its weight will end by interiorising to the point that he is his own overseer, each individual thus exercising this surveillance over and against himself. (Foucault, 1986: 155)

This constant invasion of the individual space has been made easier in the Chinese situation by a cultural backdrop which had – in the social condition – never included individual space as a 'need'. The system of the extended family ('three generations under one roof' was regarded as a social virtue worthy of emulation and indicative of social stability that rests on the correct ordering of paternal authority) denied the individual any respite from the social 'gaze'. As marriage was not considered a union of two individuals but of two families, symbolising the coming together of appropriate social and economic values, the marital state also provided little protection from the social sight (see Han Suyin, 1970).

Reinforcing this social tradition was the collectivist political ethic of Marxism as interpreted by the Chinese leadership: the collective has not been a coming together of individuals but a given reality upon which new reinforcing structures were positioned. Thus, not one student in Hangzhou University complained of the number of people in one room but almost all did about the facilities and the size of the room itself. Indeed, in interviews with Chinese students studying in Britain it became clear how 'privacy' was seen as an issue by them only after they left China. The connotations of secrecy (*si*), of hiding from others, that are attached to the word 'privacy' in Chinese prevent it from being seen as a personal, individual need. However, the identification of the individual self was put on the Chinese socio-political agenda by Deng himself with the decollectivisation of agriculture and the endorsing of the individualist ethic in the urban economy. The students too came to recognise it in the increasing competition they faced in the reinstitution of examinations at all levels of education in 1978, and the marketisation of the labour force that took shape in the mid-1980s.

The students do not participate in the day-to-day running of their living routine. The reforms of 1985 did not touch upon this. In Hangzhou University there were no student committees to look into the management of facilities and kitchens or to control quality standards, and no liaison with the academic and administrative staff of the university. One area that *had* become the responsibility of the student organisations, the Student Union in particular, is maintaining discipline in dining halls where tremendous over-crowding resulted in daily chaos, queue-jumping and quarrels. The students communicate their problems to the authorities through the class teachers (*banzhuren*) who do not have the power to deal directly with any substantive problems of the students. When asked about the improvement of dining and sanitary conditions for students, a *banzhuren* admitted: 'We can report these to the authorities, but we cannot help.' Another, when asked about her powers as a *banzhuren*, related this incident: 'There was a mouse in the students' dormitory. They [the students] complained to me. I told the caretaker who killed it with some poison.' The students know this: '*Banzhuren* does not have much power; he can only report students' problems to the department or the school leaders', said one.

After the student demonstrations of 1986–7, during which students protested against the living conditions on campuses, the universities tried to improve contact with students in various ways.

In Hangzhou University, for example, it was through a weekly 'open-office' with the president of the university. The president or the vice-president or the Party secretary of the university sat for an afternoon (every Wednesday) for students and staff to come forward with their problems. However, in such a situation the visibility of those involved in attempting to gain greater control over their living space is heightened, and the relative anonymity gained through group activity is lost, as is the coherence of the group itself. The individual student remains identifiable and vulnerable before the Party and administrative authorities. The alternative of student organisations like the Communist Youth League (CYL) or the Student Union taking up issues with authorities in a militant way is not available; these hierarchical and mobilisational structures do not lend themselves to confrontational action strategies. The confidence that students have in them is continually undermined by this inefficacy (see below).

Thus, whereas on the one hand the arrangement of daily life of students makes for a strict surveillance, the narrowness of channels of communication and the isolating impact of the controlling structures results in their retreat from activism and/or visibility of action. This is made more easily possible in a period of low emphasis on political rhetoric and mobilisation. On the other hand, it also helps students locate the 'back regions' of their environment which are less accessible to the 'gaze' of authority and, hence, to subvert that authority itself. While the overcrowding in the dormitories leads to vulnerability to surveillance, it can also form a hospitable environment for making close friendships that can be used as a protection against the attempt at 'making visible'. The university, therefore, is not a totally controlling structure: the spaces for potential and actual resistance, for withdrawal, for reworking and subversion exist and are utilised by the students.

Friendships formed in such a context also perform a function of helping students retreat from university-organised group activity to a more autonomous coming together. These form the support systems which are used by the students to construct their own area of intellectual and interpersonal relations away from official mobilisational structures. As Shirk writes about secondary school students:

> Friendships were formed by students as a haven, a 'protective environment' from the political pressure of school life . . . Friendship

relations persisted not *despite* the political pressures in the Chinese system, but rather *because* they helped people adapt to these very pressures. (Shirk, 1982: 12)

Many activists of the 1989 movement said that they joined in because of their friends. 'I had my beliefs, of course,' said Zhang Lun, a prominent member of the Committee for the Defence of Tian'anmen Square, 'but I was inspired by my friends who had participated in earlier movements as well.'

Living in the university

The system of surveillance described above requires the university to be an all-encompassing environment catering to every need of the students. This has led to a system of resident education. All students and staff of the university live either on an enclosed campus, or in university-owned living space. The entry to the campus is constantly monitored by attendants at the gate. There is a regulation that every person coming in or going out of the university must state her business and name of her contact on campus. Those on a bicycle must get off and walk through the gate and not ride past. The residential system has led to the siphoning off of funds desperately needed at the levels of primary and secondary school education. The expansion of the higher education sector has been made more difficult as a large part of the scarce financial resources goes towards providing for the maintenance of students on campus. The slow rate of growth of institutions of higher education and student enrolment can be judged from the following figures: in 1982–3 China had a total of 1,063 institutions of higher education, while India had 5,105; the student enrolment too shows disparity, with 3,136,986 students studying in the Indian higher education institutions as compared to 1,153,954 in China (University Grants Commission, 1983, Ministry of Human Resource Development, 1986, New Delhi; and Lo, 1989). As the numbers in universities have increased in the post-Mao period, so has the pressure on resources, leading to worsening living conditions.

Overcrowding of students' halls is a major problem. In Hangzhou the university provides three types of dormitory accommodation: for undergraduates, for graduate students, and for unmarried assistant lecturers. Eight undergraduate men, from

19 to 23 years of age, share a single room not more than 16′ × 9′; for women of the same age group the number is seven. The living area consists of bunk-beds and a shared space between the beds which usually holds a square table or two, which serve as working desks, as well as for eating meals. Due to overcrowding in the dining halls food is often brought into the rooms. The trunks containing clothes are stored under the beds. There is a medium-sized barred window at one end of the length of the room and the door, right across from it, opens into a usually dark and wet corridor. There is on every floor a washing area, usually a very large hall with taps down the width in rows with running basins where students wash their clothes, dishes and themselves, as hot water is a luxury that allows for a wash in the 'bed room' from the thermoses of boiling water only with some difficulty. It is an inhospitable living environment as a consequence of which students go to their rooms only for their afternoon *xiuxi* (rest) or after dark, to sit and chat till the lights go off for the night, at eleven for undergraduates (the graduates have been allowed to have their dormitory lights on all night after the demonstrations). Any study is quite impossible in such a restricted area; students study after classes in the big class-rooms or (mostly the graduates) in the library. While the facilities remain the same for the other two groups mentioned above, the graduate students live four to a room and assistant lecturers two in each room.

Another remarkable feature of the university regime is the taking over by the authorities of the students' unorganised time. For example, in Hangzhou the morning starts at 6 a.m. with the blaring of loud music over the public address system. This is repeated during the course of the day in every break between classes and is interspersed with exhortations and announcements. It is interesting to note that the selection of music is done by the CYL committee which is a much less accessible organisation because of it being controlled directly by the Communist Party, rather than by the Students' Union. During the day there are periods when most students come out of the classes to participate in organised sport like basketball and volleyball. Thus, at any point during the academic day, the students cannot get away from the presence of authority which controls both their time and their space. There is no communal space made available to students where they might relax and get together with other students, apart from the gym and an occasional tea shop. Group identity is therefore difficult to form. We have seen in Chapter 5 that any common space is also denied to the teaching staff. Thus, any interaction between the staff and the students in the department becomes difficult; visiting teachers at home is the alternative, which is necessarily limited and particular in nature and context. In Hangzhou University there are just three common rooms or TV rooms on a campus that accommodates about 6,000 students in about 15 dormitories spread over a considerable area. There are no campus tea houses where a student might spend an evening with friends. This was one of the things that the students did point to: an absence of areas of recreation that would be less demanding than a basketball court or gym.

Such an arrangement of living space also facilitates mutual surveillance among students. In every room of the dormitory there is a monitor who is in charge of keeping order and helping students solve interpersonal problems. They are also liable to be recruited by the administrative machinery for gathering information and reporting. Many students told me that they did not discuss political problems before the room monitors, especially if they were also Party members. Others, however, felt that the monitors were conduits between them and the university authorities and did not pose any threat to them. Political involvement of individual students could be the determining factor in this difference of perception. The *banzhuren*, on their bimonthly visits to student living quarters, contact these monitors to inform themselves of the problems of students and also their conduct in the dormitory.

With the reorganisation of educational structures since 1978, this system of the residential university has also come under review. Suggestions have been made that students from the local city or town should return home after classes as a means of reducing the pressure on the resources of the university. However, it is significant that not much attention has been paid in this regard, even though a rationalisation of the residential policy would be relatively straightforward.

Pedagogy

While living in the university creates frustrations and pressures for students, academic life also offers them little. With the world around them changing so rapidly, students want to be able to discuss issues arising out of this change with their lecturers and their peers, but find little encouragement in the class-rooms to do so. 'I don't like the method of teaching, the textbooks or the exams they give. They are boring', was a repeated complaint of students in Hangzhou. Combined with the dreary living conditions described above, the students face years of study shackled by ideological orthodoxy and intellectual timidity. This is especially the case with political education which forms a compulsory part of the curriculum of every course. A survey carried out among university students in Shanghai in 1988 revealed that 87 per cent of the respondents felt that university students had no interest at all in classes on Marxism; 22 per cent of these blamed poor pedagogy for this lack of interest (Rosen, 1989b: Table 2).

Pedagogy in China today resembles the 'banking' concept of education – repetitive, uncritical and anti-dialogical. The spaces left for any reworking of the texts are kept to the minimum, and there is a frightening belief in the inherent 'correctness' of the printed word. The teachers and students are not in a situation of 'co-intentionality' (Freire, 1972: 44–6). The complaints of many students at Hangzhou University concentrated on the fact that teachers in class encouraged no discussion, and no dialogue. The emphasis is on reading texts or taking down the interpretation of the texts that was offered by the teachers. One student suggested, 'Teachers should speak less in class. Students should have time to discuss and think things over . . . [it would be] much better to let us know the new trends in each course, not keep repeating the basic courses.'

A variety of reasons can explain this pedagogical style: historical, cultural and political. Apart from a history of the Confucian educational pattern of learning classical texts by rote (Mote, 1989), there are political causes affecting pedagogy. Education in post-revolutionary China has remained a prisoner of the state. The ideological conformity that the Leninist state model imposed precluded independent interpretations of texts. As we have seen in Chapter 5, intellectuals were the targets of many attempts at political 'purification' and 'remoulding' aimed at creating and maintaining uniformity in the intellectual sphere. The texts used by students in universities are prescribed by either the SEC or the PEC or selected by the university authorities. The textbooks on the compulsory politics courses are generally approved by the Party committee of the university. These approved texts then form the bulk of undergraduate teaching. Further, the teachers, until very recently, have been denied the opportunity of interpreting and explaining even these approved texts; there are 'teachers companions' to these texts: 'sometimes these are thicker than the original texts themselves', said an English language teacher in Beijing. These 'companions' give details of how to use them – how much time to spend on what, what questions to ask and what would form an appropriate answer. This takes away the enthusiasm of the teachers as much as that of the students, and education becomes a boring, repetitive process. Another reason for the archaic pedagogical styles is the inbreeding in universities. Most teachers in Hangzhou University, for example, are its alumni; this is especially true of the younger lecturers. They studied in the same environment in which they teach and have imbibed the same teaching practices as they were exposed to. As any kind of lateral mobility remains very difficult, there is no stimulus to change from outside the university but all the encouragement to conform of long-established patterns of behaviour and functioning. In the Department of Psychology, for example, only eight out of forty staff are from universities other than Hangzhou University.

The changing role of education has not led to any radical change in pedagogical practices; increased competition served to reinforce the old patterns of teaching. A traditional Chinese saying describes the process of education as *nian bei da* (read, recite, beat); a professor of Education at Beijing University said that has been replaced in most educational institutions by *nian bei kao* (read, recite, examination). In a survey carried out by the student department of the Shanghai Bureau of Higher Education, the 4,000 students surveyed in 1987 had four major complaints:

> 1) rigid teaching methods 2) backward testing methods 3) teaching theory being divorced from reality and 4) outdated teaching materials and irrational curricula. (GMRB, JPRS, 13 March 1987: 68)

Intellectuals have pointed out that:

> [there] are too few really talented people at the present. This is related to pedagogical thought and teaching methods. We invariably use a fixed measure and strictly define talent and demand outstanding [performance] in every aspect. This is very non-beneficial to the discovery and growth of talent and even stifles it. (SEC, 1985a: 40)

However, the concern for political control becomes a limiting factor in any debate on opening up areas of intellectual activity to democratic practice; the ghosts of political persecution still crowd the intellectual landscape. Further, the primary concern of the leadership today is to make up for what has been termed as the 'lost decade', in terms of creation of skill banks, for which discipline, and not experimentation, is the prerequisite. The events in Tian'anmen Square and the political backlash that has followed have resulted in further reinforcing this tightly controlled pattern of teaching. The People's Daily reported that 'after the vacation . . . the students coming back to campus will study the CPC Central Committee's documents, study and discuss Deng Xiaoping's talks and video tapes of the putting down of the rebellion and summarise their opinions in the first five weeks' (RMRB, overseas ed., 16 October 1989: 4). Military training and manual work for students are also being emphasised as correctives for the growing alienation of the students from the political leadership.

Breaking the iron rice bowl

The alienation of the students from the post-Mao state also increased with new pressures arising from the reduction in state subsidies for higher education, and greater job insecurity. Students have become anxious about the proposed abolition of the grant-in-aid system for funding their education at university (see Chapter 2: pp. 57–8). When linked to the increasing erosion of fixed family incomes by rising inflation, and to the growing fears of unemployment, students find this reform threatening. The financial pressures of their parents are acutely felt by the students. A survey carried out in 33 cities indicated that 70.9 per cent of the respondents were worried about prices, 54.0 per cent about wages, 88.7 per cent felt the income gap was widening, and 67.6 per cent that their own income was falling (Burns, 1989a: 489). As cultural patterns, economic constraints and notions of family responsibility do not allow many students the option of taking out loans to fund their university education, parents are coming under increasing financial pressures. Parents pay from 50 to 80 yuan per month to keep their children at the universities. 'This is very difficult . . . For example, my family has three children, and now everyone is in the university. The money is not enough, and my parents must do [other] jobs to earn for us', said one student now in exile in Paris. China's changing pattern of higher education system has resulted in falling enrolment from the countryside, and an increase in children of the urban middle classes, especially children of the intellectuals. This stratum is most affected by both rising expectation and erosion of fixed incomes by inflation. There is also a growing concern – perhaps born out of comparisons of fixed with entrepreneurial incomes – regarding increasing income differentials: 'In China, the poor people are very poor, the rich people are very, very rich,' said a student activist. The students themselves felt that they could not afford even small luxuries of life, and that to purchase books or occasional new clothing ate into their meagre resources substantially.

Fen pei – the politics of job allocation

By the late 1980s, the Chinese labour force was being introduced to market competition. For the students this meant a loosening up of a hitherto tightly controlled job allocation system. This created new opportunities, new pressures, and new contradictions for graduating students. While the old pattern of state allocation of jobs caused great resentment among students who felt they had little control over the most important decision of their life, the relaxation of the system has exposed the students to the dangers of urban unemployment. While the old system benefited student Party members, creating rivalries, the new favours those with family contacts; personal *guanxi* has added to the already existing political *guanxi*. The frustrations of the students remain intact.

Until 1987 graduates in China were allocated jobs by the state according to a national plan. Work units (*danwei*) in need of graduates submitted their personnel requirements to the SEC through various PECs. Together with the Personnel Ministry and the Planning Commission the SEC then drew up a consolidated plan, which was distributed to the PECs, which then passed it on to the various universities in each province, where the necessary choices were made, and jobs distributed. At the university level the jobs were generally allocated in three different ways: first, the state-allocated jobs; second, students financed by different work units (*danwei*) returned to work with them; third, self-supporting students were left to find their own jobs, unless they asked for a job allocation.

For those allocated jobs by the state, two criteria applied – the academic standard and the consideration of the native area of residence. Within the university, the allocation of jobs was carried

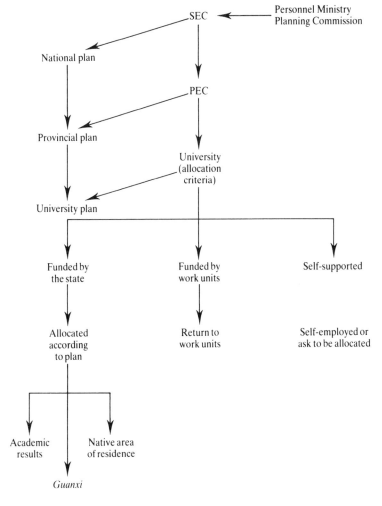

Figure 6.1 Patterns of job allocation

out by the Personnel Division which is directly controlled by the Party branch: 'In the future, maybe the president of the University might take charge [of this division] but if this happens it will take a long time', said an administrative officer at Hangzhou University. When interviewed in 1987, officials from the SEC felt that there was no plan 'in the near future' to phase out this system. '*"Fen Pei"* [is essential] to make sure the key projects get good personnel' and that the needs of underdeveloped areas continue to be met. However, since then the job allocation system has been largely replaced by an open job market – the *shuang xiang xuan ze* system, or a 'mutual benefit system' for students and employers.

The free market situation has created new problems. A survey of university students taken in ten large cities in May 1988 on job location preferences revealed that up to 40 per cent would like to work in the Special Economic Zones (SEZ) and coastal regions, and almost another 40 per cent in large and medium-sized cities (see Table 6.1). The pay and the opportunities for travel make joint-venture companies attractive to students. The joint-venture companies offer as much as 300 yuan basic pay a month, while the government organs pay at most a little over 100 yuan. In three to four years a posting abroad can be expected in a joint-venture company with no such opportunity offered by government enterprises (*Pai Hsing*, 25 August 1989, in JPRS-CAR-89-090, 25 August 1989: 55).

The officials are still concerned about the impact of this change

Table 6.1 Preferences for job location

Location	Percentage
SEZ	12.2
Coastal open regions	27.3
Large cities	20.8
Medium–large cities	18.6
Small towns and townships	2.0
Old revolutionary bases, minority nationality regions, remote border areas	1.8
Rural areas	1.8
Overseas	8.3

Source: *Pai Hsing*, No. 191, 1 May 1989, pp. 15–16, JPRS-CAR-89-090, 25 August 1989: 54.

on the spread of graduates across the country and across various economic sectors. Incentives of full scholarships are offered to students willing to work in 'border regions'.

Further, while the possibilities created by the new system raised seemingly endless expectations among the students, the slowdown of the Chinese economy in the mid-1980s, and the tremendous competition for jobs resulting from student preferences meant that many were faced with the prospect of unemployment. In a hitherto full-employment culture this came as a great shock. The graduates in China had been used to jobs coming to them; now they were having to make the running and they were not prepared for this. The position of women is even more adversely affected (see Rai, 1991, forthcoming). The problems were exacerbated by the growing corruption in the job market. 'The unfair competition stems from the students' different social relations, and at the heart of this is the difference in their family backgrounds', reported the Contemporary University Student Situation Study Group, one of the many think-tanks set up to monitor the reforms (*Pai Hsing, op. cit.*: 55). Unfair competition results both from privilege of family connections, and from a family's ability to pay bribes. Corruption became one of the biggest issues to be taken up by students in 1989. The disillusionment with this loosening of the job allocation system can be seen in the fact that more than 60 per cent of students surveyed in the poll quoted above thought that 'conditions are not ripe for [the employment] reform' (*ibid.*). Those in favour of the reform came either from entrepreneurial families, or from those with high expectations of upward mobility. Those against employment reforms, for example the high-ranking cadre and peasants either come from the formerly privileged sections, or are those with few expectations of climbing the social ladder through education (see Table 6.2).

In January 1991 the SEC revealed plans for tightening the job market, and greater emphasis on allocation of jobs to graduates. This is a response to the immediate concerns of the students faced by unemployment, bribery and corruption, and uncertainty. The party/state's own considerations are those of political control, a return on investment in the educational system, and of righting the growing regional imbalance that has increased in the last few years of the reforms. 'The majority of college students, whose higher education is financed by the government, were not allowed

Table 6.2 Attitudes towards reform of the assignment system of university students of different family backgrounds (percentages)

	Very much pro-reform	Somewhat pro-reform	Indifferent	Against	Very much against
Worker	27.1	24.9	30.4	11.0	6.6
Peasant	18.2	27.3	32.0	14.6	7.9
Intellectual	17.1	34.2	31.0	14.8	2.9
High-ranking cadre	7.1	28.6	35.7	28.6	0
Ordinary cadre	24.6	31.4	31.1	11.0	1.9
Individual householder	33.3	66.7	0	0	0
Transient worker	9.1	9.1	81.8	0	0

Source: *Pai Hsing*, 25 August 1989, in JPRS-CAR-89-090, 25 August 1989.

to find jobs on their own', said an SEC spokesman on 10 January (BR, Vol. 34, No. 5, 4–10 February 1991: 7). The SEC has guaranteed jobs to 600,000 graduates under this scheme; work units have been asked not to reject graduates assigned to them. Zhu Kaixuan, Vice-minister of the SEC, emphasised that these jobs will be allocated primarily in projects 'related to economic construction, specifically national defense projects and research institutes in China's border and remote areas. Graduates will also be placed to work in rural enterprises and collective undertakings.' (*ibid.*) Graduates from teacher training colleges 'will be required to return to their original province'. While such control over jobs gives the party/state the clout it seeks in the current situation of political uncertainty, it is also careful not to give the impression that it is reversing the trend towards the marketisation of the employment system. '[The allocation of jobs this year] does not mean we are backing away from the reform of our existing [*shuang xiang xuan ze*] system', the SEC emphasised. It has also confirmed that the 'key universities' like Shanghai's Jiaotong University and Beijing's Qinghua University were continuing with the non-allocation, market reform in employment for their graduates (*ibid.*).

Employment is also a problem for students who return to China after finishing their studies abroad. With these graduates the problem is two-fold: first, of getting a job, second, of getting an *appropriate* job. This has increased the pressure on employment opportunities in urban centres. 'Many returnees are eager to find work in places with advanced economies or better research facilities – major cities such as Beijing or Shanghai, or one of the Special Economic Zones', reported *China Today* (June 1990: 28). In order to attract students back from the West attempts have been made to give them help to get jobs of their choice. A China Service Centre for Scholarly Exchange (CSCSE) was set up in 1988 as a specialised employment agency. This service not only provides help at home, but also sends 'recruiting teams' of representatives from various enterprises to travel abroad to personally interview candidates, and make offers of jobs.

In this highly competitive employment situation students feel cynical about those who use Party membership and positions in the official students' organisations to manipulate for better jobs. 'I don't trust [student Party members]', said a graduate student at CASS in Beijing. 'They say they want to reform the Party from within but nothing happens. Except that they get good jobs!' Such resentment has further eroded the position of the official students' unions. One of the major issues that emerged during the Tian'anmen demonstrations was that of replacing these organis- ations with autonomous student unions with elected representatives. Anger about political and personal clout being used to obtain jobs has been exacerbated by the post-Mao emphasis on regularisation of standards and on academic achievement. This led to expectations among students about meritocratic advancement. These expecta- tions and the risks involved in finding employment have created a potentially explosive situation for the party/state.

Student organisations – activism, legitimation and efficacy

There is a complex network of student organisations at every level of the educational system. In the university it includes the Students' Union, the Communist Youth League, and the student wing of the CPC. The Students' Union is a mass organisation having universal membership among university students. The CYL can be called the training ground for the future CP members; this organisation is more relevant, effective and prestigious at the high school rather than at the university level. The students' Party branch is the élite political organisation at the university, comprising the most promising students who are potential cadres and are trained for leadership positions in many different fields (see Chapter 4). All three of these organisations are nationally organised with branches at every level. All of them are reinforcing organisations: they are geared not to reworking their immediate environment but to adapting to it. Their task has been to ensure minimal tension in the implementation of Party and university policies; they work as transmission belts, not as interest-representing bodies. Speaking in 1970, Mao Zedong said:

> For seventeen years since the liberation, our separation from the
> masses has been serious. The Youth Associations, Women's
> Association and the central organ of the Youth Communist League are
> all empty frames. (Liu, 1976: 16)

These organisations rest upon values of 'virtuocracy', and not of efficiency. Shirk defines this concept as:

> A revolutionary regime that attempts to bring about the moral
> transformation of society by awarding life chances to the virtuous
> many. (Shirk, 1982: 4)

The need for such a system, she writes, was felt because certain political choices were made during the earlier period of post-revolutionary China: it was seen as a means of promoting social transformation; it facilitated the leadership's efforts at mass mobilisation for economic development, and hence at political consolidation and legitimation (*ibid.*: 10). This required organisations that would primarily be tools for promoting the dominant political and personal morality; representation remained a second-ary object. It was repeatedly said by students in Party cadres in Hangzhou University that it was difficult to enter the Party because one had to be 'excellent': no distinction was made between academic, political or 'moral' excellence. Such an organisational pattern tends to ignore any 'theoretical limits to the extension of demands for political activity', and no private obligation is allowed to take precedence over the public (Townsend,

1969: 3). Thus, all aspects of student life, both public and private, become the legitimate sphere of organisational activity.

These organisations have little legitimacy among the students. They do not represent the interests of the students, or share in their concerns, and they are unable to provide students with a platform to express these concerns. They are seen as ineffective by the students; a survey carried out by the 'task group on the readjustment of the social structure and interests during reform' for the Economic System Reform Institute in May and June 1988 revealed that 72 per cent of the students are not interested in the CPC and the CYL organisations (*Pai Hsing*. No. 191, 16 May 1989, in JPRS-CAR-89-090, 25 August 1989: 52). The demand for more open and representative student organisations became prominent during the demonstrations in Tian'anmen Square.

The Students' Union

Figure 6.2 shows the basic framework of the Students' Union. The links between the various levels of the SU are loose, primarily because of the financial arrangements between different levels. While the Hangzhou University students' union constitution specifies that it 'recognises the rules of the national Students' Union' and the provincial SU (see Appendix), the national or provincial unions do not provide funds for the university-level organisations. The student union is funded by the university administration. Second, all members elected to office have to be approved by the relevant level of the Party committee; the Hangzhou University student union constitution, for example, stipulates that the 'chairperson and vice-chairpersons are elected by the committee and have to be approved by the [university] party committee' (Article 15, Section 5). This means that in the division of powers between academic administration and the Party, student organisations come under the control of the Party.

The lack of interest of students in official organisations was evident in the lack of information they had about the functioning of these associations. Many different versions of the process and procedure of election of the chairperson at the departmental level were recounted by Hangzhou University students; even the officials of these organisations seem to have difficulty in giving

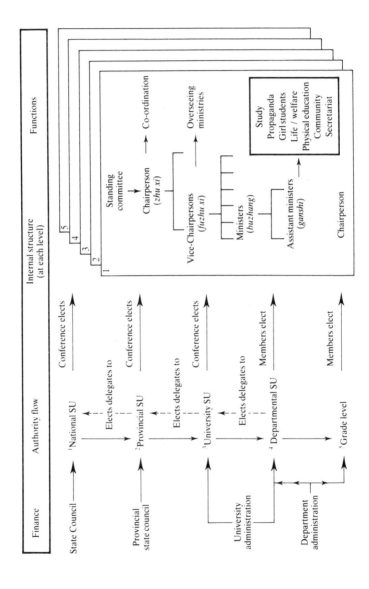

Figure 6.2 The Students' Union

clear answers. The vice-chairperson of the student union said that every department elects two representatives to the annual Students' Union Congress, where they take part in the election of the chairperson and two vice-chairpersons of the Union. The chairperson then appoints the various 'ministers' in charge of certain areas. This process, he said, was repeated every year, not once every two years as stipulated in the Student Union constitution. The account of the 'study minister' of the union differed: while he too said he had been elected for a year, he did not think that he had been appointed by the Union chairperson. Every department dean recommends a student, he said, on the basis of his 'excellent academic record, good behaviour and capabilities', to the Student Union Congress. The chairperson and the vice-chairpersons then 'talk to each of them' and draw up a list of candidates for election: the student representatives at the Congress then make their choice from among them. Another version on the tenure of the union chairperson at the departmental level was given by the departmental union chairperson at the Department of Philosophy, who said that he had a two-year tenure but that was because he would graduate at the end of that period; if he had been in junior class he would have continued as chairperson for another year. This could mean that re-election of the incumbent chairperson was automatic or that, in fact, there was no re-election until the incumbent graduated. Many final-year graduate students said that they had never voted in a student union election in the five years they had been at the university: 'We don't know who the president is', said one.

The reinforcing character of the Student Union is clear in the functions it performs. The setting out of its responsibilities and the elaborate division of these into various ministries (up to ten) illustrate this. The 'tasks' of the student union set out in its constitution include: 'adhering to the Four Basic Principles of the party and [carrying] out the party's education policy by responding to and carrying out the various tasks assigned by higher level groups'; 'uniting' the student body and 'fostering talent' among its members and 'guiding' them to be students with 'all round development'; 'representing and safeguarding students' proper rights and interests', promoting friendly and respectful relations between teachers and students, and establishing relations with similar student bodies outside the university, at a provincial, national and international level. The rights of its members include the right to elect and be elected to the union committee, and to discuss, criticise and give recommendations on the work of the committee. The duties tend towards abiding by union rules and carrying out the committee's decision (see Appendix).

The answer to the question 'What is the major function of the Student Union?' often was, 'They arrange dance parties'. Welfare functions formed the major part of the union agenda. The vice-chairperson of Hangzhou University students' union listed the activities organised by the university union in the year 1986–7: National Day celebrations; New Year's Day party; the 4 May or Youth Day activities; a fashion show; photography and calligraphy competitions; academic lectures; 'social advising' for citizens by students on 4 May; a film week; and setting up of a committee to improve the dining hall arrangements. The various 'ministries' wield little power; ordinary members were cynical about their role and seemed to feel that these were means of gaining 'points' by those in office and their friends, that might be used to get a better profile with the authorities. One rumour circulating in Hangzhou University after the 1987 demonstrations was that the Union president had identified for the authorities those students who had taken part in the student demonstrations. The anger and the cynicism of the students was quite evident when they talked about this.

The student union functions under the supervision of the CYL. The secretary of the Hangzhou University CYL said that he has the job of 'advising and instructing' the graduate student union, while the vice-secretary of the CYL looks after the undergraduate union. This places the union – the only student organisation not formally linked to the Party – at the bottom of the organisational ladder.

The Communist Youth League

As pointed out earlier, the CYL at the university level has a membership akin to a mass political organisation. The number of students enrolled in this organisation might seem surprising as it is regarded as an 'advance organisation' of 'excellent activists'. Shirk describes it while discussing activism in middle schools: 'Only the most outstanding political activists (*jijifenzi*), one half of the students at most, were admitted to this leadership group' (Shirk, 1982: 33). At the university level this figure shoots up dramatically: at Hangzhou University the figure is 90 per cent of all students. This is because those who join the university are usually among the 'politically advanced', and therefore are already members of the élite organisation (the CYL) at school level. Most of the students interviewed in Hangzhou University gave scant importance to their membership; many said they did not even remember how they became members. The élite organisation with the highest visibility of membership at the university level has been the Party, and the CYL is the recruiting ground for the Party.

Like the Students' Union, the CYL is also 'supervised' by the Party branch of the university; all appointments to offices in the CYL are made by the Party branch. In a 'Commission' of 29 members at Hangzhou University there are about eight or nine student members who are first nominated for election by the departmental CYL committee and then elected by the CYL members. These students are allocated tasks by the committee, like writing slogans, Party and administrative directives on the blackboards, and editing the CYL magazine (see Figure 6.3). An important function of the university CYL is to make arrangements for the sending of delegates to the district People's Congress. The student demonstrations of 1986–7 highlighted this role when the students of Hefei Technology University protested against the CYL vetting student nominees for the election to the Congress. This function of the CYL places both the university and the CYL in the external political environment. Hangzhou University, for example, sends two representatives to the Congress, all nominated by the Party in the university, whose names are then put up for election.

As the CYL is the agent of the Party it cannot be called the representative of the interests of the students; it might be looked upon as a representative of the Party's interests among the students. Its major tasks are to inform students about Party policies, and to pick out the brighter of its own members for recruitment by the Party. This is reflected in its structure, with no position of responsibility given to students. It is not concerned with students' immediate problems. Thus, the secretary of Hangzhou University CYL said that, if approached regarding

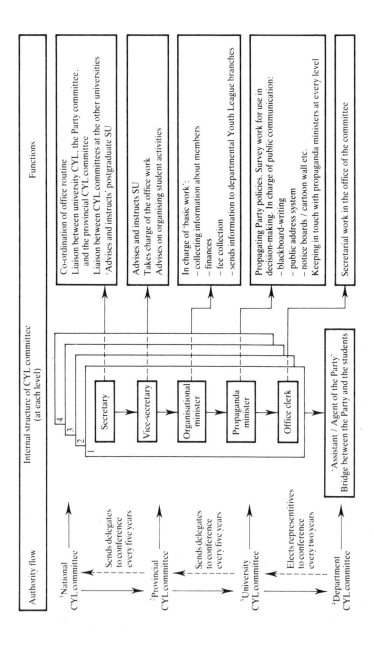

Figure 6.3   Communist Youth League (CYL)

students' problems over living conditions, he can only give 'suggestions to the University leaders. I cannot solve them.' The students do not identify with the CYL the qualities either of leadership or of power. Neither do they derive from it an identification as a group differentiated from other groups. The CYL tends to have very little relevance for the students. It is the Party branch of the university which enjoys greatest prestige among student organisations. As a consequence the students' Party branch is regarded as the most important of the student organisations. However, as we have seen, this organisation cannot be regarded as representing the general interests of the student community at all; it is an arm of the CPC among the students, constrained and limited by its rules and regulations, its goals and objectives.

Non-formal associations: renegotiating boundaries

As a result of this lack of independent representative organisations on campus, the students have been increasingly alienated from the university authorities. The control of the Party over all official student organisations has meant that in order to act as an effective pressure group, or to organise any movement of opposition to the university (and later political) authorities, the students have had to take recourse either to spontaneous, public demonstration, or to setting up independent, non-official organisations. These took many forms. Groups of students got together to practise their English language skill. Foreign students in Chinese universities became part of such groups. These groups were both university based and city based, giving them a broader educational and social foundation. Discussions among the students naturally included the progress of the reforms, the expectations and frustrations of the students themselves and, in a rapidly changing political climate, the nature of the political system itself. More organised non-formal associations were the 'salons' set up by students for discussing issues around their academic interests. For example, in Hangzhou University students organised an 'economics salon', a 'literature salon', etc. The university authorities accepted, and indeed encouraged, such associations. However, it was but a short step from these educational associations to establishing 'democracy salons' as happened during the rise of the 1989 student movement. The rise and fall of the Beijing University 'Democracy Salon' is a case in point. Established in the summer of 1988 it drew the interest both of those who wanted to participate in its activities, and of the university authorities. It held 15 sessions on the lawns of the university before it was closed down. To avoid 'rigid scrutiny' from the authorities, its organisation was not formalised; no one person was responsible for its programme. The topics that were discussed were common to most intellectual platforms – 'Commodity Economy and Democratic Progress', 'New Authoritarianism', 'China's Democratisation', etc. What caused concern to the authorities was that the speakers invited by the students included names like Ren Wanding, the editor of *Chinese Human Rights* magazine. The report of Chen Xitong, the mayor of Beijing, on 'Checking the Turmoil and Quelling the Counter-Revolutionary Rebellion' makes this fact the proof of the students' intentions to overthrow the regime:

> They invited Ren Wanding . . . to spread a lot of fallacies about the so-called 'new authoritarianism and democratic politics' . . . They also invited Li Shuxian, the wife of Fang Lizhi, to be their 'advisor'. Li fanned the flames by urging them to 'legalise the democratic salon' . . . All this prepared, in terms of ideology and organisation, for the turmoil that ensued. (Chen, 1989: 9)

It is for the establishment of this 'Democracy Salon' that Wang Dan, its organiser, stood trial on charges of 'subversion' in January 1991. The refusal of the CPC authorities to recognise these 'democratic salons', and their attempts to suppress them (and later the Autonomous Students' Union of Beijing), reaffirmed to the students in Tian'anmen the alienation of the regime. During the period of the demonstrations themselves, a more flexible attitude towards these autonomous organisations might have done much to contain the movement. However, in a press conference by the State Council spokesperson Yuan Mu on 3 May 1989 the CPC position on the question of independent organisations was made clear: 'We are always prepared to have a dialogue with the students . . . but we think it should be organised by the existing student federations because they were properly elected and approved.' (SWB/FE/0451/B2/1) Given the cynicism and indifference that the students feel about the official student organisations, this position of the authorities led to greater anger among them.

The pressures were thus building up within the university. The students were affected both by the reforms undertaken, and by the slow pace and the partial nature of these, which left old structures relatively untouched. The lack of student organisations that could represent their growing concerns and emerging interests, and the ambiguity surrounding the implementation of any reforms to the functioning of the Party in the university increased the students' sense of alienation within the system. The reactions of students were mixed – cynicism, opportunism, anger, and despair. A student at Hangzhou University expressed his bewilderment: 'I feel very desperate sometimes – nothing is under my control. I am a fatalist . . . I go forward without raising my head to look forward.' There were many others who did.

Student activism: a response to licensed participation

The student movement of 1989 that ended with the PLA marching into Tian'anmen Square was the culmination of student disaffection with the political system which had been building up for a few years. As will be clear from the discussion below, the demands of the students were neither very radical, nor even 'democratic' in nature. As university students they regarded themselves as part of the meritocratic élite of China. Their demands were centred around issues of access to information, of the curbing of political power in favour of intellectual merit, and of accountability of the political élite, not necessarily to the 'masses' who were thought too 'backward' to understand democratic principles, but to the educational/technical élite. The students were also against the corruption that threatened to undermine the very culture of market competition that the communist leadership was promoting. For these demands to be articulated, bargained for, and pressed upon the party/state, intellectuals – in this case the students – needed their own interest-representing organisations, and guarantees for their functioning. These demands *could* be met within the system; a faction within the CPC obviously thought so. What is of interest is why the CPC chose to crush the movement rather than to manage it.

While the antecedents of the movement can be traced back to the 'Democracy Wall' movement of 1978–80, it is to the more recent student activism that the links can be directly traced. In the spring of 1985 the first round of student demonstrations were organised, leading to the Party's call to fight 'bourgeois liberalisation'. In December 1986 the students of Hefei University, Anhui Province, took to the streets demonstrating for greater 'freedom and democracy'. The students were moved to action because, as one student of the University explained:

> [two] delegates were sent to the People's Congress [of Hefei] from the polytechnical university there. But these delegates were not elected; they were chosen by the university administration. When the students learned about this, they stated that these people could in no way represent their interests. We still have no democratic rights, they complained; we have no voting rights. (FBIS, no. 3, 2 January 1987: K2)

As the news of the demonstrations spread, over 150 campuses in at least 17 cities saw the students organising and demonstrating; 'every province is affected except Xizang [Tibet] and Qinghai' (FBIS, no. 13, 6 January 1987: K2). Soon Beijing emerged as the centre of the students' protest.

In Hangzhou several thousands of university students demonstrated, shouting: 'We want democracy and freedom'. At Hangzhou University, said a student activist:

> students talked about social problems like bureaucratism. Some sections want to benefit at the expense of the nation, they said. They criticised foreign trade with Japan. They held [these] discussions sometimes in the class, sometimes in their bedrooms.

The student organisations, however, seemed unaware of the increasing disaffection of the students and of their militancy: 'We [CYL officials] were taken by surprise. A day before there appeared a notice that just said "time: _____; go for demonstration". Most students were onlookers', said a member of the Hangzhou University CYL committee.

The form the demonstrations took and the speed at which they spread reveal two interesting features. First, the organisations that officially represent the students in the universities were not involved in the demonstrations; they were completely by-passed by the students who participated in the protests. 'We were surprised . . . The demonstrations came suddenly', said the vice-chairperson of the Hangzhou University student union. Second, it was obvious that the students who were organising the demons-trations in different cities were able to 'link up' with each other. An informal network was soon established and was very effective: 'A Peking University poster calls of discussions on democratisation . . . Other posters on the campus had been sent from Anhui colleges.' (FBIS/242, 13 December 1986: R1) Technology helped the students – faxes and inter-city telephoning facilities were used together with activists moving from campus to campus, city to city. This linking up with other groups is not new in students' politics in China: a similar attempt was made first during the Cultural Revolution when there was a

> sharp increase in spontaneous communications among students . . . The catchword after August 1966 was 'link up' (*chuanlian*), calling for direct interaction with other students. For example, some students in China felt they were excessively segregated by the CP, so radical students at Ts'inghua University acted first to 'link up' the different agencies on campus. (Liu, 1976: 14)

Similar 'link-ups' were made during the Democracy Wall move-ment of 1978–81 (Chen, 1984: 13). Together, these two features show that when the students acted spontaneously to support and to protest, they did so *not* through the official representative organisations available to them in the universities, but *around* these organisations, showing their lack of confidence in them and thus demonstrating their inefficacy. The organisers spread their message through the 'small path news' (*xiaolu xinwen*) – phone calls, letters and by word of mouth. The Voice of America (VOA), whose Chinese language broadcasts are normally heard by about 60 million listeners, also played a part in spreading the news of demonstrations in various parts of the country. A student at Hangzhou called VOA the 'voice of truth'. Through it the students also became aware of the international events that further sparked their enthusiasm: student demonstrations in Paris against Prime Minister Chirac's attempts at restructuring education, the emergence of an opposition party in Taiwan and peaceful elections held there, and the overthrow of the Marcos regime in the Philippines were the events mentioned by activists in 1987. In 1989 more significant trends were emerging in world, especially state socialist, politics. The 'Gorbachev phenomenon' was opening up possibilities of reforming a state socialist system from within. While the revolutions of Eastern Europe were still in the future, movement within an ossified political system could be felt in the political developments in Moscow. Further, the 'opening to the world' that the Chinese communist leadership had itself promoted also meant access to new information, ideas and opinions for the students. The anxiety felt by the Chinese on this account can be read in Chen Xitong's report:

> Reactionary political forces in Hong Kong, Taiwan and the United States and other Western countries were also involved in the turmoil through various channels and by different means. Western news agencies showed unusual zeal. The Voice of America, in particular, aired news . . . spreading rumours, stirring up trouble and adding fuel to the turmoil. (Chen, *op. cit.*: 16)

The demands that the students raised were also illustrative of the impact on young people in China of the sweeping reforms that Deng had introduced. An activist in the 1987 demonstrations pointed out, 'There were Wan Li's [Education Minister] and repeated requests by the leadership to intellectuals to speak up. Their earlier experience in the "100 Flowers Bloom" campaign meant that not many did, but the students felt enthused.' The students did speak up. In 1986–7 the demands were presented in Deng's own rhetoric; the students demonstrated in *support* of his reforms. They demonstrated to press the reformers among the leadership to accelerate the process of political reform. Demands did vary from one area to another, but two things emerged very clearly from this series of events. First, the students were aware of the loss of control and lack of participation that they had been experiencing; and second, they were aware of the need for more representative organisations through which they could liaise with university and political authorities. Under the call for 'freedom and democracy' the students demonstrated for a more open election process for delegates to the provincial People's Congress, for the right to hold public debates, to demonstrate and to put up 'big character posters' (*dazibao*), for legal guarantees for those who participated in these activities, and for a free press. The Chinese leadership claimed that the students did not know what they wanted; that their demands were too general and unspecific, and that they were not in touch with China's reality: 'Demonstrators are concerned about democracy and freedom', said Vice-minister of Education He Dongchang, 'but [there are] few concrete demands. A small number of students [are] excessive in acts and opinions.' (SWB/FE/BII, 30 December 1986: 2) To this charge one student activist in Hangzhou replied, 'Freedom of speech and of free press are not abstract demands. We were demonstrating against misuse of bureaucrats' power, and against lack of access to news of the outside world.' Freedom of press became an issue when the demonstrations were not reported in the local or the national press and when the press spoke in the voice of the Party authorities:

> Students at Peking University burn[ed] copies of Peking Daily for biased reporting of demonstrations . . . Wall posters accused Peking Daily of plotting to create divisions between the students and the Party . . . According to one student, not one reporter has come to talk to the students. (FBIS/002, 5 January 1987; R2)

In Hangzhou students demonstrated outside the offices of Hangzhou Daily for similar reasons. More specifically, the students demanded recognition of student rights by the university administration, a freeze on rising tuition and boarding costs, improvement in food quality in the university dining halls and in the poor facilities for students on campuses, freedom of choice of courses and an end to the mismanagement of scarce resources by university 'bureaucrats'. One student complained, 'Hangda [Hangzhou University] leaders spent RMB 20,000 each on five Toyota coaster vans while for all graduate students [about 1,000] there is only one small colour TV . . . the food is very bad; the dining halls are dirty and crowded.'

The rhetoric of the student demonstrators was liberal – the emphasis was on individual identity and freedom, on legal rights of individuals as a protection against state power, and a non-Marxist usage of the concepts of 'freedom and democracy' (see Schell, 1988). The post-Mao leadership itself has repeatedly employed the idea of 'democracy' after delinking it from the more orthodox Marxian idea of dictatorship of the proletariat and democratic centralism, without investing it with any new meaning. The concept of democracy has been linked to economic modernisation – 'there can be no modernisation without democracy'; this was connected to the demands of 'market forces' and the one-person management system that has been introduced as part of the economic reforms. The students supported this rhetoric, and were asking for its actualisation. Some suggested a plurality of political institutions as a means to achieving this – a multi-party system, to break the monopoly of the CPC; most limited themselves to endorsing Deng's call for curtailing the overwhelming position of the CPC in every sphere of Chinese life. The leadership, after tolerating the movement in its initial stages, started talking about the dangers of 'bourgeois liberalism' which Deng had defined in 1981, and now reiterated, as: 'opposition to the Party leadership'. The Anti-bourgeois Liberalisation campaign was launched, and with the resignation of Hu Yaobang the 1986–7 movement came to an end.

The demands of the student movement in 1989 were not very different from those put forward in 1986–7. On 4 May, the Autonomous Students' Union put forward three demands:

> One was the nature of the student movement: it must be acknowledged as a patriotic movement. The second was to develop democracy in every aspect of life, *starting on campus* [my italics]. The third was to discuss Article 35 of the Constitution and how to implement its provisions. (Li Lu, 1990: 129)

Article 35 gives the 'citizens of the People's Republic of China . . . [the right to] freedom of speech, of press, of assembly, of association, of procession and of demonstration'. Students in Canton put forward seven demands which included: 'relax press censorship, ensure freedom of the press, safeguard the people's and intellectuals' rights of political participation and consultation' (SWB/FE/0452/B2/8).

The political context of 1989 was very different from that of 1986–7. The 1980s had been years that brought with them high expectations among every section of the population. As long as the miracle of the market continued, these expectations continued to be met to a greater or lesser degree. The students and the intellectuals, basking in the positive attention of the political regime, saw themselves as partners in the programme of progress for China. The students were aware of the hardliners within the Party, but were convinced – in line with a political practice that emphasises 'good cadres' in favour of effective institutions – that they were a dying breed. Deng Xiaoping was in command, and committed to change. There was a sense of growing self-importance and relevance among the students – they were the future of China, they were needed by the country, and they had the support of the Chinese political leadership.

By the end of the 1980s the economic bubble had burst. The overheating of the economy resulted in inflation, urban unemployment grew, and with this the awareness that the political system was not geared towards open competition. Political *guanxi* remained crucial to success, which was easily explained by the political monopoly of the Party. Corruption increased, and fingers began to point at the highest echelons of the Party leadership. The factionalism within the Party was becoming more evident as the leadership struggled to cope with the twin demands of economic problems and political control. For the students all this was evidence that their efforts to bring their concerns to the notice of the leadership were unheeded. The leaders seemed too busy trying to maintain their political monopoly to listen to a conscious and critical intelligentsia. To a gerontocratic political élite the students could only seem naïve and childish. This the students came to resent bitterly as their disaffections gathered force:

> It was as if grown-ups were saying to children, 'You are still young. You don't really know anything about Party and state affairs. We have good reasons for everything we do. You don't; you're being manipulated by a few bad people. You're doing what they tell you to do, which is not what you meant to do. (Li Lu, 1990: 123)

The economic problems of the regime also led to disaffection among various sections of the population. The workers for their part felt the squeeze of inflation on their incomes. Like the intellectuals they felt they had no place in the political system through which to voice their concerns to the leadership. An activist now in exile in Paris spoke of this frustration among the workers: 'A worker said to me "the government is stupid. We are comparatively satisfied [with the system]. All we want is to be able to say what we want to say."' This was not too much to ask, except that the political system seemed reluctant to allow any institutional-isation of participative politics over which it had no direct control. The only trade union that is supposed to represent workers' interest – the All-China Federation of Trade Unions – refused to join the workers of Beijing in giving support to the students (SWB/FE/0461/B2/2). That the students were able to tap support from many different groups and interests is clear from the official report of the Beijing CPC secretary:

> This turmoil was marked by another characteristic, that is, it was no longer confined to institutions of higher learning or Beijing area; it spread to the whole of society and to all parts of China . . . Leaflets

'Unite With the Workers and Peasants, Down with Despotic Rule' were put up in some factories. (Chen, 1989: 14)

Once the student movement spilled onto the streets of Beijing, especially after the students decided to go on a hunger strike on 12 May, popular support for it grew tremendously. Journalists, teachers, media representatives, even Party members joined the marchers:

> Among those supporting the students were cadres of state organs, workers and scientific researchers, working personnel of the offices of many ministries and commissions under the State Council. [There were also] personnel of the offices of the central committees of the KMT Revolutionary Committee, China Democratic League and six other democratic parties.(SWB/B2/0461/B2/2)

On 16 May ten presidents of Beijing universities issued an open letter to the Party leaders urging them to talk to the students (SWB/FE/0460/B2/1). As the hunger strike progressed and the idealism of the students struck chords of sympathy among the population there seemed signs that not just the Party leadership, but the army was being affected by the events. On 18 May the hunger-strikers' broadcasting station relayed an open letter from a number of PLA officers to the Central Military Commission which read:

> (1) We absolutely cannot suppress the students and the masses by armed forces . . . (2) [We] urge the government and the student representatives to hold a public and fair dialogue . . . (3) Immediately take part in rescuing students who are going without food and water. (4) Beginning with the armed forces, actively promote all reforms in the units, cut military spending. (SWB/FE/0462/B2/2)

While the students appreciated this growing support, and were aware of its importance, they also showed a reluctance to let 'outsiders' participate in the demonstrations organised by the students. One reason for this was strategic: the students needed to keep a check on those involved in order to ensure that the peaceful nature of the movement was maintained. This gave them legitimacy, and was also their defence. However, the speeches, writings and interviews of the student leaders indicate that the students, in the long-standing tradition of Chinese intellectuals, did not regard the 'masses' as sophisticated enough to take part in open political practice. One student activist, now in exile, said,

It is not easy to create a political alternative for China. China is a backward country. The ways of the West cannot apply to it. Here [in the West] there is little difference between peasants, workers and intellectuals in the cultural and economic levels. This is not so in China. The economic system of capitalism is good for China. What political system China needs, I cannot say.

Another was even more explicit: 'Mao led a peasant revolution; let that be the last peasant movement in China!' The inherent élitism of this section, the images of the Cultural Revolution that had come to symbolise 'mass politics', and the intellectual debate on 'New Authoritarianism' (see Chapter 1) formed the basis of this distancing.

As the student movement grew in strength, the Party had to respond to its demands. At times a sympathetic response was made difficult by the naïve arrogance of students experiencing a sense of power for the first time. In a political system that was run on the basis of personal loyalties, party affiliations, and respect for age (which also included a respect for the revolutionary histories of certain leaders), the very tone of equality that the students spoke in caused resentment. For example, on 3 May 1989 the students spelt out 'conditions' for dialogue with the authorities which included: 'The government representatives should be at and above the positions of Political Bureau Standing Committee member, NPC Standing Committee vice-chair, and State Council vice-premier . . . Spokesmen (sic) of each side must have equal opportunities, with the same time limit on questions (3 minutes) and answers (10–15 minutes) . . . [and] Students' questions should be answered promptly, and resolved as soon as possible after the meeting.' It concluded, 'We expect a reply no later than noon on 3 May.' (*Xinhua*, SWB/FE/0452/B2/9) The students did not want to be petitioners; the Party was used to nothing else from outside its ranks.

Conclusions

The suppression of the June 1989 student movement by the Chinese regime can be read as a comment both on the limits of the reforms introduced by the leadership, and on the alienation of an important section of Chinese youth from the post-Mao regime. It was also symptomatic of the problems of reforming a centralised state and economic system from above. In the course of the reforms many new interests and contradictions have emerged that are not always compatible with the broader goals of the state. The need for the articulation of these interests has become a crucial factor in the Chinese political system. The demand for autonomous interest-representing organisations is becoming more pressing as the economic reforms progress. However, the parameters that the leadership has defined for itself in the political sphere have limited its response to this increasing pressure. A faction within the Party has thought it feasible to allow a limited, controlled participation of the intellectuals in the public sphere. A strategy of dialogue, of compromise, and perhaps of eventual expropriation into the establishment, seemed possible to leaders like Hu Yaobang and Zhao Ziyang. However, the concern of the Party has also been to manage the demand for political liberalisation so as not to jeopardise its monopoly of power. It has wanted to continue with its project of modernisation, without relaxing political control. A concern for a monopoly of power, embodied in the 'four cardinal principles' set out by Deng, has led the hardliners to be suspicious of even the licensed participation of the intellectuals.

The students themselves have been no less constrained by their own political rhetoric, *naïveté*, and social élitism. There has been little in the political discourse of the students that is creative in the Chinese political context. The students were unable to build bridges across social classes except through personal heroism during the period of the Tian'anmen Square occupation. Their suspicions of, and contempt for, the 'masses', and a belief in a political alternative that does not seem to go beyond a rejection of the CPC's right to rule has also limited the extent to which they could expand their movement. An acceptance of the marketisation of the economy as a panacea for China's economic ills without an analysis of its social consequences – some of which they themselves are uneasy about – has also meant that the student movement in China has not yet shown the potential to convert itself into a mass opposition movement. From interviews with exiled students in Paris it was evident that the repression of the state has led to demoralisation among the students in and outside China. The party/state has been able to exploit the divisions between the students and 'others'. As after the 1987 movement, the attempt is once again to distinguish between 'misled' students (except their leaders like Wang Dan) and 'criminal elements' who made the movement into a 'law and order problem'.

However, despite the suppression of the student movement, the pressures that had given rise to it remain. The very success of the reforms introduced in the system of higher education, and the determination of the political élite to continue with them despite political setbacks, has ensured that these pressures will continue to build over a period of time. The inability of the leadership to resolve them within the boundaries it has set for itself and for socio-political change will also become more pronounced. The evidence of the recurrence of student movements in the post-Mao period is indicative of the importance of these pressures and the political questions arising from them.

Conclusion

As we have seen, the post-Mao reforms in the system of higher education have been part of a larger scheme for modernising China. Educational reforms have both benefited from, and influenced, this attempt at making China a strong, industrialised nation. These reforms have been based upon certain presuppositions that are compatible with the reforms of the Chinese economy. Competition, rationality and efficiency have been the keywords used in any description of the changes in higher education (see Chapters 2 and 3). This has encouraged stratification and specialisation within the system. 'Key' institutions and 'key majors' have been introduced; examinations have been made the criterion for enrolment in universities; a market of skills has been created with the relaxation of the old system of job allocation; and significant material and non-material incentives have been given to the intellectuals. Decentralisation of the Maoist educational structure has led to the introduction of 'managerial reforms' that have given to the university administrations greater power and control over their work force and resources.

The reforms in higher education have also focused on two major political areas: the relations between the Party and the administration in the university, and the question of the decentralisation of authority. The first has led to a debate about the separation of powers between the Party and the administration to check the over-concentration of power in the hands of the Party, and to make academic administration more efficient by putting 'experts' in charge of management. However, as Pepper pointed out as early as 1982:

> The universities now appear to be relatively autonomous entities only vis a vis the local government and surrounding society. But within the educational bureaucracy, the individual universities find themselves circumscribed and constrained at every turn by the rulings of the Ministry of Education, albeit a Ministry now sympathetic to professional demands and concerns. (1982: 196)

Further, decentralisation of the structure of higher education has resulted in greater centralisation of authority at the level of the university itself. This is especially true of the more successful, and therefore financially secure, universities.

The Party at the local level has responded to these changes with caution and some suspicion (see Chapter 4). The various student movements that have accompanied these changes have given rise to further wariness among Party cadres. Suspicion of the intelligentsia, which had been in the forefront of Maoist struggles against privilege, forms the personal political history of most middle-aged cadres. Together with this, they feel threatened in their position of power by the 'experts' and sense a loss of control, leading them to resist any significant dilution of their political role. However, this resistance is counterbalanced by the recognition of the need of the nation for the expertise of the intelligentsia. These twin considerations have meant an uneven response by the Party cadres to the reforms. Local Party secretaries and Party units have negotiated their own boundaries within a changing system. Further, the national leadership has sought to distinguish between its own unassailable primary political position, and that of the local Party branches, which have been made open to criticism and whose powers have been circumscribed. This has created its own tensions within the Party structure which were evident in the aftermath of the 1986–7 student movement, and more recently after the 1989 Tian'anmen Square events. While smaller universities have shown excessive caution in implementing the more radical reforms, the prestigious ones have been reluctant to withdraw from their vanguard positions even under central government pressure. Distance from Beijing has also affected the response of the universities to central initiatives.

Crucial to the reform of higher education has been the support that the leadership has been able to mobilise among the intelligentsia – especially in the institutions of higher education – whose relationship with the party/state has been fraught with difficulties (see Chapter 5). The need for expertise to fuel economic development has underlined the party/state's response to the intellectuals in the post-Mao period. This has led to an attempt by the state to reconcile the intelligentsia by offering it various material and non-material incentives which have included improvements in their living conditions, and greater autonomy in their sphere of work. It also granted to the intellectuals a limited 'licence' to criticise government policy, propose new initiatives, and engage in public debate about the progress of the reforms. However, this project has remained circumscribed by the state's primary goal of economic modernisation. The question of the institutions that might mediate between the party/state and the intelligentsia as a social group has remained unaddressed; the very inclusion of the intelligentsia into the working class, which is legitimately represented only by the CPC, can be regarded as an expropriation of this group without creating any legal or institutional protections for its members. This has resulted in fracturing the support of the intellectuals for the reforms, as was witnessed through the spring and summer of 1989, in turn affecting the implementation of the reforms themselves.

The university students too have been radically affected by the introduction of the reforms. Their living conditions, the surveillance and control under which they live and work, pedagogy, and most importantly the allocation of jobs, have all come under scrutiny. Like the intellectuals, the students have gone through a cycle of supporting the Party leadership, becoming its critics, and opposing it as the implementation of the reforms progressed. The new pressures, expectations and disappointments resulting from the particularity of the reforms through the 1980s have created new interests in this group, the articulation of which has posed difficult questions for the reformist leadership. The situation has been made more complex by the regional and institutional variations among the universities. Local conditions have necessarily affected the response of the students to the reforms. Being caught between the project of modernising China, which requires the support of the intellectuals, and of keeping political control, the Party leadership has been unable to maintain its balancing act.

Wertheim, writing about the 'Urgency Factor and Democracy', points to the tension between the urgency of long-term economic planning and of political participation that confronts the developing states:

> popular participation appears in many cases difficult to reconcile with the magnitude and desperate seriousness of the ills from which these societies suffer and which require strong remedies (Wertheim, 1981: 18)

Indeed, this is the line of argument that Deng Xiaoping seems to have adopted. The Chinese leadership has identified the primary contradiction facing post-Mao China as between economic backwardness and the rate of economic growth. To resolve this contradiction the leadership has looked to the introduction of the market and a partial withdrawal of the state from the public sphere. It is from this perspective of rapid economic modernisation that the political and social reforms have been introduced. Speaking at the Third Meeting of the Fifth Plenary Session of the Eleventh Central Committee of the CPC in February 1980, Deng approved of the deletion of Article 45 of the Constitution that provided the citizens with the right of 'speaking out freely, airing one's views fully, writing big-character posters and holding great debates'. This he justified by pointing out that:

> While working with complete dedication for the four modernisations, we must, with equal dedication, preserve and develop a political situation marked by stability, unity and liveliness . . . And it is with this task in mind that we are proposing the deletion of the provision on the *si da* [Article 45] from the Constitution. (Deng, 1984: 261)

The political reforms have been made contingent upon the needs of the economy.

As we try to speculate what the future may hold for China in the 1990s we are faced with many uncertainties. While the reformist thrust of Party policy in China has not been entirely blunted, we are aware of a slowdown as the leadership takes stock after the student upheaval in Beijing in June 1989. Those outside China have also become aware of not only the political problems facing the country, but also its economic compulsions. The division between the Chinese reformists – inside and outside the Party – is paralleled in the academia outside China analysing the progress of the reforms. There seem to be three different responses emerging. These are an 'élitist democratic' response of the 'democracy' movement of 1989, a Marxist humanist response of some oppositional intellectuals like Su Shaozhi, and the 'new authoritarian', developmentalist response. While the first two stress the importance of representative institutions, an emphasis on citizens' rights, freedom of the media, either a rejection or redefinition of the role of the CPC, and a federative state, they have been unable to respond creatively and realistically to the problems of transforming the existing political system in China. Taking into account Wertheim's 'urgency factor', the 'new authoritarian' approach puts forward powerful arguments for the necessity of a strong state in a period of transition from a centralised economic and political system to one oriented towards the market and open government. The political instability that can accompany a process of democratisation can jeopardise the economic and administrative reforms – the very foundations upon which the political system has to be built. The economists look to the establishment of the market and the economic infrastructure, the political scientists to the separating out of a rational bureaucracy on the Weberian model, as prerequisites for a participative political system. What is overlooked by both, however, is the particular political history of China under the CPC regime.

Where the Party has been so intimately involved in both the economic and bureaucratic structures of the country, to contemplate reforming these without confronting the problem of the Party's political power would lead to a dead end. It is the very logic of the economic reforms that demands a resolution of the question of the Party's role within the system. If the market does not exist, but has to be created, it can only be through the involvement of the party/state. If the state bureaucracy has to be separated out from the Party bureaucracy, the threat to the position and power of the Party cadres is real. Given the positions of privilege enjoyed by the Party cadres, resistance to any whittling away of their power is inevitable. The question then arises how, if the economic and political reforms are to go on, this contradiction is to be resolved without interrupting the process of the reforms themselves. Further, as already pointed out in Chapter 1 and evidenced through the study of the educational reforms, the reform of the Party's position has to be seen in the context of another independent variable – the rise of new interests and interest groups seeking articulation in the public sphere. Generated by the reforms themselves, these cannot be wished away. They can be refused public space, but that will only create a political dysfunction within the system which the Party will be less able to control because of the 'informal' paths that interest articulation would then take, as happened during the student demonstrations. A further problem for the Party is its own political culture. The recognition of interests as distinct from those represented by the Party has been denied in China, as in most other state socialist countries. 'Interest' has tended to be equated with self-interest 'usually of a material kind'. This has delegitimised the concept in public political discourse.

In terms of the reforms in higher education the above debate has particular significance. One option that the Party leadership had, and exercised throughout the 1980s, was offering a suboptimal deal to the intellectuals – greater material benefits on the one hand, and allowing limited demands to be made upon the political system on the other. The problem arose when the incentives the state could offer were not enough, and the limits imposed upon the intellectuals became unrealistic in the existing political situation. This option is, of course, still open to the party/state, even though its intentions are more suspect in the eyes of the intellectuals than before June 1989. The only other option available to the party/state is that of clamping down on the intellectuals, and therefore the educational reforms, thus also injuring the progress of the economic reforms. This the state is understandably reluctant to do. Despite the trials of students and lecturers involved in the Tian'anmen Square movement, despite stricter controls over political education, and the emphasis on compulsory military training in the aftermath of the movement, there has been little real change in the higher education policy. The sentences on the leaders of the movement have been light, and the attempt continues to distinguish between a minority of 'misled' students and the majority of the 'patriotic' students who want things to return to 'normal'. There has also been an explicit commitment made to the continuation of the 'open door policy' in higher education. The Party committees have indeed become more prominent on university campuses, but their agenda continues to be the promotion of the reforms in higher education, which are premised upon a decreasing influence of the Party in administering education.

The dilemma that a theory of political participation then poses for a developing nation state is a genuine and difficult one. If political participation is based on decentralised, spontaneous mass action, it either tends to be expropriated by bureaucratic and/or political élites, or is unable to maintain its momentum in the face of lack of public space and legal protection. If, on the other hand, it is a mobilised political action, it tends to lose its autonomy to bureaucratic fiat. In the Leninist theory of political organisation and its subsequent interpretations, there has been a negation of the idea of unorganised participative practice. This could be seen in Mao's approach towards mass line politics during the Cultural Revolution. The failure to reconcile the need for efficient economic and administrative organisation with the space for individual and group participative political action thus remains the unresolved contradiction in the Chinese political system.

Appendix: Hangzhou University Students' Committee rules (draft)

Explanation: These rules and regulations were passed by the 17th Students' Representative Assembly of Hangzhou University. Now referring to the 18th Students' Representative Assembly, every delegation will discuss the document. We hope that on the basis of these regulations every delegation will raise their opinion about the amendments.

18th Students' Representative Assembly
Hangzhou University
Preparatory Group
23 March 1987

Section I *General principles*

Article 1: Hangzhou University Students' Committee is the mass organisation of the university.

Article 2: Hangzhou University Students' Union recognises the rules of National Students' Union, and joins the National Students' Union and the Zhejiang University Students' Union as a group member.

Article 3: Under the guidance of the Hangzhou University Party Committee the Hangzhou University Students' Union actively starts work in different fields.

Article 4: *Basic tasks*

(1) Adhere to the four basic principles of the Party and carry out Party's educational policy by responding and carrying out the various tasks assigned by higher-level groups.

(2) Under the guidance of the Party's educational policy, unite and guide the university's students and stick to 'take study as the dominant factor', and foster talent. Through this activity develop different suitable students, to take special care for good health and liveliness, foster students' different abilities, and guide students to develop in an all-round way.

(3) Strengthen the contacts between the Union and all students; represent and safeguard the proper interests and rights of the students; listen attentively and promptly reflect on students' demands and voice; be concerned about students' immediate interests, and make efforts to serve the students.

(4) Promote relations, exchange and unity between the students, and students and teaching staff. Make a bridge between the Party and the students.

(5) Establish and develop relations with students' groups of National Brotherly schools, including those from Hong Kong and Macao progressive students' groups, and progressive students' groups of the world's friendly countries. Strengthen the exchange and co-operation between the universities and establish friendly relations.

Section II *Membership*

Article 5: Whoever has been registered in Hangzhou University as a student in the following courses can become a member:

(1) four-year undergraduate course
(2) two- to three-year diploma course
(3) one- to two-term informal courses and
(4) the night school.

Article 6: Members' rights and duties:

(1) A member has the right to vote and the right to be elected, as well as the right to participate in any activity of the Union.

(2) A member has the right to discuss, criticise and make recommendations to the work of the Union, as well as the right to inspect the leadership and its work in the Union.

(3) A member has to abide by the rules of the Union, and carry out the resolutions passed by the Union, and accomplish the work obligations assigned by the Union.

(4) A member has the right to represent their opinions about their life, study and work and propose ways to improve them, as well as the right to inform the leadership of the Union as regards the student's opinions.

Section III   *University Students' Representative Assembly*

Article 7: The University Students' Representative Assembly is the most powerful organ of the Students' Union. It is held once every two years.

Article 8: The representatives to the Assembly are selected by members through democratic election. The number of representatives is 3 per cent of the total membership and non-elected members are 1.5 per cent of the total.

Article 9: Powers of the Assembly:
   (1) Examine and approve the minutes of the meetings.
   (2) Discuss and decide the main tasks of this meeting.
   (3) Amend the rules of the committee.
   (4) Elect a new students' union committee.
   (5) Collect and put in order proposals made by the representatives and reflect the responsibility of departmental and university leaders.
   (6) Discuss and adopt the committee's proposals; examine and approve other documents of the committee.

Article 10: The responsible person for the Students' Representative Assembly leads the students' committee work during the Assembly session until the next students' committee is selected. The students' committee in charge completes routine duties of the Students' Assembly when it is not in session.

Section IV   *University Students' Committee*

Article 11: The university students' committee members are elected by the students' representative committee and are responsible to the committee.

Article 12: The presidents of the different departments are members of the university committee.

Article 13: Rights and duties of the committee are as follows:

(1) Discuss, examine and approve the plans put forward by the Union Assembly.

(2) Guide, investigate and supervise various departmental work of the Students' Assembly.

(3) Take care of Students' Assembly work before the next Students' Representative Assembly convenes, and put out the tasks carried out by the students representative committee.

(4) Discuss and adopt organisational groups and arrange for the Students' Assembly.

(5) The committee has the right to make decisions for the managing of the Students' Union's affairs.

(6) To elect the president and the vice-president of the Students' Union.

(7) To prepare for the selection of the next Students' Union committee.

Section V   *Students' Union Standing Committee*

Article 14: The Students' Union Standing Committee is composed of the president, the vice-president, and heads of ministries.

Article 15: The Students' Union is formed by one president and several vice-presidents. President and vice-presidents are elected by the committee and have to be approved by the university Party Committee.

Article 16: A cabinet for the Standing Committee is nominated by the Students' Union president. The Standing Committee is responsible to the Union for its functioning. At the same time it is responsible for investigation and supervision of the duties (already explained in Article 4).

Article 17: Ministers heading different departments of the Union are nominated by the president, approved by the committee and can be dismissed by the committee.

Article 18: The vice-ministers of every department are nominated by the minister and have to be approved by the president.

Section VI *President of the Union*

Article 19: The president and the vice-presidents of the Union are elected/nominated (*sheng chang*) by the Union Assembly and have to be approved by the university Party Committee.

Article 20: Routine work of the Union is managed by the president of the Union who is responsible for the guidance, supervision and co-ordination of the work of different functional departments and controls the work of the Union's cadres. He also makes and keeps contacts with the student Party branch.

Article 21: The president represents the management of the Students' Union.

Section VII *Functional organs*

Article 22: There are different functional organs of the Union representing its different work necessity.

Article 23: These organs are composed of one head, several deputy heads and members.

Article 24: Their task is to warmheartedly serve the students.

Section VIII *Departmental students' meet*

Article 25: The yearly departmental students' meet is the subordinate branch of the university Students' Union.

Article 26: Under the guidance of the departmental-level Party organisation, and with the help of the departmental Students' Union the departmental students' meet starts its work enthusiastically and accepts the organisational guidance of the university Students' Union. It accepts and carries out the various tasks of the university Union.

Article 27: The departmental Students' Union is headed by a president, and various vice-presidents. It can set up various ministries according to the work need of the departmental Union.

Hangzhou University Students' Union
March 1987

The organisation of the Hangzhou University Students' Union

President

Vice-presidents (several in number)

Secretariat: Secretary, Vice-secretary and secretary (several in number)

Study department, propaganda department, social group affairs department, department for life, department for girl students, department for culture and art, sports department and security department (every department formed with one head and several numbers of deputy heads and members), intelligence development centre (general manager and several vice-general managers).

References

Almond, G. and J.S. Coleman (1960) *Politics of the Developing Areas*, Princeton University Press: Princeton, NJ.

Almond, G. and S. Verba (1963), *The Civic Culture: Political attitudes and democracy in five nations*, Princeton University Press: Princeton, NJ.

Altbach, P.G. (1990) 'Student political activism: China in comparative perspective' in *Issues and Studies*, vol. 26, no 1.

Apple, M. (1982), *Education and Power*, Routledge and Kegan Paul: London.

Ayers, W. (1971), *Chang Chih-tung and Educational Reform in China*, Harvard University Press: Cambridge, MA.

Bachrach, P. (1967), *The Theory of Democratic Elitism: A critique*, University of London Press: London.

Balibar, E. (1977), *On the Dictatorship of the Proletariat*, Verso: London.

Barber, B. (1984), *Strong Democracy: Participatory politics for a new age*, University of California Press: Berkeley, CA.

Barthes, R. (1982), *Image Music Text*, Flamingo Press: London.

Bastid, M. and R. Hayhoe (1987), *China's Education and the Industrialised World*, M.E. Sharpe: New York.

Beijing Review (ed.) (1989), *A Chronology of the People's Republic of China*, New Star Publishers: Beijing.

Bell, D. (1968), *End of Ideology: On the exhaustion of political ideas in the fifties*, Yale University Press: New Haven, CT.

Bell, R., D. Edwards, and R. Harrison Wagner (1969), *Political Power: A reader in theory and research*, The Free Press: New York.

Benewick, R. (1988), 'Political participation in China in the 1980s' in R. Benewick and P. Wingrove (eds.), *Reforming the Revolution*, London.

Benton, G. (ed.) (1982), *Wild Lilies, Poisonous Weeds: dissident voices from People's China*, Pluto Press: London.

Bereday, G.Z. and J. Pennar (eds.) (1960), *The Politics of Soviet Education*, Fredrick A. Praeger: London.

Berelson, B., P. Lazrusfeld and W. McPhee (1954), *Voting*, University of Chicago Press: Chicago.

Bernstein, R.J. (1979), *Restructuring Political Theory*, Oxford University Press: Oxford.

Bloomfield, J. (ed.) (1977), *Class, Hegemony and Party*, Lawrence and Wishart: London.

Blumberg, P. (1968), *Industrial Democracy: the sociology of participation*, Constable: London.

Borthwick, S. (1983), *Education and Social Change in China: The beginnings of the modern era*, Stanford University Press: Stanford, CA.

Bourdieu, P. and J. Passeron (1977), *Reproduction in Education, Society and Culture*, Sage: London.

Bowie, R.R. and J.K. Fairbank (1962), *Communist China 1955–59: Policy documents with analysis*, Harvard University Press: Cambridge, MA.

Brandt, C., B. Schwartz and J.K. Fairbank (1952), *A Documentary History of Chinese Communism*, Allen and Unwin: London.

Bratton, D. (1979), *University Admissions Policies in China 1970–1978* in *Asian Survey*, vol. 19, no 10.

Briggs, C.L. (1986), *Learning How To Ask*, Cambridge University Press: New York.

Broaded, C.M. (1989), 'Education and Cultural Transfer in China', in *Problems of Communism*, Sept.–Oct.

Burns, J.P. (1988), *Political Participation in Rural China*, University of California Press: London.

Burns, J.P. (1989a), 'China's governance: political reform in a turbulent environment' in *China Quarterly*, no 119.

Burns, J.P. (1989b), 'Chinese civil service reform: the 13th Party Congress proposals' in *China Quarterly*, no 120, December.

Cai Ling, (1989), *Overseas Chinese Economic Journal*, 8 June.

Carr, E.H. (1954), *The Interregnum*, Macmillan: London.

Carr, E.H. (1978), *The Bolshevik Revolution, vol. 2*, Macmillan: London.

Chan, A. (1985), *Children of Mao: Personality development and political activism in the Red Guard generation*, Macmillan: London.

Chan, A. and J. Unger (1990), 'Voices from the protest movement, Chongqing, Sichuan' in *The Australian Journal of Chinese Affairs*, no 24, July.

Chang, P.H. (1978), *Power and Policy in China*, Pennsylvania State University Press: Pennsylvania, PA.

Chen Erjin (1984), *China: Crossroads socialism*, Verso: London.

Chen, T.H.E. (1960), *Thought Reform of the Chinese Intellectuals*, Hong Kong University Press: Hong Kong.

Chen Xiaotong (1989), *Report on Checking the Turmoil and Quelling the Counter-Revolutionary Rebellion, June 30 1989*, New Star Publishers: Beijing.

Cheng Kai Ming (1986), 'China's recent education reform: the beginning of an overhaul' in *Comparative Education*, vol. 22 no 3.

Cheng Kai Ming (1990), 'Financing education in mainland China: what are the real problems?', in *Issues and Studies*, vol. 26, no 3, March.

Chossudovsky, M. (1986), *Towards Capitalist Restoration? Chinese socialism after Mao*, Macmillan: London.

Chow Tse-tung (1960), *The May Fourth Movement: Intellectual revolution in modern China*, Harvard University Press: Cambridge, MA.

Christiansen, F. (1989), 'The 1989 student demonstrations and the limits of the Chinese political bargaining machine: an essay' in *China Information*, vol. 4, no 1.

Churchward, L.G. (1975), *Contemporary Soviet Government*, 2nd edn, Routledge and Kegan Paul: London.

Clarke, C.M. (1987), 'Changing the context for policy implementation: organisational and personnel reform in post-Mao China' in D. Lampton (ed.), *Policy Implementation in Post-Mao China*, University of California Press: Berkeley, CA.

Cleverley, J. (1985), *The Schooling of China*, Allen and Unwin: Hong Kong.

Cleverley, J. (1987), 'The concept of enterprise and the Chinese universities: a cautionary tale of profit and loss' in *Comparative Education*, vol. 23, no 3.

Collins, R. *et al.* (1986), *Media, Culture and Society: A critical reader*, Sage: London.

Converse, P.E. (1964), 'The nature of belief systems in mass publics', in D. Apter (ed.), *Ideology and Discontent*, The Free Press: New York.

CPC CC (1956), *The Eighth National Congress of the Communist Party of China: Documents*, Foreign Languages Press: Beijing.

CPC CC (1965), *The Polemic on the General Line of the International Communist Movement*, Foreign Languages Press: Beijing.

CPC CC (1977), *The Eleventh National Party Congress of the Communist Party of China: Documents*, Foreign Languages Press: Beijing.

CPC CC (1981), *Resolution on CPC History – 1949–81*, Foreign Languages Press: Beijing.

CPC CC (1985), *Reform of China's Education Structure*, Foreign Languages Press: Beijing.

CPC CC (1989), *Fourth Plenary Session of the CPC 13th Central Committee*, New Star Publishers: Beijing.

Croll, E. (1983), *Chinese Women Since Mao*, Zed Books: London.

Croll, E. (1985), 'Popular participation: role and activities of women's organisations in China' in F. Lisk (ed.), *Popular Participation in Planning for Basic Needs: Concepts, methods and practices*, Gower: Aldershot.

Dahl, R.A. (1961), *Who Governs? Democracy and power in America*, Yale University Press: New Haven, CT.

Dahl, R.A. (1971), *Polyarchy*, Yale University Press: New Haven, CT.

Dai Youqing (1987), *Stones of the Wall*, Sceptre: London.

Dale, R., G. Esland, R. Fergusson and M. MacDonalt (eds.) (1981),

Education and the State vol. 2: Politics, patriarchy and practice, Oxford University Press: Oxford.

Davis, D. and E. Vogel (eds.) (1990), *Chinese Society on the Eve of Tiananmen: the impact of reform*, Harvard University Press: Cambridge, MA.

Davis-Friedman D. (1985), 'Intergenerational inequalities and the Chinese revolution', in *Modern China* no 2.

Deng Xiaoping (1984), *Selected Works*, Foreign Languages Press: Beijing.

Deng Xiaoping (1987), *Fundamental Issues in Present-day China*, Foreign Languages Press: Beijing.

Dews, P. (1986), *Habermas: Autonomy, and Solidarity*, Verso: London.

Dirlik, A. and M. Meisner (eds.) (1989), *Marxism and the Chinese Experience*, M.E. Sharpe: New York.

Dunn, J. (1979), *Western Political Theory in the Face of the Future*, Cambridge University Press: Cambridge.

Duverger, M. (1967), *Political Parties*, translated by B. and R. North, Methuen: London.

Educational Association of China (1971), *Records of Triennial Meeting: Shanghai 1883–1889*, Ch'eng-Wen Publishing Company: Taipei.

Esherick, J.W. (1990), 'X'ian Spring' in *The Australian Journal of Chinese Affairs*, no 24, July.

Etzioni, A. (1968), *The Active Society: Theory of societal and political processes*, The Free Press: New York.

Foster, K. (1990), 'Impressions of the popular protest in Hangzhou April/ June 1989' in *The Australian Journal of Chinese Affairs*, no 23, January.

Franklin, R.K. (1988), 'Macro- and micro-management reforms of China's higher education system in the People's Republic of China' in *Journal of Asian and African Studies*, vol. XXIII, 3–4.

Fraser, S. (1965), *Chinese Communist Education: Records of the first decade*, Vanderbilt University Press: Nashville, TN.

Friere, P. (1972), *Pedagogy of the Oppressed*, Continuum: New York.

Friere, P. (1985), *The Politics of Education*, Macmillan: London.

Giroux, H.A. (1983), *Theory and Resistance in Education: A pedagogy for the opposition*, Heinemann: London.

Glassman, J. (1974), *The Implementation of Education Policy in Communist China*, Ph.D. thesis, University of Michigan, Ann Arbor, MI.

Goldman, M., T. Cheek and C.L. Hamrin (eds.) (1981), *Chinese Intellectuals: Advice and dissent*, Harvard University Press: Cambridge, MA.

Goldman, M., T. Cheek and C.L. Hamrin (eds.) (1987), *China's Intellectuals and the State: In search of a new relationship*, Harvard University Press: Cambridge, MA.

Goodman, D.S.G. (ed.) (1984), *Groups and Politics in the People's Republic of China*, University College Cardiff Press: Cardiff.

Goodman, D.S.G. (1985) 'Modernisation and the search for political order in the PRC' in *Issues and Studies*, vol. 21, no 4, April.

Gordon, C. (ed.) (1986), *Foucault: Power/Knowledge – selected interviews and other writings*, Harvester: Brighton.

Gorz, A. (1975), *Socialism and Revolution*, translated by N. Denny, Penguin: Harmondsworth.

Graham, K. (1986), *The Battle of Democracy: Conflict, consensus, and the individual*, Harvester: Brighton.

Grieder, J.B. (1981), *Intellectuals and the State in Modern China*, Free Press: Hong Kong.

Gu (1989), 'The Problems with New Authoritarian Theory', in *Mingbao Yuekan*, June.

Gunn, R. (1977), 'Marxism and ideas of power and participation', in J. Bloomfield (ed.), *Papers on Class, Hegemony and Party*, Lawrence and Wishart: London.

Habermas, J. (1976), *Legitimation Crisis*, translated by T. McCarthy, Heinemann: London.

Hamrin, C.L. and T. Cheek (1986), *China's Establishment Intellectuals*, M.E. Sharpe: New York.

Han Suyin (1970), *The Crippled Tree*, Penguin: Harmondsworth.

Hao Wang (1990), 'Which way to go: strategies for democratisation in Chinese intellectual circles', unpublished.

Harding, H. (1981), *Organising China: The problem of bureaucracy 1949– 1976*, Stanford University Press: Stanford, CA.

Hayhoe, R. (1984), *Contemporary Chinese Education*, Croom Helm: London.

Hayhoe, R. (1987), 'China's higher curricular reform in historical perspective', in *The China Quarterly*, no 110, June.

Hayhoe, R. (1989), *China's Universities and the Open Door*, M.E. Sharpe: New York.

Held, V., K. Nielsen and C. Parsons (eds.) (1972), *Philosophy and Political Action*, Oxford University Press: Oxford.

Henze, J. (1984), 'Higher education reforms', in R. Hayhoe (ed.), *Contemporary Chinese Education*, Croom Helm: London.

Henze, J. (1987), 'Educational modernisation as a search for higher efficiency', in M. Bastid and R. Hayhoe (eds.), *China's Education and the Industrialised World*, M.E. Sharpe: New York.

Hinton, W. (1972), *Hundred Days War: The cultural revolution at Tsinghua University*, Monthly Review Press: New York.

Hong Yung Lee and J. Israel (1982), *Limits of Reform in China*. The Wilson Centre: Washington, DC.

Hooper, B. (1985), 'The youth problem: deviations from the socialist road' in G. Young (ed.), *China: Dilemma of modernisation*, Croom Helm: London.

Horvat, B. (1982), *The Political Economy of Socialism*, Martin Robertson: Oxford.

Hu Chang-tu (1962), *Chinese Education Under Communism*, Teachers College Press Columbia: New York.

Huang Shiqi (1987), 'Contemporary educational relations with the industrialised world: a Chinese view', in M. Bastid and R. Hayhoe (eds.), *China's Education and the Industrialised World*, M.E. Sharpe: New York.

Huntington, S.P. (1968), *Political Order in Changing Societies*, Yale University Press: New Haven, CT.

Huntington, S.P. and J.M. Nelson (1976), *No Easy Choice: Political participation in developing countries*, Harvard University Press: Cambridge, MA.

Israel, J. (1966), *Student Movement in China 1927–1937*, Stanford University Press, Stanford, CA.

Karabel, J. and A.H. Halsey (eds.) (1977), *Power and Ideology in Education*, Oxford University Press: Oxford.

Kariel, H.S. (1970), *Frontiers of Democratic Theory*, Random House: New York.

Keenan, B. (1977), *The Dewey Experiment in China: Early Republic 1919–1920*, Harvard University Press: Cambridge, MA.

Kelly, D.A. (1987), 'The emergence of humanism: Wang Ruoshui and the critique of socialist alienation', in M. Goldman *et al.* (eds.), *China's Intellectuals and the State: In search of a new relationship*, Harvard University Press: Cambridge, MA.

Kristeva, J. (1977), *About Chinese Women*, Verso: London.

Kwong, J. (1970), *Chinese Education in Transition*, Montreal.

Lampton, D. (ed.) (1987a), *Policy Implementation in Post-Mao China*, University of California Press: Berkeley, CA.

Lampton, D. (1987b), 'Chinese politics: the bargaining treadmill', in *Issues and Studies*, vol. 23, no 3, March.

Lenin, V.I. (1969), *State and Revolution*, Progress Publishers: Moscow.

Levenson, J.R. (1965a), *Confucian China and its Modern Fate*, vol. 3, Routledge and Kegan Paul: London.

Levenson, J.R. (1965b), *Liang Ch'i-chao and the Mind of Modern China*, Thames and Hudson: London.

Levitas, M. (1974), *Marxist Perspectives in the Sociology of Education*, Routledge and Kegal Paul: London.

Lewin, M. (1988), *The Gorbachev Phenomenon: A historical interpretation*, Radius: London.

Lewis, J.W. (ed.) (1963), *Leadership in Communist China*, Ithaca University Press: New York.

Lewis, J.W. (ed.) (1970), *Party, Leadership and Revolutionary Power in China*, Cambridge University Press: Cambridge.

Li Lu (1990), *Moving the Mountain: My Life in China*, Macmillan: London.

Link, P. (ed.), *Roses and Thorns: The second blooming of Hundred Flowers in Chinese fiction 1979–80*, University of California Press: Berkeley, CA.

Lipset, S.M. (1960), *Political Man: the social bases of politics*, Heinemann: London.

Lisk, F. (1985), *Popular Participation in Planning for Basic Needs: Concepts, methods and practices*, Gower: Aldershot.

Liu, A.P.L. (1976), *Political Culture and Group Conflict in Communist China*, Clio Books: Santa Barbara, CA.

Lo, L. Nai-Kwai (1989), 'The irony of reform in higher education in mainland China', in *Issues and Studies*, vol. 25, no 11, November.

Lukes, S. (1986), *Power, A Radical View*, Hong Kong.

MacFarquahar, R. (1974a), *The Hundred Flowers Campaign and the Chinese Intellectuals*. Octagon Books: New York.

MacFarquahar, R. (1974b), *The Origins of the Cultural Revolution: Contradictions among the people*, Oxford University Press: Oxford.

MacFarquahar, R. (1983), *The Origins of the Cultural Revolution: The Great Leap Forward 1958–60*, Oxford University Press: Oxford.

Mao Zedong (1964), *Four Essays on Philosophy*, Foreign Languages Press: Beijing.

Mao Zedong (1967a,b,c,d), *Selected Works, vols. I–IV*, Foreign Languages Press: Beijing.

Mao Zedong (1972), *Quotations from Chairman Mao*, Foreign Languages Press: Beijing.

Mao Zedong (1977), *Selected Works, vol. V*, Foreign Languages Press: Beijing.

Marx, K. (1975), *Early Writings*, Penguin: Harmondsworth.

Marx, K. (1976), *On the Paris Commune*, Progress Publishers: Moscow.

Mayo, H.B. (1960), *An Introduction to Democratic Theory*, Oxford University Press: Oxford.

McCormick, B.L. (1987), 'Leninist implementation: the election campaign' in D. Lampton (ed.), *Policy Implementation in Post-Mao China*, University of California Press: Berkeley, CA.

McCormick, R. (1986), 'The radio and television universities and the development of higher education in China' in *China Quarterly*, March.

Medvedev, R. (1975), *On Socialist Democracy*, Macmillan: London.

Melotti, U. (1977), *Marx and the Third World*, Macmillan: London.

Ministry of Human Resource Development, Department of Education (1986), *Extracts from National Policy on Education 1986*, New Delhi.

Molyneux, J. (1978), *Marxism and the Party*, Pluto Press: London.

Moody, P.R. Jnr. (1983), *Chinese Politics After Mao: Development and liberalisation 1976 to 1983*, Praeger: New York.

Mote, F.W. (1989), *Intellectual Foundations of China*, 2nd edn, Knopf: New York.

Munro, R. (1984), 'Chen Erjin and the Chinese democracy movement', in Chen Erjin, *China: Crossroads Socialism*, Verso: London.

Nathan, A.J. (1986), *Chinese Democracy*, Tauris: London.

Nathan, A.J. (1989), 'Chinese democracy in 1989: continuity and change' in *Problems of Communism*, Sept.–Oct.

Nathan, A.J. (1990), *China's Crisis: Dilemmas of reform and prospects for democracy*, Columbia University Press: New York.

National People's Congress of China (NPC) (1983), *The Constitution of the People's Republic of China*, Foreign Languages Press: Beijing.

Ng, Gek-boo (1985), 'Mass participation and basic needs satisfaction: the

Chinese Approach', in F. Lisk, *Popular Participation in Planning for Basic Needs: Concepts, methods and practices*, Gower: Aldershot.

Nolan, P. (1983), 'Decollectivisation of agriculture in China' in *Economic and Political Weekly*, vol. XVIII, August 6.

Oksenburg, M. (1967), *Occupational Groups in the Chinese Society and the Cultural Revolution*, University of Michigan: Ann Arbor, MI.

Olson, M. (1971), *The Logic of Collective Action: Public goods and the theory of groups*, Schocken: New York.

Parry, G. (ed.) (1972), *Participation in Politics*, Manchester University Press: Manchester.

Pateman, C. (1970), *Participation and Democratic Theory*, Cambridge University Press: Cambridge.

Pearse, H. and M. Stieffel (1980), *Inquiry into Participation: A research approach*, in UNRISD Dialogue, vol. I, UN Publications: Geneva.

Pepper, S. (1980), 'Chinese education after Mao', in *The China Quarterly*, no 81, March.

Pepper, S. (1982), 'China's universities: new experiments in socialism, democracy and administrative reform – a research report', in *Modern China*, vol. 8, no 2.

Pepper, S. (1984), *China's Universities: Post-Mao enrollment policies and their impact on the structures of secondary education*, University of Michigan Press: Ann Arbor, MI.

Pierson, C. (1986), *Marxist Theory and Democratic Politics*, Polity: Cambridge.

Pitkin, H.F. (1972), *Political Representation*, University of California Press: Berkeley, CA.

Porter, E.A. (1990), *Foreign Teachers in China: Old problems for a new generation, 1979–89*, Green Wood Press: New York.

Price, R.F. (1970), *Education in Communist China*, London.

Price, R.F. (1977), *Marx and Education in Russia and China*, Routledge and Kegan Paul: London.

Pye, L. (1963), *Communication and Political Development*, Princeton University Press: Princeton, NJ.

Pye, L. (1968), *The Spirit of Chinese Politics: A psychological study of the authority crisis in political development*, MIT Press: Cambridge, MA.

Pye, L. (1981), *The Dynamics of Chinese Politics*, Oelgeschlager, Gunn and Hain: Cambridge, MA.

Rai, S.M. (1988), 'Market merry-go-round' in *China Now*, Summer.

Rai, S.M., H. Pilkington and A. Phizaklea (1991), *Women in the Face of Change: Soviet Union, Eastern Europe and China*, Routledge: London, to be published.

Robson, W.A. and B. Crick (eds.) (1975), *China in Transition*, Sage: London.

Rosen, S.M. (1971), *Education and Modernisation in the USSR*, Addison-Wesley: London.

Rosen, S. (1985), 'Recentralisation, decentralisation and rationalisation: Deng Xiaoping's bifurcated education policy', in *Modern China*, vol. 2, no 3, July.

Rosen, S. (1986), 'Editor's introduction', in *Chinese Education 1985–86*.

Rosen, S. (ed.), (1987), 'Restoring key secondary schools', in D. Lampton (ed.), *Policy Implementation In Post-Mao China*, University of California Press: Berkeley, CA.

Rosen, S. (1989), 'Political education and student response: some background factors behind the 1989 Beijing demonstrations', in *Issues and Studies*, vol. 25, no 11.

Rosen S. (1990), 'The Chinese Communist Party and Chinese society: popular attitudes toward Party membership and the Party's image', in *Australian Journal of Chinese Affairs*, no 24, July.

Rosenau, P.M. and R. Paehlke (1990), 'The exhaustion of left and right: perspectives on the political participation of the disadvantaged', in *International Political Science Review*, vol. 11, no 1.

Rowe, W.T. (1990), 'The public sphere in modern China', in *Modern China*, vol. 16, no 3, July.

Rozman, G. (1981), *Modernisation of China*, New York.

Saich, T. (1990), 'The rise and fall of the Beijing people's movement', in *Australian Journal of Chinese Affairs*, no 24, July.

Schell, O. (ed.) (1988), *Discos and Democracy*, Pantheon Books: New York.

Schlesinger, P. (1986), 'In search of the intellectuals: some comments of recent theory', in R. Collins *et al.* (eds.) *Media, Culture and Society: A critical reader*, Sage: London.

Schram, S.R. (1969), *The Political Thought of Mao Tse-tung*, Penguin: Harmondsworth.

Schram, S.R. (1970), 'The Party in Chinese communist ideology', in J.W. Lewis (ed.), *Party, Leadership and Revolutionary Power in China*, Cambridge University Press: Cambridge.

Schram, S.R. (ed.) (1973), *Authority, Participation and Cultural Change in China*, Cambridge University Press: Cambridge.

Schram, S.R. (1974), *Mao Tse-tung Unrehearsed: Talks and letters 1956–71*, Penguin: Harmondsworth.

Schram, S.R. (1983), *Mao Zedong: A preliminary reassessment*, The Chinese University Press: Hong Kong.

Schram, S.R. (1985), *The Scope of State Power in China*, The Chinese University Press: Hong Kong.

Schumpeter, J.A. (1947), *Capitalism, Socialism and Democracy*, 3rd edn, Harper Torchbooks: New York.

Schurman, F. (1968), *Ideology and Organisation in Communist China*, Cambridge University Press: Cambridge.

State Education Commission (1983), *Education and Science*, China Handbook Series, Foreign Languages Press: Beijing.

State Education Commission (1984), *Achievement of Education in China: Statistics 1949–1983*, People's Education Press: Beijing.

State Education Commission (1985a), *Guanyu Jiaoyu Tizhi Gaige de Wen Jian*, Beijing.

State Education Commission (1985b), *Jiaoyu Tizhi Gaige Wenxian Xuanbian*, Beijing.

State Education Commission (1986a), *The Development of Education in China 1984–1986*, Beijing.

State Education Commission (1986b), *Higher Education Self-study Examinations in China*, Beijing.

State Education Commission (1986c), *China's Radio and Television Universities*, Beijing.

State Education Commission (1986d), *Post-graduate Education in China*, Beijing.

Selden, M. (1971), *The Yenan Way in Revolutionary China*, Harvard University Press: Cambridge, MA.

Selden, M. and V. Lippit (eds.) (1982), *The Transition to Socialism in China*, M.E. Sharpe: New York.

Seybolt, P.J. (1973a), *Education and Communism in China*, London.

Seybolt, P.J. (1973b), *Revolutionary Education in China*, London.

Sher, G.S. (1978), *Marxist Humanism and Praxis*, Prometheus Books: New York.

Shi Ming Hu and E. Seifman (eds.) (1987), *A Documentary History of Education in the PRC 1977–1986*, AMS: New York.

Shirk, S.L. (1982), *Competitive Comrades: Career incentives and student strategies in China*, University of California Press: Berkeley, CA.

Shue, V. (1988), *The Reach of the State*, Stanford University Press: Stanford, CA.

Singer, M. (1971), *Educated Youth and the Cultural Revolution in China*, University of Michigan Press: Ann Arbor, MI.

Siu, H.F. (1989), *Agents and Victims in South China: Accomplices in rural revolution*, Yale University Press: New Haven, CT.

Smith, T. (1987), *Thinking Like a Communist: State and legitimacy in the Soviet Union, China, and Cuba*, W.W. Norton: New York.

Strand, D. (1989), *Political Participation and the Political Reform in Post-Mao China*, Copenhagen Discussion Papers no 6, University of Copenhagen, Copenhagen.

Su Shaozhi (1983), *Marxism in China*, Spokesman: Nottingham

Su Shaozhi (1988), *Democratization and Reform*, Spokesman: Nottingham.

Su Shaozhi (1990), 'A macrocosmic study of China's attempts to reform its political system', unpublished.

Sweezy, P.M., *The Post-Revolutionary Society: Essays*, Monthly Review Press: New York.

Talmon, J.L. (1961), *The Origins of Totalitarian Democracy*, Mercury Books: London.

Tan, C.C. (1972), *Chinese Political Thought in the Twentieth Century*, David and Charles: Newton Abbot.

Taylor, R. (1981), *China's Intellectual Dilemma: Politics and University Enrolment*, University of British Columbia Press: Vancouver.

Thogersen, S. (1987), 'Senior middle schools in a social perspective: Yantai District, Shantung Province', in *China Quarterly*, no 109, March.

Townsend, J. (1969), *Political Participation in Communist China*, University of California Press: Berkeley, CA.

Unger, J. (1982), *Education Under Mao*, New York.

University Grants Commission (1983), *Annual Report 1982–83*, New Delhi.

UNRISD (1980–4), *Dialogue About Participation*, UN Publications: Geneva.

Vogel, E.F. (1968), *The Structure of Conflict: China in 1967*, in *The Cultural Revolution: Review*, Michigan Papers in Chinese Studies, University of Michigan Press: Ann Arbor, MI.

Waldron, A. (1990), 'Warlordism vs federalism: the revival of a debate?' in *China Quarterly*, no 121, March.

Wang and Wen (1984), 'The nest egg', in P. Link (ed.), *Roses and Thorns: The Second Blooming of Hundred Flowers in Chinese Fiction 1979–80*, University of California Press: Berkeley, CA.

Wang Juechi, 'Campus businesses – A source of finance for mainland China's higher learning institutes', in *Issues and Studies*.

Warner, S. (1990), 'Shanghai's response to the deluge', in *Australian Journal of Chinese Affairs*, no 24, July.

Wei Zhi (1985), 'Actively reform the enrollment source plan', in *Chinese Education*, no 4.

Weiner, R.R. (1981), *Cultural Marxism and Political Sociology*, Sage: London.

Wertheim, W.F. (1981), *Urgency Factor in Democracy: a theoretical contribution to UNRISD debate on participation*, in UNRISD Dialogue, vol. I, UN Publications: Geneva.

Wertheim, W.F. and M. Steiffel (1982), *Production, Equality and Participation in Rural China*, UN Publications: Geneva.

West, P. (1976), *Yenching University and Sino-Western Relations 1916–1952*, Harvard University Press: Cambridge, MA.

Williamson, P.J. (1985), *Varieties of Corporatism – Theory and Practice*, Cambridge University Press: Cambridge.

White, G. (1981), *Party and Professionals: The political role of teachers in contemporary China*, M.E. Sharpe: New York.

White, G. (1987a), 'The impact of economic reforms in the Chinese countryside', in *Modern China*, vol. 13, no 4.

White, G. (1987b), 'The politics of economic reform in Chinese industry: the introduction of the labour contract system', in *China Quarterly*, September.

White III, L. (1987), 'Thought workers in Deng's time', in M. Goldman *et al.* (eds.), *China's Intellectuals and the State: In Search of a New Relationship*, Harvard University Press: Cambridge, MA.

World Bank (1983), *China: Socialist economic development, vol. III*, World Bank: Washington, DC.

Ye Diqun (1986–7), 'Further probe into the assessment of investment in higher education', in *Chinese Education*, vol. XIX, no 4, Winter.

Yeh, M.D. (1987), 'The CCP's policy towards intellectuals', in *Issues and Studies*, vol. 23, no 1, January.

Young, G. (ed.) (1985), *China: Dilemma of modernisation*, Croom Helm: London.

Zeng Delin (1987), 'Several questions concerning the trial implementation of the system whereby the President assumes full responsibility', in *Chinese Education*, vol. XIX, no 4.

Index